Harriet F. Woods

Historical Sketches of Brookline, Mass.

Harriet F. Woods

Historical Sketches of Brookline, Mass.

ISBN/EAN: 9783337141769

Printed in Europe, USA, Canada, Australia, Japan

Cover: Foto ©ninafisch / pixelio.de

More available books at **www.hansebooks.com**

HISTORICAL SKETCHES

OF

BROOKLINE, MASS.

BY

HARRIET F. WOODS.

BOSTON:
Published for the Author, by
ROBERT S. DAVIS AND COMPANY.
1874.

Entered, according to Act of Congress, in the year 1874, by
HARRIET F. WOODS,
In the Office of the Librarian of Congress, at Washington.

This work is printed for Subscribers, only.

RIVERSIDE, CAMBRIDGE:
PRINTED BY H. O. HOUGHTON AND COMPANY.

PREFACE.

THE sketches of which this volume is composed, do not claim to be an exhaustive Town History, but are principally a series of articles written under the title of "Brookline as it was," and published in the "Brookline Transcript," during the years 1871-2. They are chiefly descriptive of the oldest streets and houses, with biographical sketches of some interesting persons, and local anecdotes and events. These papers have lately been carefully revised and corrected by the author, who has added new matter, including a chapter on Brookline in the late war.

She has been largely indebted for material, to the writings of Rev. Dr. Pierce (whose biography is contained in this work), to old family records and legal documents, and to verbal information from old inhabitants of the town. Deacon Thomas Griggs, Benjamin B. Davis, Esq., the late Dr. S. A. Shurtleff, George Craft, Esq., A. W. Goddard, Esq., the late Otis Withington, the Misses Heath, and many others, have contributed valuable information. The various publications of the New England Historic Genealogical Society have been frequently consulted, as also the genealogical works of Bond, Savage, and others.

In the winter of 1873–4, Miss Abby L. Pierce (daughter of Rev. Dr. Pierce above-mentioned), desirous of seeing these sketches preserved in a permanent form, voluntarily undertook the labor of obtaining subscribers for this object, and to her industry and perseverance the success of the undertaking is chiefly due. To this lady, and to Robert S. Davis, Esq., who has kindly arranged for the printing of the work, the writer herewith tenders her heartfelt thanks. Also to all who have in any way contributed to the interest or correctness of the work, or to the enterprise of placing it before the public, she gratefully acknowledges her indebtedness. It is hoped that it may be read with as much pleasure as it has been written.

H. F. W.

Cypress St., Brookline, *April*, 1874.

CONTENTS.

CHAPTER I.
EARLY SCENES, SETTLEMENTS, AND EVENTS. — SEPARATION FROM BOSTON. — OLD FAMILIES AND THEIR LANDS 9

CHAPTER II.
THE "PUNCH BOWL." — FIRST PUBLIC COACHES. — J. DAVENPORT. — THE "WHITE" HOUSE. — VILLAGE DOCTORS. — WYMAN AND DOWNER HOUSES 18

CHAPTER III.
THE DEPOT GROUND. — THE DAVIS ESTATE. — SAMBO. — DANA TAVERN. — TOM COOK. — THE BAPTIST CHURCH . . 39

CHAPTER IV.
HARRISON PLACE. — ST. MARY'S CHURCH. — LINDEN PLACE. — THOMAS A. DAVIS. — ASPINWALL AVENUE, OR, "PERRY'S LANE" 59

CHAPTER V.
THE ASPINWALL FAMILY. — THE COLONEL. — THE DOCTOR. — THE OLD SCHOOL-HOUSE ON SCHOOL STREET . 67

CHAPTER VI.
THE SHARPS. — CURIOUS OLD PAPERS. — THE SEWALLS. — EDWARD DEVOTION. — CAPTAIN WINCHESTER. — THE GRIGGS FAMILY. — HARVARD STREET, CONCLUDED . . . 98

CHAPTER VII.

WASHINGTON STREET. — HOLDEN'S HILL. — THE LEEDS PLACE. — THE PUBLIC LIBRARY 125

CHAPTER VIII.

THE FIRE DEPARTMENT. — THE DANA PLACE. — MISS ANNA DANA 135

CHAPTER IX.

THE HALL HOUSE. — THE TOLMAN HOUSE. — THE CROFT HOUSES. — "BLACK SUSY." — MISS HANNAH ADAMS. — DR. WILD. — THE BLAKE PLACE. — THE ASPINWALL PLACE 148

CHAPTER X.

THE ROBINSON, WITHINGTON, AND COREY PLACES. — CYPRESS STREET. — BOYLSTON STREET. — GIDEON THAYER. — DR. SHURTLEFF. — BRADLEY'S HILL 175

CHAPTER XI.

BOYLSTON AND BRIGHTON STREETS. — WALNUT STREET. — HOUSES ALONG THE LOWER PART. — THE WALLEY OR BIRD HOUSES. — THE CLARK HOUSE. — THE CEMETERY 199

CHAPTER XII.

THE OLD BRICK SCHOOL-HOUSE. — MASTER ADAMS. — THE STONE SCHOOL-HOUSE. — THE FIRST CHURCH. — REV. MR. ALLEN. — REV. MR. JACKSON 225

CHAPTER XIII.

REV. DR. PIERCE: BIOGRAPHY. — MR. PHILBRICK AND THE ANTI-SLAVERY MOVEMENT. — POLLY HATCH: ANECDOTES, HER MARRIAGE AND DEATH 251

CHAPTER XIV.

THE GARDNER FAMILY AND HOUSES. — THE BOYLSTON, OR HYSLOP PLACE (COLONEL LEE'S). — THE ACKERS PLACE. — OLD INDIAN BURIAL PLACE 284

CHAPTER XV.

THE HOUSE OF SAMUEL WHITE, ESQ., AFTERWARDS THE HEATH PLACE. — "AUNT WHITE." — THE WINCHESTERS . . . 313

CHAPTER XVI.

HEATH STREET, CONCLUDED. — WARREN STREET. — ANECDOTE OF JOSHUA BOYLSTON, DEACON CLARK, MISS PRUDY HEATH, COLONEL PERKINS. — GODDARD AVENUE. — THE GODDARDS IN THE REVOLUTION. — A PATRIOTIC FAMILY. — COTTAGE STREET. — THE LEE PLACE 344

CHAPTER XVII.

CLYDE STREET. — NEWTON STREET — "PUTTERHAM." — THE CRAFT PLACE (NOW THE DENNY PLACE). — THE OLD SAWMILL. — SOUTH STREET. — ANCIENT HOUSE ATTACKED BY INDIANS. — JAMES GRIGGS. — THE KENDRICKS . . . 373

CHAPTER XVIII.

HIGH STREET CHURCH. — CHURCH OF OUR SAVIOUR. — GOSPEL CHURCH. — LOCAL INDUSTRIES 396

CHAPTER XIX.

A BRIEF SUMMARY OF THE MILITARY HISTORY OF BROOKLINE . 406

BROOKLINE SOLDIERS WHO LOST THEIR LIVES DURING OR IN CONSEQUENCE OF THE REBELLION 422

HISTORICAL SKETCHES

OF

BROOKLINE.

CHAPTER I.

EARLY SCENES, SETTLEMENTS, AND EVENTS. — SEPARATION FROM BOSTON. — OLD FAMILIES AND THEIR LANDS.

LOOKING westward from the hills of Boston in Governor Winthrop's time, Charles River Bay was spread at high tide, an unbroken sheet of water from Cambridge shore to Roxbury Neck. Our present Brookline lay in full view, with its wood-crowned heights, now Corey's and Aspinwall's hills, lifting themselves up against the sunset, and its green slopes and winding brooks lying between.

It was but two miles across the bay, and here the thriving colonists of Trimountain, " which was bare of wood except here and there in clumps," came in their boats for house timber, as their successors did for ship timber.

Here, too, they found " arable grounds and meadows," and soon availed themselves of them for pasturage. The early Shawmut settlers soon explored Charles River, and no doubt its tributary Muddy River, which was navigable as far as our present boundary line near Pond Avenue. Across the broad bay, the stealthy Indians in their birchen canoes, glided from their coverts along the woody shores of the two rivers, fishing perhaps where the Public Garden at present spreads its attractions; or startling a wood-cutter with the twang of an arrow aimed at a wolf, which howled where the steam whistle now shrieks. In the "forest primeval" which shaded the site of our beautiful Longwood, on a knoll in the centre of what the early settlers called "the great swamp," the Indians had one of their forts, or strongholds, and here probably were encamped "the ten Sagamores and many Indians," which gave Governor Winthrop his first occasion to mention the hamlet of Muddy River. The oft-quoted record reads thus, under date of 1632: —

"Notice being given of ten Sagamores and many Indians being assembled at Muddy River, the Governor sent Captain Underhill with twenty musketeers to make discoveries, but at Roxbury they heard that they were broken up."

The old fort, which remained an object of historic interest in a tolerable state of preservation until 1844-45, was built of palisades, inclosing about an eighth of an acre of ground in square form and surrounded by a ditch about three feet in depth, and a parapet three feet in height, with an opening or gateway on each side, one of which was toward the swamp. The residence of William Amory, Esq., is located upon the site of this fort.

The next notice of this place in "Winthrop's Journal," is in vol. i., p. 290, as follows: —

"In this year (1633), one James Everett, a sober, discreet man, and two others, saw a great light in the night at Muddy River. When it stood still, it flamed up and was three yards square. When it ran, it was contracted into the figure of a swine. It ran as swift as an arrow towards Charlestown and so up and down about two or three hours. They were come down in their lighter, about a mile ; and when it was over they found themselves carried quite back against the tide to the place they came from. Divers other credible persons saw the same light, after, about the same place."

The editor of the " Journal " in a note, says of this phenomenon : —

"This account of an ignis fatuus may easily be believed on testimony less respectable than that which was adduced, Some operation of the Devil, or other power beyond the customary agents of Nature, was probably imagined by the relators and hearers of that age ; and the wonder of their being carried a mile against the tide became important corroboration of the imagination. Perhaps they were wafted, during the two or three hours astonishment, for so moderate a distance by the wind. But if this suggestion be rejected, we might suppose that the eddy, flowing always in our rivers, contrary to the tide in the channel, rather than the meteor. carried their lighter back."

In 1633, " It was ordered that a sufficient cart bridge shall be made in some convenient place over Muddy River," which was the first bridge at the crossing of the present town boundary line.

A more substantial bridge of stone and gravel was built by the town of Roxbury in the following century.

In 1635, it was ordered " that the poorer sort of inhabitants, such as are members, and likely so to be " (of the church probably) " and have no cattle, have their proportion of planting ground, laid out at Muddy River . . . . those that fall between the foot of the hill and the water to have four acres upon a head, and those farther off to have five."

From ancient records it seems that grants of land were often made here in those early times to induce settlement.

On the 30th December, 1639: —

"It was agreed that five hundred acres be laid out at Muddy River for perpetual commonage to the inhabitants there and the town of Boston, to begin at Mr. Hibbons's lott, and so go into the countrey as the land will afford before any other allottments are layd out hereafter.

"A true Coppie as entered with the records of the Town of Boston.   Examined per
JOSEPH PROUT, *Town Clerk*."

In 1640, the boundary line between Muddy River and Cambridge was fixed, and has so remained; but the boundary between Brookline and Roxbury, and between Brookline and Boston, has been subjected to several changes.

In 1675, Wood, in his "New England's Prospect," alludes thus to this locality: —

"The inhabitants of Boston, for their enlargement, have taken to themselves farm houses in a place called Muddy River, two miles from their town,* where is good ground, large timber, and store of marsh land and meadow. In this place they keep their swine and other cattle in the Summer, whilst corn is on the ground at Boston; and bring them to town in the winter."

In 1686, the inhabitants of Muddy River hamlet petitioned for school privileges and the right to maintain them, and the following order was passed in compliance with their request: —

"That henceforth the said Hamlet be free from Town Rates to Boston, they henceforth maintaining an able reading and writing master."

This arrangement was gladly accepted, and the people

* Across the bay.

of the hamlet agreed to pay the schoolmaster £12 per annum, and tax the individuals who availed themselves of the school for the balance necessary for the support of the master, abating in part or wholly the school rates of the poor. This is the first entry upon the records of the town. Three men were annually chosen at the Boston town meeting to manage the affairs of the hamlet, which began to be called Brookline about this time, though still a part of Boston. A committee of three men was chosen to decide where the centre of the town was to be found, that the school-house might be located there, and they fixed upon the triangular piece of ground in Walnut Street, just west of the present Unitarian church. The town fathers of those days having "tasted the sweets of liberty," soon came to a vivid perception of the inconvenience of having their local affairs managed by Boston, and on the 11th of March, 1700, they presented a petition to be set off as a town by themselves, as follows : —

"*To his Excellency, the Governor, Council, and Assembly.*

"The humble petition of the Inhabitants of Muddy River. *Humbly Sheweth,* That they are a Hamlet belonging to Boston, have been lately settled there and sometime since in the year 1686 being grown to a good number of inhabitants represented to the Government then in being, praying to be acquitted from paying duties and taxes to the Town of Boston, being then willing to bear their own public charges of Bridges, Highwaies, and Poor, and were accordingly then released and ordered to maintain a Reading and Writing Schoole as the order annexed will show, which accordingly we have ever since done, and now further humbly pray that being grown to a greater number of good settled inhabitants we may be allowed a separate right to have Selectmen, and all other rights belonging to a Township, which may further encourage us as we are able to settle a minister and other benefits amongst us, and we shall ever pray.

SAMUEL SEWALL, JR.,	BENJAMIN WHITE,
THOMAS STEADMAN, SEN'R,	JOHN WINCHESTER, SEN'R,
THOMAS GARDNER, SEN'R,	SAMUEL ASPINWALL,
JOSEPH WHITE,	JOSIAH WINCHESTER."

This gave great offense to the town authorities, and a town meeting was called, the petition was read and the reasons therefor debated, which resulted in a negative vote, and moreover the laying on again of the town taxes, from which they had been for some years excused, though they did condescend to allow them a schoolmaster who should be appointed by the selectmen and paid out of the town treasury.

This, however, did not quiet the inhabitants of Brookline. In 1704 the subject was renewed, but no favorable action was taken, and in 1705 another petition was sent in, signed by thirty-two of the inhabitants, to the Assembly and Council, as follows:—

"*To his Excellency, the Governor, Council, and Assembly, in General Court convened. The humble petition of the inhabitants of Muddy River, sheweth.*

"That at a session of this honorable Court, held at Boston on 13 August, 1704, the said inhabitants exhibited their humble petition praying, that the said Muddy River might be allowed a separate village or peculiar, and be invested with such powers and rights, as they may be enabled by themselves to manage the general affairs of the said place. Which petition has been transmitted to the Selectmen of the Town of Boston, that they may consider the same; since which your humble petitioners, not having been informed of any objection made by the Town of Boston, aforesaid, we presume, that there is no obstruction to our humble request made in our petition.

"Wherefore we humbly beseech your Excellency, that this honorable Court will be pleased to proceed to pass an Act for

SEPARATION FROM BOSTON.

the establishing of the said place a separate village or peculiar, with such powers as aforesaid, and your petitioners shall ever pray.

SAMUEL SEWALL, JR.,
THOS. GARDNER,
BENJAMIN WHITE,
THOMAS STEDMAN,
JOHN WINCHESTER,
SAMUEL ASPINWALL,
ELEAZER ASPINWALL,
WILLIAM SHARP,
EDWARD DEVOTION,
JOSIAH WINCHESTER, JR.,
JOHN ELLIS,
JOHN WINCHESTER, JR.,
THOMAS WOODWARD,
—— HOLLAND,
—— GARDNER.
JOSEPH WHITE,
JOSIAH WINCHESTER,
JOHN DEVOTION,
JOSEPH GARDNER,
THOMAS STEDMAN, JR.,
JOHN ACKERS,
JOSIAH STEDMAN,
THOMAS GARDNER, JR.,
RALPH SHEPARD,
ABRAHAM CHAMBERLAIN,
PETER BOYLSTON,
JOHN ACKERS, JR.,
WILLIAM ACKERS,
BENJAMIN WHITE, JR.,
CALEB GARDNER,
JOHN SEAVER,
HENRY WINCHESTER."

The "prayer" of the above petition was granted on the thirteenth day of November, 1705, as appears by the following record of the town grants: —

"*Anno Regni Annæ Reginæ Quarte.*

" At a great and general Court for her Majesty's Province of the Massachusetts Bay, in New England, begun and held at Boston upon Wednesday, 13th May, 1705, and continued by several prorogations unto Wednesday, 24th October, following and then met 13th November, 1705.

" *In Council.*

" The order passed by the Representatives, upon the Petition of the inhabitants of Muddy River, a Hamlet of Boston, read on Saturday last,

" *Ordered,* That the prayer of the petition be granted; and the powers and privileges of a Township, be given to the inhabitants of the lands commonly known by the name of Muddy

River, the Town to be called BROOKLINE; who are hereby enjoined to build a meeting-house, and obtain an able Orthodox minister, according to the direction of the Law, to be settled amongst them, within the space of three years next coming.

"Provided, that all Common Lands, belonging to the Town of Boston, lying within the said bounds of Muddy River, not disposed of, or allotted out, shall still remain to the proprietors of said lands.

"Which order, being again read, was concurred, and consented to. JOSEPH DUDLEY.

"Taken from Mr. Addington's copy sent to the Town.
"A True Copy Examined by me,
ISAAC ADDINGTON, *Secretary.*
"Recorded by me,
"SAM'L SEWALL, JR., *Town Clerk.*"

Thus, the General Court and Governor Dudley, having taking the matter into their own hands, established our identity as a town. For a hundred and sixty-five years we believe no one was found who regretted the separation from Boston, or desired to relinquish the liberty of an independent town.

The old boundary line of the town, on the side next to Roxbury, came down what has till recently been called Village Lane, from the direction of Chestnut Street and the Lee place, and the lot known as the Oliver Whyte place was in Brookline, while the house lot of J. A. Guild and all the houses on that side of the street were in Roxbury. The line crossed the street at the present entrance of Pearl Street, and the brick blacksmith's shop and all the rest of the village below it were in Roxbury. The line followed the brook, now the sewer, and then all the windings and turnings of Muddy River till it met the corners of Boston and Cambridge in the channel. When Brookline Avenue was built, a person going from the corner, by the gas works, to the junction, would go in and out of Roxbury eight times. The "crooked things have been made (comparatively) straight," in this direction.

The town became a part of Norfolk County in 1793, and according to a survey in 1844 contained 4,695 acres.

The first census of the town on record, was, in 1790, 518 inhabitants; in 1800, 605; 1820, 900; 1840, 1,265; 1860, 5,164; 1870, 6,650.

The centre of the town was also the centre of population for many years, there being in 1796 thirty-eight houses above the church and school-house, and thirty-four below. In 1844, by a census taken by order of the selectmen, there were found eighty-eight houses and one hundred families above the centre of the town, and one hundred and twenty-four houses and one hundred and fifty-six families below; in the whole, two hundred and twelve dwelling-houses and two hundred and fifty-six families. All that part of Boston Highlands from Muddy River for a half mile or more east, including Parker's Hill and Heath Street, and what was on this side of Muddy River till it met the old Brookline boundary, was called "Roxbury Precinct."

In this area lived several families, whose lands lying along the borders and some of them partly in both towns, had many interests in common and whose histories are blended and identified with both. Among these were the names of Craft, Heath, Griggs, Wyman, Downer, and Brewer.

The old "Punch Bowl" Tavern was the nucleus around which "the village" gathered, partly in Brookline and partly in Roxbury, and from this as a starting point the various houses and families of interest, in former days, will be successively described.

CHAPTER II.

THE "PUNCH BOWL." — FIRST PUBLIC COACHES. — J. DAVENPORT. — THE "WHITE" HOUSE. — VILLAGE DOCTORS. — WYMAN AND DOWNER HOUSES.

FROM the first settlement of the town, until the Milldam was built, the present Washington Street was the only road to Boston in this direction, and the heavy teaming from the country towns west of us necessarily came through Brookline. There was an immense amount of travel of this kind, as there were no railroads then in existence, and thus the ancient Punch Bowl Tavern was a necessity of the times; here all the teams stopped for "refreshment for man and beast," and this old building as a nucleus, gathered around itself the village which took its name. Even to this day this place is remembered by old men in New Hampshire, Vermont, and the back towns of this State as "the Punch Bowl Village."

The original house, built by John Ellis long before 1740, was a two-story, hipped-roof house, to which, as increasing patronage made it necessary, the proprietor made additions from time to time by purchasing old houses in Boston and vicinity and removing them hither. The result was in the aggregate a curious medley of old rooms of all sorts and sizes, connected together in a nondescript manner and presenting an architectural style, which, if we might apply a geological term to it, we should call a *conglomerate*.

The rafters of the original house were cedar posts,

just as they came from the woods with the bark on. This old tavern and its outbuildings occupied all the space on the street from the brick blacksmith's shop, now occupied by J. Madore, to the provision store of Brown Bros. It was of a yellowish color, and had a seat running along the front under an overhanging porch, or rather projection of a part of the second story, where loungers congregated to discuss the news of the day. In front of it and near each end was a large elm tree; under the westerly one stood a pump. This tree and pump remained until within a few years, the other was long ago destroyed. The ancient sign, suspended from a high, red post, gave a name to the tavern and the village, and swung its hospitable invitation creaking in the wind for nearly a hundred years. The design was a huge bowl and ladle overhung by a lemon tree, resplendent with fruit, some of which lay around the bowl as if fallen from the tree.

Here the Selectmen of the town used to have an annual supper, and on one of these occasions the old building came near being destroyed by fire. They had sat round the table smoking, after the repast, and probably dropped fire upon the table-cloth, which was gathered up and thrust into a closet by a servant. Soon after retiring, the family were wakened by the smell of smoke, and flames arising from the closet burst through to the chamber overhead, where the landlord's children slept. The frightened children rushed out in their night clothes to the neighbors' houses; the night was bitterly cold, and the ground covered with ice, and but for the landlord's promptness and presence of mind, the whole establishment would have been speedily reduced to ashes. Without stopping to put on a single garment, just as he sprang from his bed, he gave the alarm and seized a bucket of swill which he dashed upon the burning mass in the closet, closed the doors carefully after him, and brought water from the pump, directed the labor of others who came with their buckets, and put the fire out and saved the building, though the flames actually reached the attic. There was at that time an engine in the village kept in a house which stood in what is now the front yard of the Oliver Whyte estate. It was owned by Brookline and Roxbury in common, as the south side of the street from Village Lane to the creek below Pond Avenue was then a part of Roxbury. The extent of the patronage of the old " Punch Bowl " may be roughly estimated from the fact that it was common for a row of teams to occupy the side of the street above and below the tavern, from what is now Harrison Place, to the gas works in a continuous line, while the men and horses were being fed and rested. The " Punch Bowl " was not patronized by this class alone, however, but was a famous place of resort for gay parties, not only from the surrounding towns, but even from Boston, and was much frequented by British officers just before the Revolution.

The mill-dam, the bridges, and the opening of the Worcester railroad, at last took all the business away from the old " Punch Bowl." It was bought by Mr. Isaac Thayer about 1833, and torn down. Much of the material was of solid oak, and was used in building nine houses which he erected on the site of the old buildings. These are all standing, including the four buildings between the brick blacksmith's shop and the brick house next to Lyceum Hall, the houses occupied by J. Darragh and J. Dustin, and the first three houses on the left in White Place.* These last were built on the site of the

---

* Since this was written some of these buildings have given place to new ones, and some have other occupants.

present stores of Russell, Brown, Doherty, and De Frees, and were afterwards moved to their present situation. The spot where Lyceum Hall stands was vacant for several years.

The first line of coaches which was established between Brookline and Boston, was owned by a Mr. Spurr. Perhaps we should have said the first public carriage, as there was but one, a sort of small stage which went to Boston and returned twice a day, and the rate of fare was fixed at twenty-five cents.

Mr. Spurr built and occupied the house now used as the Massachusetts Infant Asylum, and his stage started from the " Punch Bowl." This was about 1816 or 1817. For want of patronage it was discontinued after a year or two.

Perhaps if that generation had been less hardy or less energetic, Mr. Spurr's enterprise would have succeeded better, but some of the brave women of the times thought twenty-five cents altogether too much to pay the stage-driver, and so they walked to Boston, after their house-work was done, over Roxbury Hill and the Neck, made their purchases, and walked home with their parcels in their hands. The mother of one of our prominent citizens made a practice of doing this, though in possession of abundant means for riding, had she chosen to do so.

The New York mail stage passed through the town once or twice a week; the Uxbridge stage three times a week, but these did not accommodate Brookline travel. After a few years another line of Brookline stages was started, and with more or less success struggled along for several years; and then a regular stage from Brighton was established, which was driven by Mr. Sumner Wellman, a gentlemanly and accommodating man who soon won the respect of all his Brookline patrons.

When Mr. Wellman gave up driving, he was succeeded by Mr. B. W. Hobart, so long known as an affable conductor, and now station master at the Boston and Albany Railroad Station. There were other regular Brookline stages after awhile, which accommodated the town till the Brookline Branch Railroad was opened.

On the left or south side of the street as one enters the village from Boston, lay the Ward farm, for many years the property of John, Samuel, and Henry Ward. It remained a part of Roxbury till this family was nearly extinct, at least in name, in this vicinity, and was sold by the heirs to the Brookline Land Company in 1860. A part of the land and the old buildings remained in possession of Sylvester Kimball, who had married into the Ward family; but within a short time has been sold for house lots. It was a beautiful tract of land, finely watered and wooded, and during its existence as a farm cultivated with great care. It included nearly all the land from Pond Avenue to Chestnut Street, and once nearly all from Washington Street to Jamaica Pond, being a part of Governor Leverett's allotment.

Among the old places of interest in and about the village, was once an old chocolate mill. This was accessible from the street by the lane through what was lately the estate of S. Kimball, passing the old Ward house, lately burned. It was situated where the water finds its outlet from Willow Pond. There was a large pond there then, receiving surplus water from Jamaica Pond; also a dam and flume, parts of which are still to be seen. After some time, the old mill having ceased to be used for its original purpose, a forge was established here, and the water-power used to run a trip-hammer. An Englishman named Montague kept the place, and manufactured hoes and shovels. About the beginning of the last war with England, a Mr. Faxon of Roxbury hired this property, and cast cannon, which were used during the war.

The old flume is on the right of Pond Avenue, is well grass grown, and partially concealed by bushes; and the old dam has a row of willow trees growing upon it. The aqueduct subsequently built to convey Jamaica Pond water to Boston, took all the surplus water, thus reducing the pond on the Ward place, and destroying the water-power. The place has since undergone many alterations under the hands of the Brookline Land Company. Mr. Faxon, who made the cannon, removed his business to Roxbury, where he built the first stone building on "Faxon's Hill," so called, in front of the stone quarries. It was originally but one story high, and of its present length, but was subsequently carried up two or more stories.

On the street in the village, on the site of the house and yard of the Barnard place, stood until a few years ago, a long, old house, of the style called a "ten-footer." This house was originally a part of the barracks used by the Americans at the siege of Boston, and after the dislodgment of the British was bought by Mr. James Pierce, and removed from its location on Parker's Hill to this spot, where it stood till torn down by the late Mr. Barnard. Some excellent people, now passed away, and others still living in our town, were born beneath its roof.

Mr. Pierce was a native of Dorchester, and a brother of Rev. Dr. Pierce, and long a member of the choir of the First Church. Whether living in a house which had once served the Revolutionary soldiers as a barrack inspired him with patriotic fervor or not, we do not know, but when he was seventy years of age he walked to Concord, Mass., and back, on the occasion of the laying of the corner-stone of the battle monument, to hear Webster's oration, a distance of eighteen miles each way. Mr. Pierce died in 1826. His widow, a much beloved lady of the olden style, survived him several years.

As all the residents on that side of the street were citizens of Roxbury, they were obliged to send their children to its distant schools, and go there also to "Town Meeting." It was very inconvenient; and in the year 1844, Mr. J. Lyon and other citizens petitioned to be annexed to Brookline. The request was granted, and the town lines so adjusted as to include the whole village. There was no post-office in Brookline until after 1820. It is a little singular that the first Brookline post-office was kept in Roxbury, at the tailor's shop of Mr. Phippen, for two or three years. It was the building next west of the Metropolitan Railroad stable and car house.

After Mr. Phippen, the late Oliver Whyte, Esq., was postmaster; and the office was kept in the grocery store of Whyte & Sumner, in the building which was removed two or three years ago to make room for Whyte's Block ; and here it remained till 1840. Mr. Whyte's successor was S. S. C. Jones. Mr. Whyte also held the office of Town Clerk for over thirty years. He is still well remembered by all who knew him for his venerable presence and courteous manners. And here, in passing, we cannot forbear an allusion to his beloved and honored widow, who has so recently passed from among us. Long will her memory be green in the hearts of all who knew her ; and the recollection of her cheerful, unselfish, and beautiful old age, cheer and sustain others whose faces are turned toward the sunset, and who feel their steps growing tremulous as they approach the silent river.

Another of the venerable houses of the village, fast going to ruin, is the old house next east of the brick blacksmith's shop. It takes something like a flight of imagination to recall the time when this house and the one next it were attractive abodes; yet there are many who can remember when it was a pleasant family mansion, with fresh paint and green blinds, and a grassy yard in front inclosed with a neat white fence.

This house was probably built for Edward Devotion, who was a prominent man in the town, in the early part of the last century, as he moved hither from what is now known as "the old Babcock house," and died here in 1784.

The house was next occupied by Mr. Thomas Brewer, who was a blacksmith, and built the brick shop before the Revolution. In this old house Mr. Brewer lived for many years, and his children intermarried with other old Brookline families. Now, the very name is extinct in Brookline, as of many another old family. One member, a nephew, bearing the name of Thomas Aspinwall Brewer, still lives, a resident these many years in Macon, Ga. The old house, after the Brewers ceased to occupy it, passed into the hands of Mr. Lemuel Foster, who for many years carried on blacksmithing in the shop adjoining. He built the modern house on Walnut Street opposite Whyte's Block, and resided there several of the last years of his life.

Contemporary with these families was that of the Davenports, the elder Mr. D. having married a Miss Brewer. The old house at the entrance of Walnut Street was built by him, and his long life was passed there. Mr. Davenport was a tailor by trade; and on the site of the block next east of the Brookline House, so called, he had a store; at first, a sort of tailor's shop, with small wares in the dry goods line for sale. Mr. Davenport had no children, but adopted a nephew, who rejoiced in the Scripture name of Jerathmiel, but which was mercifully shortened into "Jerry," for common usage.

As the old gentleman grew feeble with advancing years, the nephew took the shop, which he stocked with dry goods and groceries, the tailor's business having been taken up by a Mr. Phippen, in the next building east. The store was an old gambrel roof building one story high, gable end to the street. In this building a singular accident occurred which is said to have caused the death of the elder Mr. Davenport. At that time, a slaughter-house was kept on the Ward place; and one day an ox, which had been struck but not killed, broke loose from the slaughter-house, rushed madly up the street and dashed into this store, knocking down the old gentleman and so injuring him that he never recovered from the effects, but died not long after.

Some years afterward, Mr. Jerry Davenport tore down the old store and built a modern two-story one which has since been remodeled to its present form. In front of the old store were two very large buttonwood trees, a pump, and a long watering-trough. Shade trees and plenty of fresh water by the way-side for man and beast, were a part of the good old customs that should never have been allowed to fall into disuse.

Jerry Davenport, as he was familiarly called, was as much one of the village institutions as the old "Punch Bowl." His ruddy face, erect figure, short steps, and ready jokes are well remembered, and also his twenty-seven years' courtship, his slyly-planned marriage so quickly detected, and the Calithumpian serenade which followed, making night hideous, from Heath Street to Corey's Hill. Neither will his sudden death be soon forgotten; nor the singular circumstance of his body being taken from the tomb a day or two after burial, and set upright in the coffin to be photographed. "Alas! poor Yorick."

The two buildings next west of the old grocery store above mentioned were, when new, occupied the one by Dr. Downer's family, the doctor having died, and the other by Mr. Hancock's family. A generation later there was intermarriage between these families. About the year 1819, two young men, Mr. J. Lyon and Mr. W. H. Brown, commenced business in the village — Mr. Lyon being a wheelwright, and Mr. Brown a harness-maker — in a shop which was built for them in the westerly end of the old " Punch Bowl " out-buildings, by Mr. Laughton, for many years the proprietor of this famous old tavern. When the time came for the destruction of these buildings, these young men removed their business — Mr. Brown to a new shop, next to Baker's present paint-shop, and Mr. Lyon to the opposite side of the street up the yard to the Hancock house, as it was then called, which he had hired and was occupying. Subsequently this house and the one now called the " Brookline House," became Mr. Lyon's property. Here he became widely known and well patronized in his business, and earned the reputation of making wheels that would "*never wear out*," so thoroughly was his work done. Mr. Lyon, after many years of faithful toil in Brookline, sold out and retired to Lancaster, Mass.*

Mr. Brown purchased the house at the foot of Village Lane of a Mr. Barry, a hatter, who was its original owner; and here he spent the remainder of his days. Mr. Brown was for many years identified with the First Parish, as a musician, before an organ was aspired to, and contributed his share unfailingly from Sunday to Sunday through summer and winter, in the stirring melody with which the old congregations worshipped.

* He died in February, 1873.

The old house now called the Brookline House has had a multitude of tenants, in various useful callings, in its better days, it being for several years the location of the post-office, under the care of Mr. S. S. C. Jones.

We will now retrace our steps a short distance, to the corner of Brookline Avenue. Before the Mill-dam was built, for nearly a hundred years there stood, in the rear of the present gas-works a dwelling-house, with a large yard in front of it; east of this, where the roadway is now, was a small school-house belonging to "Roxbury Precinct." The ground sloped down, till the grassy upland joined the marsh on this side of Muddy River, which was then from forty to fifty feet wide. In the rear of the dwelling-house above mentioned was a bit of orchard or garden place which sloped northward to the marsh, which was overflowed with deep water at every tide. This house, with all the land adjoining on both sides of Muddy River, was in ancient times the property of the Griggs family. As early as 1635, the name of George Griggs appears in the annals of Muddy River. From that time downward the name is constantly found in the records of the town.

On the opposite side of Muddy River, nearly opposite Heath Street, stood another ancient house which is barely recollected by some of the oldest inhabitants, and this was also the property of one of the Griggs families. George Griggs, the doctor previously mentioned, inherited the ancient house on the site of the gas-works, and built early in the last century, or at least before the Revolution, the old house, now for these many years a tenement house, and known sometimes as the "Tontine," but of late years as "the long house." The western half, with the ornamental portico over the front door, was afterward added by Dr. Downer. Dr. Griggs did not remove the old house which he had inherited, and at his death it became the property of his daughter. He lived to a great age, and died in the latter part of the last century.

A curious old paper, dated 1721, contains the autograph of George Griggs, who if he was the same who was afterwards the doctor, must have been quite a young man at that time. This paper is a bond or agreement between Joseph Craft, George Griggs, and William Heath (afterwards the General), to " build a dam ajoyning to Muddy River Bridge." This must have been where Washington Street crosses " the creek " or Muddy River, now the boundary line separating Brookline from Boston, as there was no other bridge over Muddy River at that time. The road was low, and the tide-water went far up the marshes and lowlands.

The Heath property lay along both marshes and uplands west and south of Heath Street, abutting upon what is now " the Ward farm," or Brookline Land Company's property. Where the Craft lands lay we are not informed, except that it included all that lay on both sides of the street, for some distance above and below the old house on Tremont Street, which bears the date of 1709 on the chimney.

George Griggs' part of the agreement read as follows: —

" In order to building a dam ajoyning to muddi River Bridge I Gorge Griggs of Roxbury do hereby offer and Ingage one half rod wide next sd Rode which shall be for Building a dam on and that I will pay one pound to the proprietors Besides my Equail proportion to aid in Building sd Dam provided the Northeron face of said Dam shall be made with a good stone wall four feet high so far as is needful to make a Dam."

" *February* 24, 1721. GEORGE GRIGGS."

It would be interesting to know whether this dam was ever built, and if so, when it was removed. The meadows south of the street were formerly flooded, and as before stated there was water power enough from Willow Pond to run a chocolate mill, and afterwards a trip hammer in a blacksmith's shop at the point where the brook flows from the pond. But the dam now surmounted by a row of willows, next Willow Pond, is not "ajoyning Muddy River Bridge," and we have sought in vain for information among the old inhabitants and old documents respecting it. The only reason for thinking of this dam in connection with Willow Pond, is that William Heath agrees in his part of the document that "the stones shall be taken out of the west end of my pasture Lying on the south side of the Great hill, taking all that is movable that I shall appoint." Perhaps the dam was eventually built thus far up the meadows, instead of "ajoyning Muddy River Bridge."

Dr. Geo. Griggs left one child, a daughter, who became the wife of Capt. Wm. Wyman; and the house and land now occupied by the Gas Company, including some land now covered by Brookline Avenue, some marsh land and many acres now on the Boston side of Muddy River, all originally belonging to this estate, were long known as the Wyman property. The descendants of this branch of the Griggs family are still in existence under various names.

Mary Griggs was very beautiful, and quite an heiress. A large tract of land belonged to her in Brookline and Roxbury, and much more in Brighton, Newton, and Needham. She married in opposition to the wishes of her parents, and lived an uncongenial and most unhappy life. It was by marriage with her daughter that Dr. Downer became connected with this family and its possessions.

The original Griggs house, which the old doctor would not have removed when it became untenable, was held with equal tenacity by Captain Wyman, who would neither sell, repair, nor destroy it; and it stood until it leaned over with age and fell piece by piece into the cellar. A gale of wind (some say the September gale of 1816) finished it. There are persons now living who can remember playing among the beams of it in their childhood.

When the Mill-dam was built and the Brookline branch of it opened, in 1821, it cut off Captain Wyman's yard. Afterwards a blacksmith's shop was built on the east corner of the avenue, which was after a number of years moved across the street into the lot now bordering on Pond Avenue. After Captain Wyman's death and the sale of his property, the old house now owned by the Gas Company was kept as a tavern for several years, with the sign of the Punch Bowl; but it had little except local patronage, and that of the lowest sort, and was finally given up.

The houses of Captain Wyman and Dr. Downer both originally set back further from the street than at present, as the widenings which have taken place from time to time have cut off the yards. Captain Wyman's house had cherry trees about it; and on the east side, before the street cut off his ground, there were green grass and flower-beds. Many persons can remember when "the Downer house" or "long house" had a broad green yard shaded by tall buttonwoods and two Lombardy poplars, while a beautiful elm was between the two houses. The whole village was beautifully shaded from one end to the other, until within thirty years, with fine large elms and buttonwoods.

Dr. Downer was a skillful surgeon, though a hard,

rough man. A story is related of him which proves that he was a man of mettle. On the day of the battle of Lexington, in returning home toward night he met with or overtook a straggling British soldier in the field. They had a hand-to-hand fight, which resulted in the doctor's pinning the poor fellow to the ground with his bayonet, though he plead for mercy.

For several years there was a brewery kept in one end of this old house, and an old malt-house stood on the opposite side of the street. After Dr. Downer's death, a Dr. Sylvan came to the village, and took up his residence in this same house. He is best remembered as "the rain-water doctor," as he professed to cure nearly all "the ills that flesh is heir to" by the use of rain-water. Like more modern quacks who deal in more dangerous, though quite as useless nostrums, he found plenty of dupes for two or three years; but at last public opinion became so excited against him that he was forced to take speedy leave of the town.

Lyceum Hall was built in 1841 by a stock company of Brookline gentlemen, and subsequently passed into the hands of Samuel A. Walker, its present owner. The post-office was removed here and kept for several years by different postmasters, and with the exception of a brief interval there has always been a well-kept grocery store in this building.

The hall was for several years quite a fashionable resort; and balls, concerts, and Lyceum lectures were well sustained here by the *élite* of Brookline.

Near the old elm which stood in front of this building a skeleton was once dug up in the street. It was found in a sitting posture facing the east, and was thought to have been an Indian. This was during the excavations made by the Boston Water Company for the laying of the main pipe in 1848. The bones, which were much broken by the workmen who removed them, were delivered to Dr. Edward A. Wild.

The fact of this solitary skeleton being found under this great tree, would seem to indicate that the tree itself was of great age, and of all the fine trees which once ornamented the village this was the only one which was allowed to die a natural death, all the rest having been ruthlessly destroyed when in full vigor.

An old landmark, quite recently removed, was the double house between Boylston and Walnut streets, on the site of Whyte's block. Its original owner was Mr. Thomas White (the family name was originally spelt White, but was changed by one branch of the family to Whyte). The estate comprised not only all the buildings and land bounded by three streets in the village, but also all the meadow, between Boylston Street and the north side of White Place, and west from Washington Street nearly to Dr. Shurtleff's line, and much woodland elsewhere.

The original house was the easterly building, and at first fronted on Washington Street; a grocery store was kept for many years in the lower story, and dwelling apartments on the second floor. A long shed extended from the east side of the store as far out as the great elm, which was cut down two years ago when the block was built. Here was a pump in an excellent well of water.

The other part of the house extending westward was built by Mr. White for his daughter, who resided there for a while, but subsequently that branch of the family left town, and Mr. White occupied it himself, having let the store and apartments over it.

The store was kept for many years after Whyte and Sumner, by Mr. George W. Stearns, the father of Messrs.

John G. and George W. Stearns of this town, and who is remembered as an honest, kind, and most worthy citizen. After Lyceum Hall was built and the grocery opened in that building, this old house was remodeled, the shed and pump removed, and a large and beautiful yard, adorned with shrubbery and vines, occupied the place of the old out-buildings. The village probably was in its best attire from 1840 to 1855, or thereabouts; the old houses were all in good condition, and the yards tastefully kept, while the more modern houses were then so new as to look fresh and agreeable. In the front or easterly part of this house lived for several years Dr. Joseph Hobbins, a most skillful English physician, who won the warm regard of his numerous patients. He was succeeded by Dr. Wm. Dexter, who afterwards removed to Jamaica Plain.

Another physician, a Dr. Barrus, lived for several years in the old house called " the Brookline House ; " and in more recent times Dr. E. A. Wild, now more widely known as " the General," was for a while a boarder in the house of Mr. Lyon.

Our present excellent Dr. Francis was located at the entrance to Walnut Street during the first three years of his practice in Brookline; so that until within a comparatively few years there has been most of the time some physician in the town below the railroad bridge.

To return to the White estate. After the death of the venerable widow, who lived to an advanced age in the westerly part of the house, the property was let to any tenants who would occupy it without repairs, year after year, till some minor heirs should come of age ; and thus deteriorating from year to year it became an unsightly nuisance, till it was separated into two sections and carried off, one part up Boylston Street and the other down to " the marsh."

It would have been a blessing to present and future generations if some wealthy and philanthropic person had bought the whole area occupied by these buildings and the stable and blacksmith shop, and bequeathed it to the town to be forever kept open as a public common. A breathing space for the neighborhood and a perpetual play-ground for the children, in any growing suburb like this town, thus secured, would be a nobler donation for all coming time than a hundred thousand dollars to Harvard College. Is this thing never done by individuals because towns might do it but will not? Whoever provides a public play-ground for the boys is a benefactor to his race. Had ten such little parks in the course of a century past been secured to the densely populated portions of New York, or three or four to the north part of Boston, with grass, shade trees, and drinking fountains of pure water, who can doubt that the health, taste, and morals of the city would have been better promoted than by all the labors of the Tract Society?*

Before the railroad was built, or White Place projected, there stood on the site of Guild's block two small ancient houses, fronting on Boylston Street. One of these must have been one of the oldest houses in town. The sills were great oaken timbers from which there was a step *down* into the rooms on crossing the threshold, without entry or porch.

It was owned and occupied by Major Edward White, the father of Thomas White, and ancestor of many Brookline people of the same name, though spelled differently by some descendants. He was major of militia in King George's service, and was an honored citizen of this town in those old days when Massachusetts was a colony.

* Since the above was written this town has secured two pieces of ground for public play-grounds.

Major White owned three other houses near the one he occupied, all of which long since ceased to exist. One stood on the ground where Mr. Royal Woodward's house now stands, one where the shop of Beals & Jones stands, and one about where De Frees' dry goods store is located. The Major finally built and occupied, until his death in 1769, the house on Washington Street lately occupied by the family of our late respected townsman, James Bartlett. We return to the one first spoken of, on the site of Guild's block.

This old house was occupied in Revolutionary times by a branch of the Aspinwall family. The other house was wholly remodeled about fifty years ago; and Mr. Elisha Stone, so long the undertaker and sexton of the town, occupied it for many years.

Behind this house were two very large trees and a well, with a curb and a "sweep," the long pole reaching high up into one of the trees. Both these houses, quite rebuilt, are now in White Place, the fourth and fifth on the left side. A little steep driveway went down from Boylston Street to Washington Street between these houses and the row of trees which extended eastward, of which now there is but one left, — the old buttonwood at the end of the bridge.

Under this row of trees were the hay-scales, the platform on a level with Boylston Street, and doors below on the north side. These mysterious doors were seldom open when we were straying by in our childhood, but when they were, we used to pause and look at the dark recess underneath from the opposite side of the street with something of the same feelings with which we might now approach the portals of the Mammoth Cave.

The meadow which we have before alluded to, which is now divided by the railroad, and includes White Place and Kerrigan Place and all the houses on the north side of Boylston Street from Guild's Block to the last mentioned place, was, until about the time the railroad was projected, a green and open field. The beautiful brook which is now walled up alongside the railroad, then wound through grass and wild flowers at " its own sweet will," and coming out from the meadow through two arched openings in a low stone wall it spread itself along beside the street for a space at least twenty feet wide and more than twice as long, and then flowed under the road through a broad culvert. On the east side, where it came out, exactly where Mahoney's building stands, it was covered by the engine-house which the town built, after the old one at the foot of Walnut Street was torn down. This house was destroyed by an incendiary fire more than twenty years ago. The brook as it stretched along beside the road over a stony bottom, was clear and not very deep, and its sparkling water invited the great droves of cattle which came from Brighton on market days; and few drivers were so heartless as to hurry them through without allowing them to drink their fill. Often in our childhood we paused to note the eagerness with which they would plunge in at the upper end of this grand watering-place and their reluctance to leave it at the other. The railroad bridge and the street covers all the space the brook thus occupied, and the driveway to the depot is where the old roadway used to be.

The meadow before alluded to included a piece of grassy upland on the north side where now is White Place; and here was one ancient little cottage, a quaint affair, half chimney and fire-place; it sat far back from the street and was approached by a grassy path through a turn-stile. This was one of Major Edward White's houses, and like the one he occupied had a well with a sweep under an elm tree. It was whitewashed and half covered with woodbine. When White Place was planned this picturesque old cottage was removed and remodeled, its enormous fire-place and chimney furnishing bricks enough to build a basement story ; and it now stands, a commonplace affair, in the rear of Mahoney's building in front of the depot.

The brook in those days having plenty of room, often turned the meadow into a temporary lake, without intruding into cellars and basements as of late, and in winter it made a fine skating-place for the boys. Alas, for the necessity which has turned this once beautiful stream into a common sewer. " To what base uses do we come at last! "

CHAPTER III.

THE DEPOT GROUND. — THE DAVIS ESTATE. — SAMBO. — DANA TAVERN. — TOM COOK. — THE BAPTIST CHURCH.

ON the spot where the railroad depot now stands, and on the vacant ground north of it, formerly stood the large square house now in the rear of the Colonnade Building. This house was built some time in the latter part of the last century by Mr. John Howe, father of the late John Howe, Esq., of this town. For many years Mr. Howe had a tannery south of his house, but he subsequently gave up this business and went into the lumber trade in Boston. The tannery was removed, and a garden occupied the place of it, until the place was invaded by the railroad.

The house stood upon a high bank shaded by large elm trees, of which the only vestige remaining is the forlorn stump covered with woodbine, in front of the depot.* It was a very pleasant situation, and through the garden a small branch of the brook flowed. Here were fine fruit trees, and currant and gooseberry bushes.

The railroad tracks, the bare space south of them, and a part of Mahoney's building, cover the site of this garden, running back to where the turn-table is located. In front of the house the bank projected beyond the fence into the street, and as it was high and narrow on the top, outside the fence, no child passing by could resist the temptation to go up one side and down the other. A clump

* Even this has since been removed.

of wild rose bushes grew on the top, outside the fence, and lilacs within. So a narrow little path was worn there, year after year, by many childish feet that have since grown old in treading our streets, or perchance wandered into steeper ways uncrowned with roses. This bank was removed to widen the sidewalk many years ago.

After Mr. Howe's day the house was let for so many years to a Mr. Marshall, that it became known as "the Marshall house" for a long time. Since then it has had countless tenants, among whom were the late David R. Griggs, Mr. Harrison Fay, and Mr. Twitchell, all of whom occupied it while their own houses were being erected.

The house was moved to its present location when the railroad was laid ont. The alterations in that vicinity have been so great, that could any former resident of Brookline, who had not seen the place since the railroad and the bridge were built, be brought unexpectedly to a view of it, he would not have the faintest idea of his whereabouts.

On April 24, 1847, the railroad was completed to this village and opened for travel. On that day, by the generous courtesy of the directors of the Boston and Worcester Railroad, fourteen trains of cars were run *free*, and more than two thousand persons passed over the road. No accident occurred even of the slightest nature.

An account of the opening was written by S. A. Walker, then a resident of Brookline, for the "Boston Journal," in his usual glowing style.

Mr. B. W. Hobart, who was then well known to the people of Brookline, was appointed conductor, an appointment which gave general satisfaction, and which office he filled till appointed to a more lucrative situation on the long route from Boston to Springfield. The railroad was not continued beyond the depot in the village for several years, and therefore there being no necessity for a bridge, the old road and the watering-place beside it remained as we have before described it, a few years longer, excepting that White Place was begun, by the removal there of three houses which formerly stood below the depot.

The land north of the depot on the east side of the street as far north as Aspinwall Avenue, had not a single house upon it until within forty years, except the ancient house between Andem and Harrison places, nearly opposite the Catholic Church.

Probably few people among the present generation know anything of the great age and interesting history of this house, as, though in apparently good condition, it is one of the three oldest houses in town, dating back at least two hundred years.

In the early days, when this town, then called "Muddy River Hamlet," was apportioned out among certain residents of Boston, a large tract was assigned to the Rev. John Cotton, the second minister of Boston. This included all the land from Muddy River as far west as where the estate of Mr. George B. Blake is now, and perhaps even farther; bordering on what is now Harvard Street, then called the Newtown Road (Cambridge being called Newtown), and on what is now Walnut Street, called for many years "the Sherburne Road." This great tract of land the Reverend John Cotton probably never used for aught else than a cow pasture, as there is no evidence that he ever made this place his residence; but he left this whole property to his heirs, Rowland and Thomas Cotton. Deacon Thomas Cotton built the ancient house now standing, above mentioned, about two hundred years ago, and subsequently sold it to Deacon Ebenezer Davis, and took his departure to the then wilds of Connecticut. Deacon Davis was the son of

Ebenezer and Rachel Davis, who emigrated from Wales to this country in the latter part of the seventeenth century, and settled in Roxbury. The parents died young, and left the farm to their son, whose only sister, Rachel, kept his house, though but a child of thirteen. Subsequently Mr. Davis married a sister of Moses White of Brookline, and Moses White himself married Rachel. With this house was also transferred to Deacon Davis all the land from Harvard Street to Walnut Street, as far west as Cypress Street and School Street, though School Street was only a lane, and Cypress Street not even that. Whether Major Edward White, spoken of previously, purchased of the Cotton heirs, or of Deacon Davis, we have not been able to ascertain, but he was contemporary with the first two generations of Davises, and his land was a corner of this great estate. Deacon Ebenezer Davis had a son of the same name, and this son still another, so that the name was perpetuated through three generations in this same house. The next descendant who inherited the homestead was Robert S. Davis, the father of the present bookseller of that name, now a resident in Cypress Place.

During his lifetime, about seventy years ago, the house was thoroughly renovated and repaired, and the immense chimneys taken down, by which ample space was obtained for a pantry and bedroom. It would seem as if it must have been necessary for every man to own a brick-yard in those ancient times, when as many bricks were put into one stack of chimneys as would build a small modern house. Where they found clay enough, workmen enough, and time enough to accomplish such solid results, must forever remain among the mysteries.

Besides the chimneys which were rebuilt, this old house had also another built up from the ground, wholly outside of the house, like a buttress, so that only the great fire-place opened into a room, in the style still to be seen in Maryland and Virginia. These chimneys were all laid in clay, instead of lime, and became unsafe as it crumbled with age, and when their reconstruction became necessary other alterations were involved, and the buttress-like chimney was dispensed with. Behind, and a little south of the house, was a large, long barn which in comparatively recent times was divided, one half being used to build the house with, which is now the next in the rear of the Davis house and occupied by Mr. Tyler, the other half was moved near to the depot, and was lately torn down. On the southeast, the brook now the sewer, formed the boundary of the orchard, and was so excellent a fishing place for smelts, that as we have been informed by one who well remembers, it was not uncommon for half a bushel of these little fishes to be taken there in a morning before breakfast.

Deacon Ebenezer Davis was, according to all accounts, an excellent farmer, and his estate was adorned with splendid peach and cherry orchards, to say nothing of apple trees in great variety. He also ventured upon an experiment in horticulture, for those times, and raised the first musk-melons that were ever offered for sale in Boston market. It was a success, and gave him such a notoriety that his portrait was painted *with a musk-melon under his arm*. The picture was subsequently carried to England, where it is still preserved in a collection. Under it is written, "An American Farmer." A unique ornament would the portrait of this ancient farmer of Brookline be for our Public Library, or our Town Hall. In the rear of the old deacon's house and barn was a little house for negro quarters in the old days when slavery existed in Massachusetts; and one old negro named Sambo, figured for many years in the experiences of this household. The deacon resigned his office in the First Church in 1770, and died in 1775, at the age of seventy-two. Sambo continued to live in the family with the son and grandson of the deacon. There are many amusing anecdotes of his sayings and doings still extant among the descendants of the family. He seems to have been one of those curious combinations of wit and stupidity which are occasionally to be met with.

His master gave him a patch of ground to plant and cultivate as he pleased for his own profit. Sambo planted a goodly supply of beans, and when they came up, in true bean style, Sambo went to work, and with infinite labor re-set the whole of them with the beans under ground where he thought they belonged. He was the butt of so many jokes for this exploit that he was rather sensitive upon the subject of beans afterwards.

But Sambo had all the laugh on his own side sometimes. Some blacksmiths, one first of April, seeing Sambo coming along the road from Boston, walking beside his team, threw a hot horseshoe into the road, expecting to find a victim. But the old fellow saw it fall and knew the joke was meant for him, so he quietly took his shovel from his load and tossed the horseshoe upon the top, and went on his way chuckling over the fact that they "did n't fool 'dis darkey dat time."

At another time this old servant accompanied the deacon to Boston where he called to pay a lawyer who had transacted some business for him. Mr. Davis overpaid the lawyer, who, greatly to Sambo's indignation, refused to return any change, saying that he never returned money in such cases. There seemed to be no help for it and the matter was dropped, but Sambo revolved the subject over and over in his thick head, and "bided his time."

Some months afterwards he carried a load of melons to market, and as he stood retailing them on the street who should appear as a purchaser but this very lawyer. He bought a water-melon, worth ninepence, and gave Sambo a dollar, which he serenely pocketed. "Where's my change?" asked the lawyer, seeing it was not forthcoming.

"Hi!" said Sambo, "you gib massa no change, I gib you none," and he brought home the dollar.

Sambo lived in celibacy, and died when more than ninety years of age. It was winter when he died, and the ground was covered with deep snow. His body was carried to the Brookline Cemetery upon a pung, and laid near his old master.

Long afterwards, when the old chimneys were taken down, a stout silver spoon, marked with a quaint old " E. D." was found, with the handle bent double, and Sambo's agency in the matter was strongly hinted at by those who knew his faults as well as his virtues. " *Requiescat* " Sambo.

The third Ebenezer Davis who occupied the old house, married into the Aspinwall family, and had a son born there of the same name, who many years ago removed to the State of Maine, where he still lives.

Another son, I. Sumner Davis, was a minister, and still another, Thomas Aspinwall Davis, was for some time Mayor of Boston. Of him more will be said hereafter.

The son Robert Sharp Davis, was named for two ancestors of the same name on the maternal side, who had distinguished themselves in the old French and Indian wars. He married a granddaughter of one of our old Revolutionary patriots, Phinehas Stearns, of Watertown, who was one of the famous Boston tea-party. The son of this marriage, who bore the name of P. Stearns Davis, in honor of his plucky old ancestor, was born in the old house, and brought up in Brookline schools. He was sent elsewhere to finish his education, and then returned to his native town till his marriage, after which he resided in Cambridge.

When the Rebellion broke out, the blood of the brave old heroes burned in his veins and he could not rest. Day and night the conviction of duty was upon him, till finally a reluctant consent was wrung from those who loved him best, and he left home and a circle of devoted friends, for the battle-fields of Virginia. His honorable record as Colonel of the Massachusetts 39th Regiment prepared the way for his promotion, and he was soon distinguished as a Brigadier-general. On the 11th of July, 1864, he was killed by a rebel shell in front of Petersburg, and his distinguished name was added to the list of heroes and martyrs for liberty. On the day he took his farewell of his aged mother, she said to him, " My son, how can you *want* to go ? " He replied, " Mother, if I should live to see the end of this war *without* going and doing my whole duty for my country, I should never rest." And he went with her blessing.

His venerable mother still lives among us in an honored and beautiful old age.* May the memory of what he was, ever be the consolation of all who are bereft of his loving care.

Another descendant of Deacon Ebenezer Davis, who deserves honorable mention, was Mr. Isaac Davis, born in the old house, and a resident there till his early manhood, when he took up his abode in Roxbury, on land which he inherited from his father, and to which he added by purchase.

* This much beloved lady died May 4, 1874, at the age of nearly 89 years.

This worthy farmer was Town Treasurer of Roxbury for thirty years, and Representative to the State Legislature for seventeen years. Miss Sarah Davis, a missionary to Burmah, a sister of General Davis, also born in the old house, will be mentioned in connection with the Baptist Church.

A few years after the death of Mr. Robert S. Davis, Senior, the family mansion, and what remained of the land near it which had not been disposed of to other purchasers, was sold by the heirs to Mr. Moses Andem, who resided here for several years.

After Mr. Andem's death, the house was occupied by Captain Isaac Taylor, till his present handsome residence was completed. Until this time the spacious yard in front of the old house remained ornamented with trees and shrubbery, and a straight gravel walk, bordered with the stiffest of fir trees, led from the street to the front door. Soon after, the two houses which now stand in front of it were built, and the old house was quite excluded from a view of the street.

From that time to the present it has been occupied by various families, two at a time.

We will now cross the street to follow another branch of the Davis family. A son of Deacon Ebenezer Davis, born 1765, by the name of Benjamin, inherited as his portion of his father's large domain, all the land on the west side of Washington Street, beginning at the north side of White Place, and extending on that side as far as Cypress Street. He had built for his own use the house long known as "Mr. Benjamin Davis's old house," and married Elizabeth Baker of Roxbury, in 1791. On the opposite side he owned all the land from where Panter's Building stands to School Street, extending across from Harvard Street to Washington Street. This was a high hill sloping down to the three streets above named.

As new residents came to town one lot after another was sold off it, which we shall allude to hereafter.

This Mr. Davis, like his father, was a farmer. South of his house, where the shop of the Kenricks now stands, was an immense elm tree, said to be as large as the famous Aspinwall elm. This tree was cut down, sorely to the regret of Mrs. Davis, because it shaded a desirable garden spot. Afterwards a row of elms which sprang from the seed of the old tree, grew along beside the wall; and one which Mrs. Davis set out with her own hands grew to be the great elm which was cut down, on the corner of Davis Place, when the block of stores was to be built. The tree was not only the chief ornament of the neighborhood, but a grateful shade in a hot and dusty place, and its destruction was a public loss.

On the piece of ground above alluded to, was set out a peach orchard, which remained until within the recollection of the present Mr. B. B. Davis, his son, who with his own hands cut down the old peach trees, some of which were a foot in diameter, and over thirty feet in height. The same gentleman, to whom we are indebted for much valuable information, informs us that in his school-days there was such an abundance of peaches of fine quality raised in Brookline, that the boys had a standing permission to go into the orchards daily and carry off all they could eat, loading their caps and pockets, and that even then the hogs were turned in to devour the quantities of fruit which were left on the ground.

If by the result of any subtle chemical analysis of the soil, a happy experiment in horticulture could produce such an abundance again, there could possibly be found enough of the " rising generation " to take care of them all without calling in the swine.

The first Benjamin Davis died suddenly while in the prime of life, of lockjaw, caused by a cold taken by sitting upon the ground to rest during over-fatigue from mowing. His son, of the same name, occupied the house which he inherited; and thus three generations of the same name occupied this house, as was the case with the one on the east side of the street.

In Revolutionary times, a part of a company of Connecticut soldiers, who assisted in the siege of Boston, were quartered in this house, much to the discomfort of the excellent housekeeper, who used to tell in after years of their cutting up their rations of pork *on her front stairs.* The soldiers were subsequently removed to the barracks on Parker's Hill.

A few years since Mr. Davis removed to his present residence, and the old homestead was sold.

Mr. Davis is too well known to need mention in this place; yet we trust one may allude, without apology, to his services as a selectman of the town; and he will ever be identified in the annals of the Handel and Haydn Society as one of its most enthusiastic members during the greater part of his long and useful life. During fifty years, Mr. Davis was at his stand in Faneuil Hall Market three hundred times a year.

In this neighborhood there stood another ancient house, when as yet the houses of the two Davises, on either side, were the only other dwellings fronting on the Square.

This building stood upon the site of a part of Panter's building, Hunting's grocery store,* and Mrs. West's house. It was known as "Dana's Tavern," and was kept for many years by Mr. Jonathan Dana. It was a large gambrel-roofed house, with a row of sheds and out-buildings behind it reaching nearly across from Washington Street to Harvard Street.

* Now Howe's furniture store.

This tavern was a great resort for country produce dealers, but never had as large a local patronage, or entertained as much fashionable company as the Punch Bowl, — as the latter had a large dancing-hall, which the Dana Tavern had not.

The easterly end of this building had a shop attached to it, in which Mr. Peter Parker, the original owner of the building, had a shop in which he worked at shoe-making. His son, John Parker, born in that house, became a very wealthy man, and his name is still perpetuated by "Parker's Hill," on which he lived, and "Parker Street," which passed his house. He held important and very successful contracts under the United States government during the second war with England.

There is an amusing incident connected with the old tavern which may not come amiss in this part of our record. There was a notorious thief, well known in Brookline and the adjoining towns, by the name of Tom Cook. He had many eccentricities, among which was a habit of stealing from the rich to give to the poor. In horse-stealing he was specially expert. He was frequently arrested, tried, convicted, and sentenced to short terms of imprisonment at "the Castle" (now Fort Independence), that being then the common prison for all offenders in Boston and vicinity.

On one occasion Tom stole a goose from a countryman's wagon, which was under the shed, at Dana's Tavern; not, however, with generous designs for any of his poor *proteges*, but for the satisfying of his own appetite. But as an uncooked goose would be about as unsatisfactory as no goose at all, Tom resorted to the old school-house — school not being in session — to cook and devour it. The school-house was in what is now School Street, at the corner of Prospect Street, then concealed from observation on the east by a high hill. The nearest house was the great square old house on Harvard Street, which was removed two or three years ago from the corner of Harvard Avenue. It was occupied by Esquire Sharp, the School Committee and Justice of the Peace. The Squire with his *sharp* eye on the interests of the town, discovered a smoke arising from the school-house chimney, and as " where there is smoke there must be fire," he proceeded to reconnoitre, and caught Tom in the very act of roasting the goose. Laying the strong hand of the law upon him, he made him confess where he got the fowl, and march back with it, under his own escort, to the tavern ; and before the assembled inmates of the bar-room, gave him his choice to take, then and there, a public *whipping*, or be tried and sent to the Castle. Tom considered briefly, and decided to *take the whipping*.

The countrymen agreed, and flourished their long whips upon him with such vigor, that Tom's appetite for roast goose was abated in a summary manner, and the punishment proved more effectual than his various sojourns at the Castle.

The same causes which tended to reduce the " Punch Bowl," caused the Dana Tavern to be discontinued as a public-house, and for several years it was let as a tenement house.

It was destroyed by fire in January, 1816. It was in the night ; and Benjamin Bradley, afterward the owner of " Bradley's Hill," saved the life of a woman and child by mounting a long ladder and taking them from an upper window.

Let us hope this good deed was set down to his account.

In front of the old Dana Tavern, on ground that is now Harvard Square, there stood for many years the only hay-scales in the place. (This was prior to the days of those alluded in the previous pages.) These were placed there by Dr. Aspinwall, Senior. They presented almost exactly the appearance of a gallows, there being a vertical beam with a horizontal one extending from it. To weigh a load with this clumsy contrivance the horses were detached, the wheels chained, and the wagon and its contents lifted bodily off the ground by the use of fifty-six pound weights successively applied till the result was reached. How they ascertained the fractional parts of fifty-six pounds we are not informed. This apparatus may have been useful but could hardly have been ornamental to the neighborhood.

With the exception of the hay-scales the ground formerly occupied by the tavern and out-buildings remained vacant for several years after the fire. It was owned by the heirs of Jonathan Dana, one of whom was a minor child living in Maine, the other a youth following the sea. The property was of course under guardianship.

In the year 1827, the few Baptists living in Brookline began to hold meetings in private houses in this neighborhood. There had been for several years before, gatherings of persons calling themselves " New Lights," who mostly met in the upper part of the town, who drew in all who for any reason had lost interest in the old or First Church. There were many shades of belief among these people, some of whom came out on the strong ground of Orthodoxy, and connected themselves with the churches of that faith at Brighton or Roxbury, while others became Baptists, and joined the church of Father Grafton at Newton, or the churches at Roxbury or Cambridge.

The meetings held by the Baptists were soon too fully attended to be accommodated in private houses, and they began to think of securing a piece of ground on which to build a chapel.

But the spirit of the times was averse to religious toleration, and the old animus which drove Quakers behind carts in Boston, and banished Baptists to Rhode Island, had not wholly died out; and an opposition was raised which aimed to prevent the success of the enterprise, if possible.

The principal movers in the Baptist interest were Deacons Elijah and Timothy Corey, Deacon Thomas Griggs, David Coolidge, and Elijah Corey, Junior. This committee were desirous of securing the land owned by the Dana heirs, and after some trouble and a visit to Eastport, finally succeeded in hiring on a three years' lease that part of the land which belonged to the heir in Maine. They in the mean time had their timber got out for a chapel, and all ready to put together, hoping that when the other heir returned from sea they should be able to get possession of the remainder of the land.

The chapel was raised in the early part of 1828, and occupied in March as a place of worship, greatly to the surprise of the opposition, who little imagined how energetically their Baptist neighbors were at work. It scarcely seems credible, yet it is true, that a wealthy gentleman then residing in town, whose zeal for his own sect was more active than his love for his neighbor, actually sent his carriage and horses regularly to the door of the Baptist Chapel, at evening service, to convey to Brighton to the Congregational meetings, any who could be induced to go.

In the mean time the heir returned from sea, and the guardian purchased for himself the much desired residue of the land.

On the 5th of June, 1828, thirty-six individuals, eleven

males and twenty-five females, were publicly organized as a church. The congregation at once became so large that their little new chapel would not hold them, and steps were soon taken to build a church. The five gentlemen above mentioned agreed to build it at their own expense, and each give a certain percentage of the whole cost, whatever it might be.

Deacon E. Corey pledged forty per cent., Deacon T. Corey and Deacon Griggs each twenty per cent., and the others each ten. The church was built at a cost of about six thousand dollars; a few friends who had moved in gave from ten to a hundred dollars each, and the work was paid for. But there was no room for sheds, and hardly room enough to walk around the church on the west side, on their own ground which they had now bought.

At last the owner of the much desired piece of land, seeing that the church was built, signified his willingness to sell for a sufficient bonus.

Deacon Corey offered fifty bushels of corn, in addition to what was asked in money, and his offer was accepted. The land was secured, the sheds built, a strip west of them now in Mr. Panter's yard was sold to Mr. Holden, the next owner on that side, and thenceforward the Baptist ship sailed in smooth water.

The meeting-house was dedicated November 20, 1828. But the little chapel stood in front of it, and the gallows-like hay-scales in front of that. The hay-scales were bought and taken down, the chapel moved to the rear of the church and altered over into a parsonage; it still stands with additions and improvements, next south of the present church. The green in front of the church was fenced and planted with trees, and soon became a very attractive spot.

THE BAPTIST MEETING-HOUSE.

The meeting-house had a brick basement for a vestry, partially under ground, and was entered by a door from the side next Harvard Street.

The building was painted white on the outside, but inside it was unpainted and uncarpeted, except the pulpit and front of the gallery. The pulpit being white, had a green blind behind it as a back-ground, and the reading-desk was draped with red damask in folds which were hung with tassels like a fringe. The counting of these tassels beguiled many a weary juvenile who could not appreciate the strong doctrine on which the seniors were fed. The gallery, on the southerly end over the vestibule, was occupied by a volunteer choir, of which Mr. David Coolidge was for many years the leader, while his daughter was "head singer," among the female voices. The instrumental music was furnished by a bass-viol, or sometimes a violin, in the hands of an eccentric old man by the name of Humphrey, and irreverent urchins were only too ready to laugh at the sawings and scrapings of what they termed " Daddy Humphrey's fiddle."

The house was heated by a square box-stove, the funnels extending over each aisle and hung with little tin pails to catch the drip of the steam generated by the wood fire.

In the vestibule hung a frame in which from time to time the " publishments " of parties about to marry were hung for three weeks, to be read by all who chose to avail themselves of the interesting information.

In the year 1830, the Rev. Joseph Driver was settled as the first pastor. For some reason his stay was short, and he was succeeded the following year by Rev. Joseph A. Warne, an Englishman, who was said to be " mighty in the Scriptures."

Sixty-five persons were added to the church during the

six years of his pastoral labors. Mr. Warne had an acquaintance, an Englishman, living in another town, who was something of an organ-builder, and he was very desirous that his friend should have an opportunity to exercise his skill on behalf of his parish. Accordingly he built a small organ (which proved to be a miserable affair), and Mrs. Warne was organist. Mr. Humphrey's bass-viol was banished to the vestry, where he had abundant opportunity to use it. This old man invariably carried with him to church a good-sized round bundle, in a red pocket-handkerchief. It lay upon the seat beside him and was carried away by him to his home after service. What it contained was a mystery to the youngsters which was never explained.

Mr. Warne was an irritable man and very abrupt in speech. On one occasion when his friend's organ gave a prolonged squeal instead of the desired harmony, he called out to his wife across the church, " Emma, stop that organ! It makes me nervous!"

A lady parishioner entered one Sunday, and as there were others behind her whom she expected would follow, she left the door open. She had not reached her pew before she was startled by Mr. Warne, calling out sharply, "Go back and shut that door!" an injunction hardly conducive to devotional feelings we should judge.

On another occasion, not in church, he told his excellent senior deacon, who used to sing in the vestry "with the spirit and the understanding also," that his singing always reminded him " *of a pig under a gate*."

Mr. Warne's soundness of doctrine was thought by many to be a sufficient offset for his lack of "the sweet charities" and social amenities, but not all his mental acuteness, or vigor in expounding the Scriptures could make him popular with the young people, and after nearly six years, his connection with the church ceased.

He was succeeded the same year, 1837, by Rev. Wm. H. Shailer, now of Portland. Mr. Shailer was pastor of the church sixteen years and was much beloved. The next year after Mr. Shailer's ministry began, the attendance became so large that it was found necessary to enlarge the church edifice. It was raised higher, several new pews were added, a mahogany pulpit took the place of the pine one, the whole house was painted, inside and out, the aisles were carpeted, a new organ bought, the damp and mouldy vestry was enlarged and made lighter and dryer, a furnace was put in, and altogether the place assumed a modern air.

In February, 1854, Mr. Shailer having been repeatedly invited to Portland, resigned his charge here, and removed to that place. Under his ministry the church here received two hundred and four additional members.

In Mr. Warne's day the rite of baptism was at first administered in the open air in the salt water at the lower end of the village. Where Muddy River passes under the street, now narrowed to a scanty stream, and almost covered with the houses of the Irish population, was then a broad, clear stream, or " creek," as it was generally called, at certain states of the tide, convenient for this purpose.

Some large flat stones were arranged as stepping stones for the minister and candidates.

The same spirit that would have prevented the building of the church if possible, prompted some ill-disposed person to remove the principal stone one Sabbath, when a baptism was to take place, and the result was that Mr. Warne took a deep step into the stream unexpectedly and somewhat ungracefully. He recovered himself, however, and the ceremony proceeded, but after that a baptistery was provided in the meeting-house.

During Mr. Shailer's ministry the church frequently resorted to the beautiful bend of Charles River always known as the "bathing place." Since then, Jamaica Pond has been the favorite resort for open air baptism, but this is less frequently practiced of late years than formerly.

The bend of the river alluded to above was bordered by a pebbly beach, half screened by overhanging trees and clustering bushes on either side of the farm road by which it was approached. The trees and shrubs are now gone and the whole place for half a mile is covered with a network of railroad tracks.

CHAPTER IV.

HARRISON PLACE. — ST. MARY'S CHURCH. — LINDEN PLACE
THOMAS A. DAVIS. — ASPINWALL AVENUE, OR, "PERRY'S
LANE."

BEFORE proceeding further up Harvard Street in our description, it will be necessary to turn aside a little and mention briefly the " Places," leading off from it along the easterly side.

Harrison Place was originally nothing but a cart-road leading across the Davis farm by the old house and barn, down to the marsh which was then undreamed of for any other use than the production of salt hay.

Could one of the old proprietors awaken from a sort of Rip Van Winkle sleep and see the roads and dwellings and people that now cover the once green acres where the tide rose and fell, and the wild ducks swam, and the sea-gulls came sailing in on their white wings before a storm, he would be quite as amazed as at any other discovery his astonished eyes might make.

Nearly down the slope of the upland this cart-road led to a beautiful, clear spring of cold water which was overshadowed by a great oak tree.

Under its wide-spreading branches the men of the village used to assemble on " Election Day " and " Fourth of July," to celebrate and make merry with unlimited quantities of punch. There are people among us, not very old, who speak of having seen "a bushel of lemon rinds " at a time as the *débris* of such a festivity.

The attractions in Boston were not so great as in more modern times; no long steam-trains rolled shrieking and smoking into the city on holidays, swarming with their living freight, neither did crowded horse-cars afford their patrons the opportunity to pay for the privilege of hanging up by a leather strap during a four miles' ride.

On the contrary, Boston parties of Masons in regalia, or truckmen in their white frocks, with bands of music, and sometimes a military escort, used to make equestrian trips through Brookline, stopping often at the "Punch Bowl," and returning through Brighton and Cambridge on Independence days. So those who stayed at home solaced themselves with the sights that came out to be seen, and vented their patriotism in punch and gunpowder under the old oak. The boys found it a favorite resort in their games, and the hay-makers in summer noons rested under its shade.

But the punch drinking proved the bane of many who indulged in it, and one of the proprietors not liking the idea of having that sort of rendezvous on his place, cut down the grand old tree, and ended the sport of those who frequented it.

After the farm was sold, the first house built upon a lot purchased from it, was the one formerly owned and occupied by the late David R. Griggs, now (1871) owned by Dr. Lowe. Mr. Griggs occupied the house till a few years before his death. He was so long identified with the neighborhood, and so much beloved as a superintendent of the Baptist Sabbath-school for many years, that he will be well remembered and long missed by all connected with that society and living in that vicinity; and hosts of other warm friends will ever cherish his memory with tenderness.

Mr. Griggs' house was built in 1833, but the road-way

was not opened to its present length till 1837, when the house now occupied by Mrs. Phillips was built for Mr. Luther Thayer, who soon died, and the house was purchased by Mr. Mellen, who occupied it for several years. The name of Harrison Place was first given it in 1840 in honor of President Harrison.

Andem Place was not opened until some ten years later, and was named for Moses Andem, who lived for many years in the old Davis house. For some little time the Catholics of Brookline had held services on Sundays in Lyceum Hall. In 1854 the Church of "St. Mary" was built in Andem Place, and was first occupied for regular services on Christmas Day of that year. Rev. Mr. O'Bierne was the first priest of the parish, and was succeeded by Rev. J. M. Finotti in 1856.

In 1855, on Thanksgiving Day, November 27th, the church narrowly escaped being destroyed by fire, from some accidental cause. It was repaired and has since been enlarged and improved. The great increase of this congregation made it necessary that there should be an assistant in the clergyman's duties, and for some time Rev. J. C. Murphy was associated with Father Finotti as colleague. The latter gentleman closed his labors with this church at Easter, 1873, leaving the parish in charge of Rev. Mr. Lamb. This young man was much devoted to the interest of the young people in his church, and was highly popular. But greatly to the regret of all, his health failed, and he went South hoping for restoration. He died in New York on his way home, July 5, 1873, and his body was brought to St. Mary's Church, where impressive funeral services were held, attended by an immense congregation. Father Lamb was succeeded by Rev. L. J. Morris, the present pastor.

A branch of the great Catholic Temperance organization, called St. Mary's Total Abstinence Society, is connected with this church.

Webster Place, named for the great statesman, is of more recent date than either of the others, the only house built previous to 1850 being the first on the left, built by Mr. Bela Stoddard and now occupied by his son-in-law, Mr. A. L. Lincoln.

To picture Harvard Street as it was previous to 1843, it will be necessary to recall briefly the description respecting the entrance to this street, from the "square," so called, — on the right there being no house, after Mr. Griggs' residence on the corner, except Mr. Stoddard's just mentioned, as far as Aspinwall Avenue. On the left, after the old Baptist Church, with the sheds and parsonage behind it, were Mr. Seaverns' buildings on the top of the hill, accessible only by a rather steep driveway, or numerous wooden steps in a terraced bank, the common sidewalk going up over the lower terrace. From there to School Street was no building. The street, dug somewhat below the level of the hill, was much higher than at present, and bordered by high banks on either side, with a low stone wall on the top of each, overhung all the way on the left side by barberry bushes, with here and there a wild cherry or apple tree. On the right, the bank was overgrown with blackberry bushes, and other wild shrubs and vines, and some young buttonwoods which had sprung up from old stumps, for Brookline was luxuriant with buttonwoods until a comparatively recent date.

These trees made a litter with their falling bark and downy round balls, but they were picturesque, with their bare white spots, and made a grand shade when the mercury was rampant among the nineties, for they often towered to a great height besides being spreading, and thickly set with their fan-like leaves.

The site of Linden Place was formerly an extensive cherry and apple orchard. An old barn stood where the entrance is, with a pair of bars beside it, where a cart-road began. This ground remained the property of the Davis family till 1843, though often called "Holden's farm," a Mr. James Holden having married the widow of Mr. Eben Davis, 3d. It was then laid out in house lots and sold at public auction. It was the first land thus sold in Brookline, and the highest price paid for any part of it was *five and a half cents a foot.*

Times have changed since then, and it is perhaps possible, that there are children now living in the town who will see it five and a half *dollars* a foot.

The central lot was taken by Mr. Thomas Aspinwall Davis, and for him was built the house now occupied by Mr. Goodnow.

Hon. Thomas Aspinwall Davis, who built the house in the centre of Linden Place, was born in the old Davis house in Harrison Place, in December, 1798, and was baptized in infancy by Rev. Dr. Pierce, then the only minister in Brookline. He was the child of Eben Davis, 3d.

His name was given him in honor of his maternal grandfather and great-grandfather, his mother being of the Aspinwall family and the Gardners, two of the oldest families on record in the town. He was a bright and interesting boy, ready to learn according to his opportunities in the Brookline schools, and full of the activities of boyhood, nutting in the Aspinwall woods, hunting and fishing along the marshes and creeks, and ingenious with tools. A little cider-mill of his construction is remembered by the playmates of his childhood. While a boy rambling over the marshes one day, he was accidentally shot in the breast by a Brookline gentleman who was aiming at a flock of plovers on the wing. Much alarm was felt at first, but no permanent injury resulted from it, and the gentleman made all the restitution possible. When the boy was fourteen years of age he was placed in a jeweller's shop in Boston to learn the business, coming home only on Saturday nights, which occasions were looked forward to with the greatest pleasure by the family. He soon became acquainted with a young Parisian who could speak no English, and they became mutual teachers, each thus learning the other's language.

Few young men in High School or College devote themselves more assiduously to culture than did young Davis. Instead of rushing into wild gayeties as soon as business hours were over, as too many did then as well as now, he turned his attention to his beloved books, and read and studied upon the various sciences, writing out a synopsis of each book as he progressed, the better to fix it in his memory.

When he had an interval of leisure from business, he procured a complete set of Blackstone and studied law. Some changes in business, and openings at the South made it necessary for him to be sent to New Orleans, and before he was twenty-three years of age he had twice made a tour from Boston to New Orleans, chiefly in a private carriage, attended with some fatigue and hardship, but giving him fine opportunities for observation and a knowledge of men.

After his return from the second trip he established himself with Mr. Julius Palmer in the jewelry business in Boston, in which he continued until chosen Mayor of Boston in 1845. At that time he was living in Linden Place and devoting his leisure to ornamenting his grounds with choice trees and shrubbery.

He was not a very robust man, and the duties and

cares of his office were too great a tax for his physical endurance.

He was taken sick in the autumn, and after a few week's illness died November 22, 1845. He had been in his early manhood a member of Park Street Church, Boston, but at the time of his death was connected with the Winter Street or Central Church. Rev. Mr. Rogers, his pastor, being in Europe at the time, Dr. Pierce of Brookline, the pastor of his youth, was requested to preach the funeral sermon.

Mr. Davis was greatly beloved and most sincerely lamented. He was buried in the family tomb in Brookline, where five generations of his ancestors had been laid away. Like the good men of old he was literally "gathered to his fathers." Mr. Davis left a widow but no children. His house and grounds were sold; and this property has changed owners more frequently than any other in Linden Place. There are now but three of the original owners of houses in that place still living there.

Leaving Linden Place we pass up "the Cambridge Road," as Harvard Street was called, between its bush-grown banks till we come to Aspinwall Avenue, only a narrow lane with a gateway. On the left as we enter, the brook which comes through under the road (Harvard Street), makes a sweeping curve and goes under the lane. Beside the low stone wall on the left, on the grassy bank beyond the brook stand two great willow trees whose pendent branches, overhanging the brook and the lane, droop so low that the children can reach them as they come there to play during the "nooning," from the old school-house in "School-house Lane." The brick store now covers the place where we used to swing on the old willows and hunt for "Jack in the Pulpit," in the meadow behind the wall, in the early spring. The side of the lane where the "blue eyed grass" grew, is covered by a row of houses, and the brook where we dipped up the froth, and traced the musk-rat by his perfume, and sailed our freighted chips, is concealed by stone and gravel and is no longer a brook but a sewer.

Further along on the left, near the old house which Mr. Melcher has tastefully rejuvenated, was a great butternut tree, where the children hunted for butternuts in the autumn. Another stood upon the right, and the field in front of the old mansion which yet overlooks its green acres is still almost unchanged. This ancient house was once no doubt by far the finest in the town.

CHAPTER V.

THE ASPINWALL FAMILY. — THE COLONEL. — THE DOCTOR. —
THE OLD SCHOOL-HOUSE ON SCHOOL STREET.

IN 1660, Peter Aspinwall built the house which still stands, the most ancient in our town, or probably anywhere in this vicinity, and from him it passed to his son Samuel, who was quite a military hero. In 1690, when Sir William Phipps took possession of the fort at Port Royal, and of the coast as far as the Penobscot River, Samuel Aspinwall served under him as lieutenant in the expedition.

Afterwards he was captain of a Brookline company. The muster-roll of this ancient company would be an interesting document.

In 1727, at the age of sixty-five, the Captain was drowned in Charles River, not far from his farm. One can imagine something of the sensation this event must have produced in this thinly settled town; the loss of so prominent a citizen, the search for the body, — the military procession, for he was buried under arms, — the long funeral sermon, probably in the little church then only ten years built, — the vacant seat in the square pew, "in the northwest corner," — the muffled drums, and the volley fired over the grave.

And how it was doubtless the topic of conversation among neighbors when they met for weeks after, and with what superstitious awe they looked upon the forerunner or "warning" as they probably considered it, that he should have selected for his morning reading at family devotions the 27th chapter of the Proverbs, beginning, "Boast not thyself of to-morrow, for thou knowest not what a day may bring forth."

One of the Captain's sons, Thomas by name, was a lieutenant in the company commanded by his father. He lived and died upon the farm. His wife was Johannah, daughter of Caleb Gardner, and thus the connection of these two ancient families was formed to which we have heretofore alluded. His son, William, the celebrated physician (of whom more hereafter), married a daughter of Captain Isaac Gardner, who was killed at Lexington.

Of the seven children of Lieutenant Thomas and Johannah Gardner, another besides the doctor deserves particular mention. This was Thomas, who bore up the military fame of his father, grandfather, and great-grandfather by efficient service in the War of the Revolution.

He held a colonel's commission and commanded the fort in this town at Sewall's Point.

The fort mounted six guns, which commanded Charles River, and was built to prevent the British from ascending the river in their boats, and this, with old Fort Washington on the Cambridge side, doubtless saved the country along the river from many depredations. A water-battery mounting two guns was on the present site of the Longwood School-house near St. Mary's Street.

The family of the Colonel lived in a large two-story house which stood near the residence of the late Marshall Stearns, on Sewall Avenue. The Colonel probably regarded his house as in an exposed situation, in case the fort should be taken, and he sent his family away to Sherborn, where they remained till after the British evacuated Boston.

The old fort remained in good preservation till the Worcester Railroad was built, and as that was laid out directly through it, and Abbott's wharf was afterwards built upon the water-front of it, nothing was left but the well on the left of the driveway to the wharf and the old ovens in a corner of the estate of A. A. Lawrence, Esq., and even these have now disappeared.

A venerable lady of this town, long since dead, who remembered the battle of Bunker Hill, and Washington when in command at Cambridge, used to speak of a visit of inspection which Washington made to the Brookline Fort. Several Brookline boys, full of eager curiosity to see the new commander-in-chief, pressed quite near, when an orderly peremptorily drove them back. This attracted the General's attention, and beckoning the boys towards him, he laid his hand kindly upon the head of a little fellow who approached with hat in hand, and told the orderly to allow the boys to see all that was to be seen. We do not know that this anecdote has ever been in print before, but it was current among the old inhabitants of Brookline and there is no reason to doubt its authenticity.

The house in which the Colonel lived was afterwards occupied by his son John. Through some misfortune of his it passed out of the possession of his family, but his widow lived in it with a son, William, who is still remembered as a patient, bed-ridden sufferer, for over thirty years. His devoted mother attended him with unfailing care till his death, when she was over eighty years of age. She did not long survive him, and soon after her death the old house was destroyed by fire.

A great-grandson of the Colonel, and grandson of the John above mentioned, bearing his name, has kept up the military character of the family by good service in the War of the Rebellion, and daily walks our streets bearing trace of rebel shot or shell received in the fight at Hatteras Inlet where he served as engineer of the Minnesota.

We turn now once more to the ancient house in Aspinwall Avenue. The youngest brother of the Revolutionary colonel, still well remembered by many of our townspeople as "the Doctor," was born in 1743.

He entered Harvard College in 1760, received his degrees in the usual course, and then went to Connecticut, where he studied medicine under Dr. Gale, then a celebrated physician.

Having completed his course by attending a series of medical lectures in Philadelphia, he returned to Brookline, and commenced practice at the age of twenty-six. It was seen by those who had his education in charge that he was a young man of more than ordinary promise, and the certificates given him, and still preserved by his family, are unusually commendatory.

The young doctor was not only a man of learning but a man of principle, — he not only "regarded man" but he feared God, and he took up his life work in an earnest and faithful spirit. His personal appearance was commanding, as he was a fine figure and over six feet in height. He had lost the sight of one eye in childhood by an accident with an arrow, but judging from his portrait this was but slightly noticeable. A portrait of him by Stuart when far advanced in life so resembles the portraits of Washington, that when the house of his son-in-law, Lewis Tappan, Esq., was sacked by a pro-slavery mob in New York, many years ago, this portrait was the only picture spared. Probably the rioters mistook it for that of Washington and forebore to lay their desecrating hands upon even the painted semblance of "the Father of his country."

The Doctor's practice grew rapidly, and extended far

and wide, so that he frequently rode even forty miles on horseback to visit his patients, carrying his medicines in saddle-bags, as was the custom of those times.

When the War of the Revolution broke out we hear of the Brookline doctor first, at the battle of Lexington. Regardless of personal danger he was hastening to the fight in the red coat he was accustomed to wear, when he was reminded by a friend that he might be taken for a British " red coat " and be shot by his friends, so he hastily laid that garment aside and donning one which would prove him unmistakably a Yankee, he joined the eager throng who had dropped plough, spade, hammer, or pen, to rally at the insulted country's call. The road was too circuitous for men on such an errand, and taking a short cut across the fields and " over the river," they were soon in the deadly fray. Captain Gardner, of Brookline, was killed, and the Doctor, after assisting in chasing the retreating British to Charlestown, returned through Cambridge and had the body cared for that night, and in the morning Mr. John Heath, of Brookline, went to Cambridge and brought it home to the bereaved family.

Dr. Aspinwall being blind in one eye, was obliged to fire from the left shoulder, but he proved himself a sharp shooter on this occasion, being seen to lay one if not more of the enemy in the dust.

He applied for a commission, but by the advice of his friend, General Joseph Warren, himself a physician, he decided to serve in the medical department and save Yankees instead of killing the British. General Warren's brief and brilliant career was speedily closed at Bunker Hill, but Dr. Aspinwall's knowledge and skill were in requisition not only through the war but long years after.

In 1775, Dr. Aspinwall was surgeon at St. Thomas' Hospital in Roxbury. In 1778 we find by his letters to his wife, that he was with the army under General Sullivan in Rhode Island.

To this wife, with whom he lived most harmoniously thirty-eight years, he wrote most devoted and charming letters. We make one brief extract which sounds refreshing in these days when we hear so much of conjugal infelicities.

Alluding to a letter which he had received from her the day before " with great joy and satisfaction," he says : —

" I did not much expect you would write me, but assure you it was very agreeable to hear from the chief or sole source of all my earthly happiness. . . . . I have at times, almost been tempted to return and relieve your anxious solicitude about me, by reason of the dangers I may possibly be exposed to. But my duty and honor, the kindness I am treated with by the officers, their great desire and persuasion to have me tarry, and the importance of the cause I am engaged in, forbid me to harbor a single thought of returning at present. I rely on the protection of that beneficent Being under the shadow of whose wings I have trod the dangerous and thorny paths through life with safety. On Him I trust, and to Him I pray, that I may be returned to the arms of the dearest and most deserving of women."

Time passed on and " the dearest and most deserving of women " received in safety her affectionate and high-minded husband, who forthwith settled himself again to the work of a village doctor, — laborious enough at best with all the modern appliances and conveniences, but in those days of poor and unlighted streets, scattered population, and bulky medicines imported slowly and with difficulty and expense, — with the cumbersome saddle-bags, the prejudices and the poverty of the people, his must have been a life of fatigue and anxiety beyond anything in the range of modern experience.

The small-pox, then the terror of the whole country, had been introduced here by foreign armies, and the practice of inoculation for it, was beginning to gain a strong foothold in spite of the prejudices which it encountered.

This was not *vaccination*, but a regular inoculation with the virus of the real small-pox, that the patient might have the disease by appointment instead of unexpectedly, and thus be relieved of all future apprehensions respecting it.

It was the custom of those times to carry off a person showing symptoms of the dreaded disease, to the most remote place possible, shut him up there with one attendant, put out a red flag to keep all passers by at a distance, and there let the poor victim die or recover according as Providence decreed.

After Dr. Aspinwall's army experience he conceived the idea of establishing on his own premises a hospital, to which patients should be received and where they should be inoculated, and stay during their sickness under his personal attention and that of experienced nurses. Accordingly, he erected a building for that purpose upon his farm, and patients began to come. He was very successful in his treatment, and the fame of his hospital so extended that he soon had to build another, and afterward still a third. One of these buildings was situated about where Perry Street joins Aspinwall Avenue, the others not far from Longwood Station on the left from Aspinwall Avenue near the marsh. Of course some of the patients died, and there are Brookline people buried in the marshes, as well as others who came from a distance, who perished under the horrible scourge in spite of the skill of their wise doctor.

But the majority recovered and went to their homes gratefully rejoicing. One of our oldest inhabitants remembers being in this hospital for treatment almost eighty years ago, and retains a more distinct recollection of trying to drown a squirrel by turning water into a hollow stump where he had hidden, than he does of the small-pox.

One can imagine something of the feelings with which an adult patient must have entered the fearful portals of this institution, and the strength of nerve it must have taken to sit down and calmly receive into the system the virus which must mean suffering in a most loathsome form, and *might* mean death. Yet parents sent there whole families of children, of whom some returned to them, and some, alas! never came.

But a new order of things was about to be established. Vaccination, as a means of prevention of the dreaded disease, was first introduced in this country by Dr. Waterhouse, of Cambridge, about the beginning of the present century. Dr. Aspinwall had then been devoted to the treatment of the disease by inoculation, and had spent much money, no doubt, in building and fitting up his hospitals.

Dr. Waterhouse invited all the physicians of Boston and vicinity to see the first cases of vaccination ever practiced in the United States. Of course it was a matter of vital interest to Dr. Aspinwall, and he gave it the most keen and critical examination. He took home a portion of the virus, tested it in the most thorough manner, and with Dr. Waterhouse's consent took to his hospital, some little time after, all of Dr. W.'s family who had been vaccinated and there tested the genuineness of the new treatment, "to the verge of rigid experiment."

He satisfied himself of the value of the new discovery, and with generous and noble spirit he said to Dr. Waterhouse and others, "this new inoculation of yours is no sham. As a man of humanity, I rejoice in it though it will take from me a handsome annual income." Dr. Waterhouse gave this voluntary testimony to the honorable course pursued by Dr. Aspinwall in this matter, in a paper published in the " Medical Intelligencer."

Dr. Thacher also, in writing of him on this subject, calls him " an honest man and a faithful physician." Had he, for selfish motives, chosen to throw the weight of his strong influence against vaccination, it would doubtless have affected public opinion for several years, and brought him further profit. As it was, in less than two years he took down his hospitals.

The talents and energy which distinguished Dr. Aspinwall were by no means confined to the profession to which his life was devoted. He was a man of culture and sagacity and practical wisdom, ably fitted to be a legislator, and as such he represented Brookline in the State Legislature, was three times chosen Senator for Norfolk County, was a member of the Council and a Justice of the Peace.

In the year 1803 the Doctor built the fine large house upon the hill, now occupied by his grandson, and removed thither. A year or two ago a carpenter making repairs, had occasion to remove some clapboards or shingles, and in the boards thus uncovered, he noticed names of several persons, with dates in the last century, and residence in distant States, deeply cut in the wood. On making inquiry respecting them he learned that the Doctor had used more or less of the timber and boards of the hospital in constructing his house, and here were the *autographs of his patients*. Poor fellows! Did they recover and return to the distant homes from which they came, lighter hearted for having met the foe and conquered, or do they sleep in unknown and unmarked graves, in the Brookline marshes? Who can tell?

It will be remembered that the Doctor had but one eye for all his study and writing, and of the latter there is abundant evidence of the unflagging industry of more than half a century. In his later years a cataract began to form over the one precious eye, and fearing that it too would become useless, he submitted to a surgical operation by a distinguished Professor of more than one medical school. The operation was a failure, and sight was destroyed forever.

With heroic philosophy and Christian resignation the brave old man bore up under this great affliction, and devoted himself to thought and reflection and "preparation for death," as he expressed it. He had always been religious, and had religiously brought up his family; his memorandum book gives evidence of his daily desire in the midst of the activities of his most crowded and busy years, to live in fidelity to God and man. And what better preparation than such a life could any man make for entrance upon a higher and holier one? Yet this brief pause on the threshold of the great unknown, he consecrates to calm reflection and faith and trust, and closing his sightless eyes upon the things of earth, at the end of almost eighty years he passed away, let us hope where all "shall see eye to eye," and know even as they are known. He died April 16, 1823, and was buried in Brookline cemetery.*

The beautiful oriel window in the chancel at St. Paul's

---

* We are indebted to our townsman, Wm. Aspinwall, Esq., for papers containing full and valuable information respecting his honored ancestors, and from them have drawn materials for this brief sketch.

Church, Aspinwall Avenue, was placed there as a memorial by his children, and contains an inscription in Latin, on the lower margin.

DR. WILLIAM ASPINWALL, JR., COL. THOMAS ASPINWALL.

The eldest son of Dr. Aspinwall who lived to manhood inherited his name, studied and graduated at Harvard College, and having prepared himself to succeed his father in his profession, settled in Brookline, and already had begun to practice, when his father's blindness caused him to retire from professional life altogether.

But the blind father, with the infirmities of age upon him, outlived the vigorous young son, who died in April, 1818, at the age of thirty-four. The next son, Thomas, who was also a graduate of Harvard, and had been admitted to the bar, found the whole career of life changed for him, by the second war with England.

During that war he held a colonel's commission and served the country gallantly and faithfully; was in the battle at Sackett's Harbor in 1813, commanded Scott's Brigade in the defense of Fort Erie, in August, 1814, and on the 17th of September of the same year he led Miller's column in the storming of the British entrenchments.

This engagement cost him the loss of his left arm.

In June of the following year, Colonel Aspinwall was appointed U. S. Consul at London, which important office he held with great honor to himself and the country which he represented for *thirty-seven years*, and was then removed; not for any fault or failure or mistake, but simply because it pleased Franklin Pierce, then the President of the United States, to fill that important situation with one of his own political supporters.

This event caused much indignant comment on both

sides of the ocean, and the result was doubtless to cause fresh disgust with that miserable theory of "rotation in office," which has so often been unfortunately illustrated by the placing of inexperienced men in important situations under Government.

When Colonel Aspinwall left England, the Barings, the Rothschilds, George Peabody, and other distinguished individuals in London, presented him with an unusually magnificent service of plate, accompanied by a letter bearing most cordial and grateful testimony of respect and appreciation.

The Colonel returned to his native town, and after spending some time here, removed to Boston, where he still lives, and although more than eighty-four years of age, is vigorously at work daily on literary matters.

The venerable Colonel Thomas Aspinwall is the only surviving child of Dr. Aspinwall. His son Augustus, who succeeded him in the occupancy of the mansion house on the hill, has so recently passed away that his erect figure and handsome countenance are still fresh in the memory of all who knew him, and shared in the admiration of the exquisite roses for which he made his fine estate justly celebrated.

The ancient homestead in Aspinwall Avenue was leased for many years after the Doctor ceased to occupy it. Mr. Daniel Perry was a tenant there for many years, and both himself and wife died there in old age.

The house now occupied by Mr. Melcher was built more than a hundred and fifty years ago by Dr. Aspinwall's father, no doubt for the use of some of his children, and was occupied by various members of the family.

It was afterwards let for some years to Mr. Peter Banner, who built the old Unitarian Church (the second edifice) in 1805. After him, many other tenants successively occupied the house till Colonel Aspinwall sold it to its present owner.

The magnificent elm which overshadowed the old house, and of which now only a portion of the trunk remains, was said to have been set out in 1656. This statement may be found in the "North American Review," for July, 1844, but Rev. John Pierce, D. D., from whom any native of Brookline who should dare to differ on dates would be audacious indeed, stated that the "tradition of the oldest and best informed inhabitants has uniformly been that it was set out by Deacon Samuel Clark" (great-great-grandfather of the present Samuel Clark of Walnut Street,) who served his boyhood in the Aspinwall family, which, if true, would probably fix the date of the setting out of the tree, about 1700. About thirty years ago nearly half the tree fell, under its great weight of leaves, and four or five years since the rest of it followed, breaking a hole through the roof of the house.

Two splendid elms from the seed of this ancient one now grow, one near the front of the old house, the other close to the Avenue. May no ruthless "widening" hasten their destruction for a century to come.

The ancient elm measured twenty-six feet in circumference near the surface of the ground, and sixteen feet eight inches at five feet from the surface.

One cannot but look regretfully upon the fast hastening ruin of a house which for two hundred and eleven years has borne a conspicuous part in the annals of our town, and has sheltered under its low roof so many distinguished individuals. For long ago —

"In that mansion used to be
Free-hearted Hospitality;
His great fires up the chimney roared,
The stranger feasted at his board.

. . . . —

> There groups of merry children played,
> There youths and maidens dreaming strayed,
>
> . . . .
>
> From that chamber, clothed in white,
> The bride came forth on her wedding night,
> There in that silent room below
> The dead lay in his shroud of snow.
>
> . . . .
>
> All are scattered now and fled,
> Some are married and some are dead;"

and of those who once frequented it there are none to come again.

The beautiful grove in the rear of the farm on the high ground bordering the marsh, though nearly obliterated, is well remembered by all middle-aged persons who grew up in Brookline, as a great resort for local picnics. The place acquired the name of "Perry's Woods" for several years when Farmer Perry was the lessee; in "Perry's Woods" lovers rambled and children played unmolested. The long, high, green ridge, with shade trees on each side whose arches met overhead, seemed as if planned for a natural dining hall, and when long tables were spread there with white cloths and ornamented with flowers, and the music of a band awoke the echoes, it was a most attractive spot. But perhaps nothing was looked forward to with more eager anticipation or more thoroughly enjoyed than an annual visit to the grove, in an informal manner, by the teacher and pupils of the old Primary School in "School-house Lane."

The memory of the race from the upper to the lower end of that long green ridge, — the great swing on the oak, the game of "Hunt the Squirrel through the woods, I've lost him, I've found him," how we all remember it still! Most of us have been hunting our squirrel ever since; some have lost him, and a few have found him, and some tired out with the weary chase have lain down and abandoned it forever.

ST. PAUL'S CHURCH, ASPINWALL AVENUE.

This beautiful little building with its picturesque surroundings, from whatever point it is approached, is one of the pleasantest objects upon which the eye rests in the whole vicinity. Through the summer the dark green clustering vines almost conceal the walls, and in autumn they hang out their flaming banners of scarlet and crimson, gracefully festooning porch and gable. It is often a pleasant reminder of lovely bits of English scenery to those who have made themselves familiar with the pleasant places of that country.

The society was organized in 1849, and prominent among its earliest members were Messrs. Eliakim Littell, James S. Amory, Augustus Aspinwall, William Aspinwall, Harrison Fay, John Shepherd, Moses B. Williams, James S. Patten, Theodore Lyman, Frederic P. Ladd, and others. On the second Sunday in July of that year, the first service was held in the Town Hall, Rev. Thomas M. Clarke (the present Bishop of Rhode Island) generously volunteering his services as pastor during his vacation of that summer.

A few months later, during which the society had been without a regular incumbent, it was decided to call the Rev. William Horton, of Newburyport, as Rector. That gentleman accepted, and for three years, during which the society steadily increased in numbers and prosperity, he faithfully discharged his parochial and ministerial duties. In the fall of 1850 it was decided to build a substantial church. A subscription was raised for the purpose. Among the contributors were Messrs. James S. Amory, Moses B. Williams, John S. Wright, Benjamin Howard, Theodore Lyman, William Appleton, Augustus Aspinwall, Harrison Fay, and others. The two gentlemen last named were the largest subscribers, Mr. Aspinwall giving $2,000, and the land now belonging to the church, at that time worth about $1,500. Mr. Fay gave $5,000. The total amount subscribed was about $12,000, which was sufficient to build the body of the church only, the addition of the tower involving a further outlay of about $13,000, which was paid equally by Messrs. Aspinwall and Fay. T. C. Leeds, of Boston (a native of Brookline) gave the bell, worth nearly $1,000. The beautiful memorial window in the chancel was presented by the Aspinwall family, the rest were given by Mr. Fay. Mr. Augustus Aspinwall bequeathed to the church in his will several pews belonging to him at the time of his death, the proceeds of the sales of which should be applied towards the building of a parsonage.

Richard Upjohn, Esq., of New York, was the architect, and Messrs. Aspinwall, Fay, and M. B. Williams were the building committee. The church was built with remarkable solidity and very economically, the whole cost not exceeding $26,000. It was entirely paid for when completed, and since that time has had no lasting debt. In May, 1852, Rev. Mr. Horton resigned, and Dr. John S. Stone, of Brooklyn, formerly of St. Paul's Church, Boston, accepted a call as his successor. The church was formally consecrated in December, 1852, and Dr. Stone entered upon his duties as Rector. His eloquence and great worth are well known and fondly remembered by those of his parishioners who survive his pastorate, as well as by many others in this town who heard and knew him.

He continued here for ten years, and resigned in the fall of 1862, to accept a professorship in the Episcopal Theological Seminary, at Philadelphia. After an *interregnum* of a few months, Rev. Dr. Francis Wharton of

Kenyon College, Gambier, Ohio, was installed as Rector, and continued until the summer of 1869, when he resigned, and was succeeded in the spring of 1870 by Rev. Wm. W. Newton, the present young and talented Rector.

During Dr. Stone's ministry (in the summer of 1857) the chapel adjacent to the church was built. One thousand dollars was contributed towards its erection, by Mrs. Mary Rogers, of Boston, on condition that it should contain a mural tablet in memory of her daughter, who had died in Egypt the previous year. The remainder of the sum necessary for its completion (about $4,000), was raised by the ladies of the parish. The condition annexed to the donation of Mrs. Rogers was complied with, and the chapel has on its western wall a beautiful marble tablet with a tasteful design representing Mary sitting at the feet of the Saviour, under which is the line, "Mary sat at Jesus' feet and heard his word," also an inscription commemorating the death of Mrs. Rogers and her daughter.

Prominent among the past members of the society were Colonel Wilder Dwight and his brother Howard, and Henry V. Stone, a son of the former Rector, all of whom lost their lives in the War of the Rebellion.

THE OLD SCHOOL-HOUSE ON SCHOOL STREET.

Leaving Aspinwall Avenue, we turn aside before going further up Harvard Street, to take a glance at the "School-house Lane," as it was formerly called, — now School Street, — as there was but one building upon it until within thirty years, and that was the school-house.

The lane was narrow, not much more than a cart road, and bordered on either side by a low stone wall overhung by trees, and on the east side by a thick, natural hedge of barberry bushes, which nearly concealed the wall.

A school was kept in this lane from a very early period, probably the only school in the town while it was a part of Boston. The original school-house was a very small and low, square, hipped-roof building, on the spot where the Williams block of houses now stands. Some of the oldest inhabitants can just remember it as a mere hovel going to ruin, in their early childhood.

The second school-house was the same style of building, a little larger, and stood on the spot now forming the corner of School and Prospect streets. There is a tradition that this bit of ground was given to the town for a school-house lot, *forever*, by one of the ancient Davises.

The arrangements in and about this ancient edifice of learning, for the accommodation of teacher and pupils, would hardly satisfy modern tastes and requirements. On each side of an alley through the middle of the room, the seats were arranged facing the alley, like seats in a street car, only they were long, narrow benches, with a plank in front upon legs, running the whole length of the room (except a space for admission at the ends), and this plank served the purpose of a desk. A sort of drawer underneath served to hold the books, which were not numerous. The Bible, the Psalter, the Spelling-book, and the Arithmetic being all that were used, and not all those at once. Perhaps they feared softening of the brain. The teacher's desk was in the left hand corner farthest from the door, and the right hand corner was occupied by an immense fire-place with a chimney to match. On the wall the clothing was hung.

The wood, of cord length and often unseasoned, was deposited outside the school-house, and autumnal rains and winter snows fell unchecked upon it. The winter school, taught by a man, used to begin with the Monday after Thanksgiving, and the boys took turns, week by week, in sawing and splitting the wood and making the fire. Friction matches were one of the blessings reserved for modern times, so the luckless wights who made the fires had to bring live coals in an iron skillet, kept for the purpose, from " Squire Sharp's," the nearest neighbor, and for some time the schoolmaster.

On one occasion, a boy who lived with " Parson Jackson," as he was called (the predecessor of Dr. Pierce), after laboring over a green and knotty stump without much success, hit upon the bright idea of blowing it up with gunpowder.

Accordingly he drilled a hole, filled it with powder, and applied the fuse or tinder, and in his great interest stood close by to watch the result of his experiment. He did not stand there long, however, and a lame leg proved to him convincingly how very active and powerful an agent gunpowder will become under the influence of fire, even in a green stump.

One morning, on the arrival of teacher and pupils, the room was found filled with the densest smoke. Opening doors and windows did not produce much effect; the chimney could not be persuaded to *draw* that day, study was impossible and school was dismissed. An investigation as to the sudden foulness of the chimney revealed the fact that the top was closely covered with a board, and there was an understanding among the boys that one of their number who lived with Squire Sharp had thus secured them the holiday.

For many years the town appropriated money for two terms of school in the year, three or four months each, in summer and in winter. The people of the district then contributed somewhat more, that a few weeks might be added to the terms. Thus the schools were kept nearly as many weeks in the year as at present, only the vacations occurred in the comfortable weather of fall and spring when the children were in good condition to study, and through the whole of the sweltering dog-days, teachers and pupils were kept at their tasks.

"Squire Sharp," of whom further mention will be made hereafter, was teacher of the winter school several years, as was also Dr. Aspinwall. Three teachers by the name of Allen (not brothers), also served for several winters. One of them was afterwards President of Bowdoin College, Brunswick, Me., if our information is correct, and another became subsequently a Unitarian clergyman.

Among the old school-masters was one who at times indulged in various strange freaks, and was strongly suspected of stimulating the inner man too largely with doses of something more exciting than water. About eleven o'clock every day he retired to the entry, and one day as he returned through the alley, a little fellow raised his hand and called out, "Master! master! your bottle's sticking out of your pocket!" It was too true; not only was the bottle out but the truth was out also, and the story flew about town.

It came to the ears of the School Committee, who were also the Selectmen at that time, and they decided that it was best to call on the master in a body (of three) and remonstrate upon the errors of his ways. Accordingly that formidable trio presented themselves on a certain evening at the master's boarding place for an interview.

Instantly on their arrival the master suspected the reason of this surprise party, and quietly asked his host to prepare a bowl of punch and bring it in immediately. In the meantime he entertained his guests most cordially and socially, calling on all his resources of wit and anecdote. Presently the punch came in and was passed around with most cheerful liberality, the master talking on all the while, and among the rest of his good stories he told of a schoolmaster, a friend of his, who was suspected of indulging too much in the use of liquors, and was actually called upon by his committee for the purpose of reprimanding him, but he treated them so well with excellent punch that they went away without saying a word!

The baffled Committee knowing too well that the wily schoolmaster had the advantage, as they had already each taken a draught, actually retired from the field, and left him the victor, and he finished the winter school unrebuked for either his intemperance or his impudence, and we have been informed was even employed again.

Among the female teachers of those days were two sisters, Nabby and Joanna Jordan, who lived with their parents in the little house which we described as formerly standing in the meadow about where the upper end of White Place now is. Many good people now far advanced in life, learned their A, B, C, in that little old building of Miss Nabby or Miss Joanna. Another of the female teachers, for many successive years, was Miss Lucy Aspinwall. A little bit of the economy of those old times is preserved to extravagant moderns in an anecdote of this lady's habits. A lady, who attended her school more than seventy-five years ago, remembers that her old teacher used to wear a long dress to school and take it off and hang it up, on her arrival there, and put on a short, loose gown and skirt, to keep school in. The one long dress thus carefully preserved did service a long time. It will be remembered that this economical teacher was from one of the first families in town. What would our ancestors have thought if they could have foreseen a Saratoga trunk, or a modern dressmaker's bill?

Early in the present century the old school-house being seriously dilapidated, at town meeting an appropriation was asked for to repair it. On examination it was found to be so unsound that the best judges recommended the erection of a new building.

Then out came the conservatives to the battle, for they never lack a champion or a reserve force. All the ancient and time-honored arguments so familiar to modern ears were set in array. The present building could be "fixed up" for a small sum and answer its purpose for years to come. It would increase *the taxes*, and here came in the cry of the veterans who had plenty of money but no children; and so on, *ad infinitum*. But the men who believe that nothing is economical which stints education carried the day so far as to secure an appropriation of twelve hundred dollars for a new building. This much conceded, Mr. Thomas Griggs (now the Deacon), who was then one of the School Committee, represented to the assembled wisdom of the town the better policy and economy of adding a few hundred dollars more and making the building two stories high. Audacity, indeed! Had they not just voted away the town's money with unparalleled extravagance, *twelve hundred dollars* to build a *new* school-house when a respectable minority thought the old one might do for a dozen years to come, and now to be asked to build it *two stories* high! Oliver Twist's petition for "more" did not evoke more surprise. Two stories high indeed! and where were the children coming from to fill it? No! the matter was settled, so far as the town was concerned, twelve hundred dollars and not a cent more.

But the Deacon, nothing daunted, called a meeting of the inhabitants of the district, and urged the matter upon them, proposing that they should raise a few hundreds more, and put on the second story. He drew up a paper and began the subscription list there, and in a few days four hundred dollars were subscribed. It was sorely opposed by some who were well able to give, and one man who had several children to send to school absolutely refused to give a cent. Finding, however, that the four hundred was nearly subscribed and the work would be done, he finally handed in *ten dollars*.

So the school-house was built two stories high with a place for clothing in the entry, and a little room for fuel in the rear of each room. A platform ran across the end on which was the teacher's desk, opposite to the door. The seats were arranged to face the teacher, six in a row, the desks being all under the same board for one row, but separated inside from one another. A square box stove for wood heated each room. On each end of the platform were three more seats, and in front of the desks a narrow board was placed a few inches from the floor for a seat for the *little children*. Who that ever sat upon those seats will forget their hardness? We have heard mention made of " the soft side of a plank." That there was no soft side to those planks none who sat there will deny their testimony. Poor little urchins of four years and upwards sat there from nine to twelve in the forenoon, and from one till four in the afternoon, summer and winter, to read the alphabet once through from A to Z, each half-day, with five minutes recess only in each session, and a smart application of the rattan or ruler if they turned round or whispered.

What would some of the tender mammas of present times think of this course for their darlings, who imagine the present *regime* of the public schools " hard," for children of six or seven years to stay under, five hours a day, divided by two recesses of fifteen minutes each, and with all the resources of slates, picture books, singing, and an endless variety of pleasant exercises in reciting. But unreasonable parents were not unknown fifty years ago. For some time a Miss Wheelock was teacher of the school, and among the pupils was a somewhat wayward girl, the child of a woman known as "Mother Marean," who used to go out by the day washing. It became necessary for Miss Wheelock to punish this pupil one day, and she did so, not unreasonably however, but the maternal wrath was excited. "Mother Marean" was quite sure her child was punished only because she was the washerwoman's daughter, and thereupon she proceeded to the neighborhood of the school-house, and when school was out pounced upon the unsuspecting teacher as she turned the corner of the street and tumbled her into the brook, administering at the same time a smart castigation with a bunch of nettles on face and neck, an exploit for which she was tried, convicted, and served a term in Dedham jail.

It was not long before it was found necessary to occupy both school-rooms in the winter, as the farmers' boys attended school then, under the master, and the girls and young children were numerous enough to need the female teacher the year round.

There were abundant facilities for amusement about the vicinity of the old school-house both in summer and winter. We have alluded above to the shady brook at the entrance to Aspinwall Avenue, which was a favorite place for the children to play. Besides this the open brook on the south side of Harvard Street, which came out from under the low stone wall and spread itself out over a shallow pebbly bottom before it made the dark plunge under the road, was always a safe and pleasant place for those who loved to paddle in its waters. This was where the unfortunate teacher took her involuntary bath.

Then under the barberry bushes, near by, were cosy little nooks where the girls made themselves happy with dolls and bits of broken china or glass, and very proud were those who could bring small pieces of board and bright squares of carpeting to cover them, for seats in these play-houses. Of course ball, hoops, jump-ropes, and kites were as popular then as now, but these other amusements filled up the intervals.

But the great source of winter amusements was "the long coast." The hill, east and south of the school-house, extended to a point about half way between the present High and Grammar school-houses, and the Public Library; and was about the height of the roof of the Grammar school-house. From that high ridge it sloped gradually down close to the school-house and then came a sudden depression which the boys called "*the jounce.*" This slope formed the long coast, and the new impetus given by "the jounce," sent the sleds to the corner of Harvard Street. Here the wall and the bushes prevented further progress, as one of our young men, if not more, probably remembers, having tried the calibre of that wall with his head, seriously to the damage of the latter.

Below *the jounce*, on the right of the coast, was a deep hollow, which contained water enough to be called "the pond," the greater part of the year, and when the spring rains and snows melting from the hill filled up the pond till it was level with Harvard Street, all sorts of rafts were improvised by the boys, and merry times were had poling about over its surface. By varying the course of the sleds a little they could be sent shooting across the icy surface in winter.

In the hottest part of summer the bottom of this hollow was about dry, and covered with great bunches of rushes. In our childhood, in hunting about among the rushes one day, we noticed a smoothly-rounded surface just above the soil between the bunches in one spot, — something hard, which did not seem to be a stone. By dint of considerable digging with a stick, it finally was thrown up and proved to be a six-pound cannon ball, well rusted. We carried it home with nearly as much reverence as we would have carried the bones of Washington, not doubting our treasure was a Revolutionary cannonball from old Fort Sewall, but were sadly disenchanted on learning that the location would have made it impossible, and our venerable relic was thenceforth old iron, " only that and nothing more."

In front of the old school-house and just where Prospect Street slopes downward toward School Street, was "the short coast," only it was much steeper than the present grade, and came out between posts where the rails had been removed. This was much frequented by the smaller children. Opposite the school-house, just across the road, there stood behind a low wall a russet apple tree which spread its low branches wide and made a good shade. Here the hard green apples were pounded on the wall till the juice flowed, when they were pronounced " mellow," and eaten with appetites such as are seldom brought to the more savory viands of later years.

But near the lower end of the street, on the west side, there stood close to the wall, on the same field, two large trees which bore tiny red sweet apples. The late Mr. Bartlett carried on this farm for many years, and always allowed the children all the fruit they could get from these trees, and lucky was the boy or girl who arrived first in the morning and secured " the lion's share " of the spoils and then practiced munificence or meanness when the rest came, as the natural disposition prompted.

Water for the use of the school was brought twice a day from Mr. Hall's, at the corner of School and Washington streets. In the large open shed to this house was the pump, and few if any children ever passed without stopping for a " drink of water ; " real thirst had little to do with it we imagine.

A pleasant excitement was occasionally created in the school-room by the downfall of the entire length of stovepipe, with a crash and a dust, only second to an earthquake, to childish imaginations. Then Mr. Hall was sent for to put it up again, and it was quite delightful either to sit and watch the process, or be sent out to play while it was going on. Anything was a godsend which broke up the routine and monotony.

In winter, when "the master's school" was kept down stairs, it was a great pleasure to the pupils of the upper school to go down occasionally to hear " the great boys " declaim, and the rounded periods of grand oratory, from Cicero to Patrick Henry and Edward Everett were rolled out and sent the blood thrilling through childish veins as the studied elegance of few orators or actors since has caused it to thrill. They were admired, those young orators, in the school-room by their youthful audience, but how they were feared when out from under the master's eye, because they wore long blue frocks, had stentorian voices, and kicked foot-ball furiously. There were many changes of masters, a new one being hired almost every winter. What would be thought in the present days of school courtesy, of a teacher who should throw an open knife across the school-room at a disorderly pupil, or launch a mahogany ruler at another, which striking upon a desk should split, and inflict so serious a wound upon the victim that a strong boy should faint at the sight? Yet such events as these have occurred within thirty years in this school-house, and the teacher continued his school through the winter, only being advised to slightly modify his methods of discipline. The rattan and the cane were in daily and almost hourly use, but the schools were far less quiet and orderly than at present.

There was no teacher so thoroughly identified with the building as Miss Catherine, daughter of Charles Stearns, Sen., of this town, who taught the year round for twenty-five years. In all this time she never lost a day by illness. The schools were of course ungraded in her time, and the pupils were from four years old upwards, as long as they chose to attend. The amount of real work, hard work, done in this school seems marvelous. There were from fifty to sixty pupils during the several years of the writer's familiarity with it, and there were four classes in reading and spelling besides "the little children."

Written Arithmetic was taught as far as simple interest. Mental Arithmetic, Grammar, Geography, History of the United States, Goodrich's Universal History, Natural Philosophy, Roman Antiquities and Mythology, Blake's Astronomy, Composition, Map-drawing, and Writing, each received attention, and there was no lack of thorough reviewing. These studies were not all prescribed by the School Committee, but great freedom of choice was left to the teacher and first class.

The elder pupils often rendered the teacher assistance in instructing the younger ones. Besides all this, needle-work was allowed, and Miss Stearns often fitted her pupils' work out of school hours, this being wholly gratuitous service. After the school had above sixty regular pupils Miss Emily Reed was appointed assistant to Miss Stearns. Soon after, she was appointed principal in another school, and for thirty years gave this town her best energies. Both these ladies were conscientious and laborious teachers, yet for many years the highest price paid them was but two dollars and a half a week.

During a period of many years, there was a Prudential Committee, but the entire management of literary affairs connected with the schools devolved upon Rev. Dr. Pierce, the minister of the First Parish for fifty years.

Rev. Mr. Shailer of the Baptist Church was also active in school matters during the entire period of his residence in the town, but Dr. Pierce being many years his senior, was always authority in all open questions, and for years was the only active committee man. He it was who visited the schools, examined the pupils in their studies, and made such suggestions as were deemed expedient.

His visits were received with great delight by most of the pupils, mingled with a sense of awe, and a great desire to please. What a hush fell upon the buzzing and restless school when his step was heard ascending the school-house stairs. He rapped upon the door with the head of his cane, and as the teacher opened the door the pupils were expected to rise, and remain standing while the venerable gentleman walked up the aisle to the platform, set his cane in one corner, hung his hat upon the top of it, and seated himself at the teacher's desk. We said venerable, for Dr. Pierce was venerable long before he was old. His snow-white hair and his dignity of manner impressed even the most careless, yet he was never *feared* by the children, as fault-finders are feared, though he was a good critic.

How he puzzled the grammar class with all sorts of intricacies, and how delighted he was when we could manage the knotty passages in parsing " Thompson's Seasons." How he brought forth an inexhaustible series of hard words for the spelling classes from his wonderful memory, and delighted in confronting us with some jaw-breaking proper name from the Old Testament. He capped the climax one day by giving out to the first class, "Honorificabilitudinitatibusque." To his astonishment one pupil had heard the word before and could spell it, in the old style, going back to the first syllable in pronouncing it after every successive syllable. Then his love of antiquities, and his wonderful memory of dates and anecdotes, made him most entertaining, as all his teaching and examining were interspersed with these varieties as they were suggested by whatever might be in the lessons. When he had criticised the classes and told his stories, and his rich sonorous voice had joined the childish ones with "Greenville" or "Old Hundred," he rose to go, and the school, rising, remained standing while he passed out, bowing right and left as he went. "Thou shalt rise up before the hoary head, and honor the face of the old man." Young America needs many a lesson to-day in common courtesy to the aged. Of the pupils who figured conspicuously in this old school, a volume might be written, but this is not the time or place, for most of them are still grappling with the problems of life. But there are still tenderly remembered, the sweet young girls who faded early from sight and fell asleep before sorrow or care cast a shadow over them ; and brave and manly boys who went forth to serve their country and whose fate is marked by a little flag and a withered wreath in yonder cemetery.

But we must take leave of the old school-house. It overflowed into the town hall, and the old stone school-house in Walnut Street, and still the children came, springing up like Roderick Dhu's men, till the town provided new and ample accommodations ; and the old building, no longer wanted, was sold to George W. Bird, the apothecary, in 1855, who moved it to its present location and altered it into the dwelling and shop now occupied by A. A. Cheney, watchmaker. One would think his clocks and watches might catch the echoes of the old walls, and be heard in the stillness of night ticking out the spelling book and striking the changes of the multiplication table.

CHAPTER VI.

THE SHARPS. — CURIOUS OLD PAPERS. — THE SEWALLS. — EDWARD DEVOTION. — CAPTAIN WINCHESTER. — THE GRIGGS FAMILY. — HARVARD STREET, CONCLUDED.

LEAVING School Street to proceed up Harvard Street, we find the first house to be that of Esquire Sharp, on the left hand side, standing now next to Cousens' Block, but formerly on the high bank at the entrance to Harvard Avenue, on the left. The only other house on that side of the street before arriving at the present site of the house of William Griggs, was the house of Captain Robert Sharp, on the site of the present house of J. C. Abbot, Esq. (We are writing now of forty or more years ago.) On the north side of the street was no house from Aspinwall Avenue to the house occupied by Charles Stearns, Sen. All the land on both sides belonged to the Sharps. This name, like that of many of the other old families, is extinct; but through a line of female descendants, the ancient Sharps "still live," in the families bearing the names of Clark, Davis, Jones, and Craft, in this town, and through the Buckminsters, in the families of Rev. Dr. Lothrop, George B. Emerson, and Judge Lowell, of Boston and Brookline.

We will go back more than two hundred years, and trace downwards something of the family history. Robert Sharp was of English origin, and came to Boston in the ship *Abigail* in 1635, from London, aged twenty years. It would seem that he lived at Dorchester for a while, as he came from there to Brookline, or Muddy River, in 1650, with Peter Aspinwall, and the two bought a great tract of land, one hundred and fifty acres, of William Colborn. The ancient deed, bearing the above date, is still preserved in the Aspinwall family. Harvard Street was not then laid out, and School Street was but a part of the lane leading to the Aspinwall house from the "Watertown road," as Washington Street was then called. Four years later Harvard Street was laid out through their farms, and the Davis property, etc.; "Peeter Asppenwall," William Davis, and others appointed by the town authorities of Cambridge being authorized to lay out the street.

The ancient dwelling house of the Sharps was near the present corner of Harvard and Auburn Streets, on what is now Mr. Harris's lawn. The old cellar, and an English cherry tree which was near it, were to be seen within the memory of persons now living. Robert Sharp died in 1654, and in 1656 we find recorded a petition of his widow, who has already consoled herself with a second husband, that "Peter Aspinwall and Thomas Meekins" be appointed guardians for her three minor children, John, Abigail, and Mary. It is proposed that Aspinwall "take ye two daughters and finde them meate, drinke and apparell, learne them to reade, to knitt, to spine, and such Housewifery, and keepe them either to ye day of marriage or until ye age of eighteene; for which said '*Peeter*' is to have ye vse and profitt of ye house and land, yt was said Sharps, only ye said *Peeter* besides bringing up ye said daughters, in consideration of ye benefit of said house and land, alow ye sonne £5 per annum. (Thomas Meekinne's had the sonne to bringe up to his trade.)" Signed January 15, 1656, witnessed by Abigail Clapp, Relicte and Administratrix to the Estate of the late Robert Sharp." Nine years later, on April 15, 1665, we find a petition of the mother that the guardians be discharged, they having fulfilled their trust. At this time John, the eldest, is twenty-two years of age and married, Abigail seventeen and Mary twelve.

We hear no more of the " sonne John," till the beginning of the year 1676, when he writes a letter to his old guardian, Thomas Meekins, which we copy entire for its exquisite quaintness.

[Address.] " This for Loving Master Thomas Meekins living at Hatfield. This deliver.

"LOVING AND MUCH RESPECTED MASTER:—

" My love is remembered to you and my dame hoping you are wel as I am at the writing hereof, blessed be God for it. My wiff desiars to be remembered unto you and my dame, and wee are yet in our habitation through Gods marsi, but we are in expectation of the enimi everi day if God be not the more marsiful unto us.

" I have been out 7 weeks myself and if provisions had not grown short we had folood the enimi into your borders, and then I would have given you a visit if it had been possibel, for I went out a volintere under Captain Wadsworth of Milton, but he is coled hom to recropt about their owne town, so I left off the desire at present.

" There is many of our friends taken from us. Cap Jonson of Roxberi was slaine at Naragansit, and Will lincoln died before his wound was cured; filip Curtis was slane at a wigwame about Mendham, but we have lost but one man with us these wars. My mother bose is ded and my sister Swift. I pray remember my love to John Elis and his wiff, and the rest of our friends, and however it is like to fare with us God knows, and wee desiare to comit all our affairs into his hands.

" So having nothing els desiaring your praiars for us, I rest,
" Your Sarvant, JOHN SHARPE.*
" Mudiriver 8 of the 1 mo. 1676."

* Dr. Pierce, in his Town Hall Address, 1845, speaks of the Lieutenant who

On the eighteenth of April following, occurred the memorable fight at Sudbury, in which Captain Wadsworth and Lieutenant Sharp were both killed. Those who are familiar with the history of King Philip's War will remember the horrible atrocities practiced upon the wounded in this battle. It is only to be hoped that poor John Sharp was killed outright, early in the contest.

The old stone which formerly marked the spot, bore the following inscription : —

" Capt. Samuel Wadsworth of Milton, his Lieut. Sharp of Brooklin, and twenty-six other souldieis, fighting for the defence of their country were slain by the indian enemy April 18, 1676, and lye buried in this place."

A few years since a tasteful monument was erected upon the spot.

Lieutenant John Sharp left four children, Robert, William, Martha, and Elizabeth. The son Robert married Sarah Williams of Roxbury. In 1690 a campaign was planned against the Indians at the north, in which he bore a part. A writing which lies before us, from his own hand, is worth transcribing. It is as follows : —

" Know all men by these presents that whereas, I, Robert Sharp of mudyriver in the county of Suffolk in newingland being bound out to the warr, and leaving some conserns behind me, doe therefore ordain and constitute my loveing father Steven Williams of Roxbury in the counti aforesaid my lawfull attorny for and in behalf of myseulf in all things to act and doe in all things both to pay and receive debts, and to plead and to be impleaded and to be discharged and to give discharges, to imprison

fell at Sudbury, as " *Robert* Sharp." This was incorrect. See Town Records of Sudbury, and Eliot Church Records of Roxbury, quoted in " New England General Register," vol. xi. p. 257. All the old writings prove his name to have been *John*.

and to be imprisoned, and in all things to act and doe as my lawful attorny for my advantage and to lett out my lands and to take rents and to sell and dispose as if it were myseulf, and in all and everi respect as is above expressed I doe leaue my conserns for the time of one yeer after the date hereof if I return not in witness of the premises I have hereunto set my hand and affixed my seal this 16 of aprill 1690.   ROBART SHARP."

"Witnes. Andrew Gardner, Samuel Craft, Sen."

Like his father this Robert "returned not;" he perished in the expedition to Canada.

The bones of Robert Sharp had not had time to whiten in the Canadian forests, before his widow married Mr. Thomas Nowell. She seems to have been unfortunate in her husbands or fatal to them, for in 1694, less than four years from the time her first husband went to the "*warr*," she was the widow of Thomas Nowell and made a will in favor of her children by Robert Sharp, of which we will transcribe one clause only.

"I, Sarah Nowell, the relict of Mr. Thomas Nowell, late of Muddy River in their Majesties Province of Massachusetts Bay in Newengland deceased, being about to intermarry again with Mr. Solomon Phipps, son of Mr. Solomon Phipps of Cambridge, & &c, I do therefore by these presents before my said intermarriage, for and upon divers good and weighty causes, reasons and considerations me thereunto moving. And also that I may testify and demonstrate the naturall love and affection which I have unto Robert Sharp and Sarah Sharp the children which I had by my former husband Robert Sharp, And that I may faithfully discharge that duty unto which both by the law of God and nature I stand obliged by providing as well as for their future good and comfort as well as for my own, and also for their decent and laudable education if it should please God to take me away from them or deprive me of doing any further for them,

I do therefore by these presents aforesaid not privately, but with the knowledge of the said Mr. Solomon Phipps make, ordain, and constitute this my will for the attainment of the ends premized in manner and form following."

The will then goes on to bequeath all " the housing and lands" to Robert, and sixty pounds in money to Sarah, with twenty additional pounds, to be paid to her by Robert at two different times after he comes of age. Sarah also was to receive various household goods, including " one silver cup, three silver spoonds, three gold rings and one silver girdle " — whatever that might be.

There lies before us the bill of sale of " a neagroe Woman named Rose," which the above mentioned Mr. Thomas Nowell purchased of a Mrs. Abigail Davis in 1693, which piece of property this enterprising widow probably retained for herself, as there is no mention made of such a chattel in the will.

As there is no occasion to follow the *widow* further, we return to the children of the Lieutenant. William, it seems, on coming to manhood removed to Pomfret, Conn., and some years afterwards sold out all his Brookline inheritance to his nephew, Robert, his brother Robert's son. He was a resident here in 1704, as his name is on the petition for a separate township from Boston. Martha Sharp was destined to be the ancestor of a distinguished posterity. She married Joseph Buckminster, a native of this town, and they removed to Framingham, then the outskirts of civilization, and lived the life of pioneers.

Her son Joseph was a colonel in the army, was a selectman of that town twenty-eight years, and town clerk thirty years. For thirty years he also represented the town in the General Court and died when over eighty, beloved and respected. Her grandson William, son of the abovementioned colonel, was a distinguished man. He, too, held the office of colonel, and commanded a company of minute men from Barre, at the battle of Bunker Hill, and was wounded there.

Another of Martha Sharp's grandchildren, a brother of the last mentioned, was a clergyman, and from him in a direct line descended the distinguished Dr. Joseph Buckminster of Portsmouth, and his son Rev. Joseph S. Buckminster, the beloved and talented young minister of Brattle Square Church in Boston, who died so deeply lamented.

His sister, Eliza Buckminster, wife of the late Thomas Lee of this town, was the author of "The Life of the Buckminsters," "Naomi," "Parthenia," and other works.

As Martha Sharp's descendants are still numerous, in most cultivated circles, others among them may yet distinguish themselves for culture or patriotism.

As we have found no record of Elizabeth Sharp's marriage it is probable she died single.

We now return to Robert, the young son of the Robert who perished in the Canada expedition. He was but two years old when his father left upon the fatal march.

As soon as we hear of him in his early manhood, after his marriage to his wife Susannah, he holds the office of constable of this town. Soon after this we find him designated as captain. Captain Robert (the third of the name it will be remembered), was a shrewd, successful man in business, as his accounts and other papers indicate. The original large tract which his great-grandfather bought had been divided and subdivided among the descendants, and it seems to have been his great aim to recover as much of it as possible, as from time to time deeds were recorded showing that he had made purchases of various lots varying from a few rods to several acres. He also boarded or pastured sheep, cattle, and horses in great numbers for people living in Boston. All the land from the corner of School and Washington streets, on the north side, to a line above Park Street, extending across beyond Harvard Street, to the Longwood marshes along the river, above the Aspinwall lands and below the present Stearns' lands was at one time his property and was probably most of it grazing land. A glimpse into the prices and customs of those early days in our own town, is afforded by these long preserved papers.

The early settlers, as is well known, were obliged to barter instead of giving and receiving cash payments, and Captain Sharp did not always get paid in money for his "Sider," as we find on his ancient parchment-covered account-book the credit which he has given one individual for "orringes," another for "naels," another for a "grenston and a pair of stillyards." In one place he allows ten pence for one "orring," and in another two shillings and eight pence for four.

The explicitness with which the expense of each item of an outfit of clothing is recorded, in the quaint old spelling of those days, is entertaining. We give a specimen.

"Paid Thomas Sharle for Cloas.

	£	s.	d.
For a hatt	3	3	0
For a shurt	0	9	0
For Britches		15	0
For Stockens		3	6
For a coat	2	0	0

Thus the "cloas," it will be seen by reckoning a little, cost a little less than thirty dollars, in United States money.

In another place is the receipt which Abigail Story, a long-forgotten school teacher, gave Captain Sharp for £3 16s. for keeping school.

Mr. Sharp had hired laborers who came and went as farm hands do now, but he also had a man who was bound by indenture to him by his master, Joseph Little, of Boston, for three years. This man is described in the indenture as " Dunkan Mackeever late of Bellenock in the county of lonon Derry," and the writing obliges Captain Sharp to " supply his said servant with Sufficient meat, Drink, washing, lodging and apparrel fitting for such a Servant, and at the end of Said Term shall Dismiss his said Servant with two suits of apparrell suitable for Every part of his body." This is signed by " Duncken Ma-Keever."

But the Captain's good wife Susannah needed help in the great farm-kitchen, and it was obtained on this wise:

BOSTON *March* 12, 1749.

Received of mr. Robart Sharp *iun* Ninety-eaight Pounds old tenor in full for a Negro girl named Luce beLonging to the Estate of Mr. Hez'h. Barber.

(Signed.) EUNICE LANERD.

An old order issued by the assessors of this town to Constable Robert Sharp in 1719, instructs him to collect the sum of thirty pounds from the inhabitants of the town for the town expenses of that year.

Captain Sharp built and occupied a house which stood on the site of the present residence of J. C. Abbott, Esq. It was a large square house, was never painted, except the window frames, which being white made the house, which was black with age, a very conspicuous object on Harvard Street. It remained there until about twenty-five years ago.

Captain Sharp died in 1765, aged seventy-seven years. He left a son Robert and four daughters.

The will left by Captain Robert Sharp proves him to

have been a man of wealth for those days, and in it he provides abundantly for his "beloved wife Susannah," and puts in a clause which allows, or enjoins her to bestow all that is over and beyond her own requirements upon such of her children as treat her best. There was real estate belonging to this family in the town of Warwick, Mass., which was then called "Gardner's Canada," it being a part of a large tract in the northwest part of the State which was assigned to soldiers (or their heirs) who served in the Canada expedition. Ashburnham, it will be remembered, was a part of the same tract and was called "Dorchester-Canada."

Among other effects which the Captain left to his wife was a negro slave, Jane, and a silver tankard. This silver tankard was presented by Mrs. Sharp to the First Congregational Church in this town in 1770 and is still preserved. She did not long survive her husband.

All the "housing and lands" became the property of the son Robert, who it seems by old papers still extant was kind to his mother, and carried out his father's intentions with regard to the property.

The fourth Robert Sharp married Sarah Payson of Roxbury, by whom he had ten children, four of whom died in infancy. The eldest, Robert, died without children, and at this point the family name of Robert ceases.

The second son, Jacob, was married, but died at the age of twenty-nine, in the year 1775, no doubt in the service of the country.

The third son, Stephen, became a prominent man in Brookline and is still well remembered by many persons now living as Esquire Sharp.

This was the person to whom allusion has been made as the owner of the large square house which stood until recently on the left of the entrance to Harvard Avenue, from Harvard street, and is now standing next to Cousens' Block, on the same street, and occupied as a tenement house. On the left side of Harvard Avenue on the site of the garden of Mr. M. C. Warren, was a house which Esquire Sharp had finished off from a shed, and afterwards enlarged for a farm-house, to be occupied by whoever he hired to carry on his large farm. This house was moved to School Street, several years ago, where it still remains, opposite Mr. Matthews' residence.

Esquire Sharp was never married. He was a teacher in the little old school-house in School Street for many winters, was a justice of the peace and town clerk for many years. It will be remembered that this was the man who brought Tom Cook to grief for stealing the goose, as mentioned in a former chapter.

The 'Squire was a somewhat stern and gruff man in his ways, and not very popular with the children of the neighborhood, and was known by them by the nickname "*Grumpy.*" He died in 1820.

From his sister Lucy, who married into the Davis family, descended Captain Robert Sharp Davis, whose son of the same name is now living in Brookline.

From another sister (Mary) descended the present Jones family of Brookline, and the Clarks of Walnut and Warren Street. The eldest daughter married Caleb Crafts of this town, and her descendants are still living, though not in Brookline.

Thus it will be seen that this ancient family, now so numerous, are all traced directly back in an unbroken line to the Robert Sharp who came from England in the *Abigail* in 1635, and beyond that the family is traced to Robert Sharp of Islington, England, as far back as 1534. Few New England families are probably able to trace their ancestry so far and so creditably.

The old unpainted house previously alluded to, on the site of J. C. Abbott's residence, was occupied after Captain Sharp's death by Major Joseph Jones who had married into the family. Several years after Major Jones's death the farm was improved by his son Stephen S. C. Jones, afterwards postmaster of Brookline. In the interval between, it was in the hands of Moses Jones, who became unrivaled as a farmer, subsequently, in Cypress Street. The old house, black with the storms of many years, was taken down about thirty years ago.

Stephen Sharp's residence passed into possession of his nephew, the late Samuel Crafts, of this town, and was occupied by him for many years, and these two estates were spoken of as "the Jones" and "the Crafts farms," until cut up into house lots and divided by many streets and avenues.

The next estate on Harvard Street, in former times was that of Chief Justice Sewall, comprising three hundred and fifty acres of land, most of it being now known as Longwood. It extended from Harvard Street to Charles River, and from the Aspinwall and Sharp Estates to Pleasant Street. This property came into the possession of the Judge by inheritance. The earliest owner of this great portion of our town was John Hull, who lived in a house somewhere in the neighborhood of the Sears Church, or Gospel Church, Longwood. He was a poor boy, but his devotion to his widowed mother caused the Rev. John Wilson, the first minister of Boston, to predict for him a prosperous future. The prediction was verified. John Hull became Master of the Mint in Boston, an opulent merchant and a large landowner. He was highly respected throughout the colony. He married Judith, daughter of Edmund Quincy, the first of that distinguished family in this country. It is said that he was the designer of the coat of arms of Massachusetts, — an Indian with a bow and arrow, — and also of the famous pine-tree shillings.

Chief Justice Sewall married for his first wife, Hannah, the only daughter of John Hull, and thus came in possession of the large estate which John Hull owned in this town.

When the marriage took place, the bride received from her father as a wedding present, *her weight in pine-tree shillings!* How heavy she was we are not informed, but at all events her dowry seems to have been a substantial one.

John Hull died in 1683. A poem written upon his death by Rev. Daniel Gookin, son of the Major-general, is entitled, " A few Shadie Meditations occasioned by the death of the deservedly honored, John Hull Esq., who was removed from his earthly tabernacle, to be an inhabitant of the house not made with hands eternal in the heavens, 30 September, 1683."

A notice of his wife's death, supposed to be by Rev. Cotton Mather, reads as follows, —

"Mrs. Judith Hull, of Boston, N. E., late wife of John Hull Esq. deceased, a diligent, constant, fruitful reader and hearer of the word of God, rested from her labors, 22 June, 1695, being the seventh day of the week, a little before sunset, just about the time she used to begin the Sabbath, aged 69.

Chief Justice Sewall was famous in his day, as one of the judges who condemned the Salem witches to death, an error in judgment of which he lived to repent bitterly, and for which he made voluntary and humble confession in public, in the Old South Church in Boston. The Judge is represented by his biographers to have been eminent for piety and learning. He died in 1730.

An interesting sketch of Judge Sewall's life may be found in the " New England Historical Register," vol. i., page 105. It would seem from this paper, that the Judge was far in advance of his age in perceiving the evils of negro slavery, and in courage to denounce it.

In writing to Judge Davenport, just before he sat upon the trial of a white man for killing a negro, he made use of language which has the true ring of justice in it. We quote, —

" The poorest boys and girls, in this province, such as are of the lowest condition, whether they be English, or Ethiopians, or Indians ; they have the same right to religion and life, that the richest heirs have. And they who go about to deprive them of this right attempt the bombardment of Heaven ; and the shells they throw will fall down on their own heads."

He wrote and published a tract in 1700, called " The Selling of Joseph," which was perhaps the first anti-slavery document published in the United States. It seems strange that a man so clear-headed in his judgment as to the rights of the weak and defenseless, could have been misled even temporarily in the witchcraft cases, but that when he saw his error he had the rare courage and the honor to confess it, does credit to his heart. The Judge left many volumes of valuable manuscript which are still carefully preserved.

Samuel Sewall, Jr., son of the Judge, lived in a house on the site of the present residence of Charles Stearns, Esq., which was built in 1703. His son Henry succeeded him in the same house. He was a farmer, and held the office of Justice of the Peace in this town. He was educated at Harvard College, as were also his own three sons, Henry, Hull, and Samuel.

Henry and Hull both died at the age of twenty-four, and little is known of them. Samuel was a young lawyer practicing in Boston at the breaking out of our Revolutionary difficulties, and he became so odious, as a Tory, that he was obliged to leave his native land, and ended his days in England. He owned real estate in Brookline in his mother's right, which was forfeited, he being a refugee, and after the war it was sold by the Government. It was purchased by Mr. John Heath, the ancestor of the present Charles Heath of this town, and has ever since been retained by that family.

The house now occupied by Charles Stearns, Esq., was built for Henry Sewall, Jr., and after his death was occupied by his daughter, who married Edward K. Wolcott.

This Wolcott built the old house on the Francis estate, near the river, north of Pleasant Street and Brighton Avenue, established a race-course there, and kept a public house for several years, and was succeeded in that business by his son-in-law Frost. It was not very successful, however, and after a while was abandoned.

About the time the Mill-dam was projected, a great part of the Sewall estate was bought up by the five gentlemen who were the prime movers in that enterprise, of whom Eben Francis was one, in expectation of a rapid growth of Boston in that direction and the consequent rise of property. But though the Mill-dam was completed, contrary to the predictions of the croakers of that generation who pronounced it a wild scheme, the expected rise of real estate did not follow, and those who bought the Sewall property died without seeing their hopes realized. It was their misfortune to be in advance of the times.

The elder Charles Stearns, who came here from Chelsea, purchased and settled upon the estate now owned by his heirs, quite early in the present century, and the Wolcotts left Brookline; none of the descendants of Judge Sewall being now left in the town, so far as we can learn, though there are a few bearing the names of Ridgway and Gilbert in Boston.

Next west of the Sewall estate is situated what has been in modern times known as the Babcock farm, but in Judge Sewall's day was the property of John Devotion.

The ancient house is no doubt at least two hundred years old.

John Devotion was a prominent citizen in Muddy River, holding various offices, and his name appears upon the petition for a separate township.

Ebenezer Devotion, probably a son of John, became a clergyman and removed to Connecticut, and from him descended "Grace Greenwood," Mrs. Lippincott, of literary fame.

After the death of John Devotion, the house was occupied by his son Edward, and Mary his wife. Edward Devotion was a public spirited citizen, and reference to the old records of the town will show that he held various offices of trust for many years. In the church he was for a long period the tithingman.

The principal duty of this officer was to keep good order during divine service, among the children, who sat in rows by themselves instead of with their parents. A long rod was usually carried by the tithingman, with which to touch any delinquent who might become drowsy or mischievous. Whether this ancient Brookline tithingman was particularly feared by the youngsters does not appear, but he was evidently not unfriendly to children, as he adopted a boy and girl, whom he brought up, as he had no children of his own.

The old house in the village, formerly known as the Brewer house, next the brick blacksmith shop, was probably built for Edward Devotion, as he died in that house in November, 1774.

He left the old house on Harvard Street to the young couple whom he had brought up, and who were then married. To the Brookline church he left a silver tankard.

He also left to the town a sum of money, which at the time of its being received in 1762, amounted to " £739 4s. lawful money," for the use of schools.

This money was borrowed by the State during the Revolutionary war, and when it was paid back to the town, it was in depreciated Continental currency. It was put at interest however, and in 1845 had accumulated to the amount of $4,531.01, which was appropriated to the building of the Town Hall, which was to have two school rooms in it.

Why would it not have been well to keep in memory this worthy patron of education, by giving his name to the old Town Hall?

Solomon Hill, the young man to whom Edward Devotion left his old house, and some money, did not prove to be very enterprising, and before many years lost his property and died, very poor, in an old house in the village. The house which Mr. Devotion left to him was sold to a man named Marshall who occupied it for a number of years, until it was purchased by one of the five gentlemen heretofore mentioned as having bought the Sewall property. It was hired for some time by the late George Babcock, who afterwards bought it, and its history since its purchase by him is well known.

The house is a curious old relic of former times, and the beautiful elms which shade it were no doubt set out by the hands of the ancient owner, whose devotion to the interests of his church and town, suggest the idea that a similar characteristic in his ancestry may have earned for the family its very uncommon name.

A sister of Edward Devotion married a Ruggles of Roxbury, and old papers are extant in which her son Edward Ruggles, of that place, presents claims for property left him by his uncle, which had not been settled.

In an ancient paper found between the floors of the old house once occupied by Deacon Benjamin White, which was taken down in 1809 (on the site of General Lyman's house), is found the order of the seats in the First Church, in 1719, where Mr. Edward Devotion's seat is mentioned " as on the men's fore-seat in the body-seats," and his wife's place in the " women's fore-seat," according to the unsocial and strange old practice of separating husbands from wives, and parents from children during religious service.

There are modern churches in which employment could be found for several tithingmen, notwithstanding the improved methods of arranging families during divine service.

THE WINCHESTERS.

The name of Winchester was a prominent one in the early history of Brookline. The family was scattered throughout the town, and Harvard Street was probably the place of the first settlement. The family was of Welsh descent and emigrated to this country at a very early date. On the site of the present residence of William Griggs, Esq., stood until some thirty years ago an ancient, unpainted house, black with age.

This house was the residence of John Winchester, the first representative of Brookline in the General Court. All the land from Harvard Street to the top of Corey's Hill, and west as far as Brighton line on that side of the street, belonged to the Winchesters. It may have extended over upon the south side of the hill for aught we know, as there was a house on the site of the stone house now owned by the Coreys on Washington Street, which belonged to Isaac Winchester, but we leave that side of the hill for a future chapter. Corey's Hill was spoken of in the early records of Boston and Muddy River as "the great hill," and it is certain that for many years the Winchesters were the principal owners of it. It was probably well wooded once, as was a great part of the Sewall and Sharp farms and the Babcock place.

Two tall trees which escaped the axe, probably only because they were buttonwoods, not good for timber, and vexatious for firewood, were left standing on the very summit of the hill till they died a natural death not many years ago. On one of these for a few of the last years of its existence, was conspicuous a bright tin signal, placed there by the U. S. Coast Survey, and discernible, when the sun's rays fell upon it, far up and down the coast.

John Winchester being near neighbor to Samuel Sewall, was one of the first to sign the petition drawn up by him for a separation of this town from its parent, Boston.

After his death, his son, Capt. John Winchester, occupied the homestead, and after him his son Isaac, probably the one alluded to above as afterwards living on the other side of the hill.

After him it came into possession of Samuel Griggs, the grandfather of Deacon Thomas Griggs now living on Washington Street, and after his death to his son Thomas. And there his widow remained, living to a great age, a much beloved and respected lady, and for her sake and during her lifetime the old house was allowed to remain.

After her death, over thirty years ago, Deacon Thomas Griggs had the old house taken down.

The branch of the Griggs family represented in this

part of the town are the descendants in a direct line from Joseph Griggs who was born in England in 1625, became a freeman, or member of the church in 1653, in Roxbury, and the same year married Mary, a daughter of Griffin Crafts. She died almost immediately after, and he married the next year Hannah Davis, likewise of Roxbury.

The children of this marriage were Hannah, Benjamin, Joseph, Ichabod, and Mary.

From Ichabod Griggs descended Thomas, grandfather of the present venerable citizen of that name. There has been a Thomas in this family ever since 1715. Joseph Griggs, the ancestor above mentioned, lived in that part of Brookline village which was then a part of Roxbury, as in the Suffolk Registry of Deeds, lib. 24, folio 279, is recorded the following Deposition : —

"Jos. Griggs of Roxbury, aged about 85 years, testifieth and saith that about three score years since he settled at Muddy River now called Brooklyne and has lived there and at Roxbury ever since, and in all that time has been very well acquainted with that tract of land now in farms and proprietys, viz., Capt. Sewall, the late Deacon Elliot's Devotions, Clarks and others lying in Muddy River aforesaid, which was commonly called a common field butting on the salt marishes. As to the fence or enclosure of said common field this deponent very well remembers that those persons that owned the upland were at the whole and sole charge of the outside range of fence the marish owners refusing to pay any part of the charge and at a meeting of the upland and marish owners about forty years since the marishmen representing their design to fence the marish from the upland desired the upland owners *to be* (?) their proportion but the upland owners utterly refused it for the reason above mentioned and told the marish owners that if they would fence out the marish they must do it at their own cost, and this depon't hath never known or understood that the upland owners ever bore any proportion of the charge of fencing off the marish, but that they did at all times maintain the outside range of fence and the marish men were at the charge of fencing the marish from the upland. JOSEPH GRIGGS, January 21, 1709."

The dispute was about the fences along the old roadway which once skirted the upland from a point this side of Chapel Station to what was called Sewall's Point, where the fort was afterwards built. Traces of this old road are still to be seen in the fringe of trees which still borders the edge of the upland north of Chapel Station.

Joseph Griggs died in 1715, at the age of 90.

Ichabod Griggs had nine children, and was probably a man of wealth for his times, as some old papers which are extant, show that his son Thomas, who came of age 1726-27, received of his guardian, James Clark, the sum of one hundred and sixty-eight pounds nine shillings as his share of his father's estate. The names of Samuel Griggs (his elder brother) and Thomas Cotton, appear as witnesses on this old receipt. Samuel Griggs settled on Harvard Street on the estate now in the Griggs family. It was formerly Captain John Winchester's. Thomas Griggs married Margaret Williams. From this marriage came Moses Griggs, from whom descended that branch of the family in this town now represented by the heirs of the late David R. Griggs, Samuel Griggs, and Deacon Thomas Griggs. From Nathaniel, the youngest son, descended another branch of the family now represented in Brighton.

An ancient letter recalls an incident perhaps long forgotten among Nathaniel Griggs' descendants. He was born in 1778. The letter referred to was written in March, 1799, by a young lady in Brookline to another belonging here but who was on a visit to the family of Dr. Goddard in Portsmouth. She tells her story as follows: —

"One day the week before last Mr. Nat. Griggs went to Boston in the morning with his team and before he got back his House, furniture and Cloaths except what he had on his back were consumed by fire. His house was all finished but one Room. The carpenter had just begun to finish that and went over to Mr. Moses Griggs' to get some tools. It is said he was not gone more than ten minutes and when he came back the House was all in flames, — he left a window open and there was a little fire on the Hearth to smoke Bacon, and it's supposed the wind blew a train of shavings into the fire which caught the house. The Housekeeper was spinning in the kitchen but did not perceive the fire till the flames burst in upon her & she jumpt out at a window and lost all her cloaths but what she had on. But Mrs. Moses Griggs and Mrs. Tom Gardner have been around the town to collect Cloaths for her so I believe her loss is in part made up if not all. . . . . When Mr. Griggs got home and found his House and all that was in it burnt up (except a few things in the cellar were saved) he was ready to sink. One hundred dollars of money was consumed some silver, some Bank Bills, the Silver was melted into small pieces like shot. But one of his Brothers and Ebby Davis went round the next morning with a subscription paper & people were very liberal, the more so because he was a very industrious young man. Judge Dana, of Cambridge gave him eighty dollars, Major Gardner forty, Mr. Mason twenty and every body according to their ability. Some gave him Timber, some boards carried to the spot, some bricks, some lime, and in short he is to have a new house raised this week and expects to be married before long to Nancy Aspinwall. He was finishing his house for her when it was burnt."

He afterwards married accordingly.

For more than two hundred years there was a Joseph Griggs in this ancient family, but this christian name seems to have fallen into disuse within the last half century. This family in its various branches has been always of high standing in the town, having hardly ever been without one or more members holding some office of trust and honor either in the town or church. One of the elder members of the family in the last century was one of the founders of the Baptist Church in Newton. The present venerable senior deacon of the Baptist Church, in this place, was active in the interests of the first church of that faith in Roxbury, and when the time came for a similar movement in Brookline, he was one of the first and most liberal in the cause. He has also repeatedly held the office of Selectman in this town to the entire acceptance of our townspeople. During the second war with England, he was in active service as Ensign of the Brookline Company on duty in Boston harbor.

A young lady of this family, Miss Helen Maria Griggs, daughter of Joseph and Sarah Griggs, was eminent as a foreign missionary, in the employ of the Baptist denomination. Her daughter Harriet is now the wife of Rev. Mr. Stephens of the Burmah mission.

Two of the sons of the former Thomas Griggs, and who were born in the old house now occupied by David Coolidge, removed to Sutton, Mass., in their early manhood, and there became honored and influential citizens. Their descendants are scattered among the towns in that vicinity. One or more of them are physicians by profession. Moses Griggs, who was before mentioned as one of the sons of this Thomas Griggs (father of the late D. R. Griggs), settled just within the edge of Brighton, the house being the first after crossing the town boundary on the north side of Harvard Street. It is not now standing. The house which his brother Nathaniel built on the site of the one that was burned, is the house which still stands nearly opposite the one just mentioned. In these four houses, two in Brookline and two in Brighton, but so near the boundary as to be all neighbors, four or five generations of Joseph Griggs' descendants have lived, and here many of them have died. Samuel Griggs, Jr., brother of the present Deacon, removed to Rutland, Vt., where he lived to a great age, one of the most earnest and faithful pioneers in that town in all matters of local interest and church labor and prosperity. Stephen, the youngest brother, was for many years a merchant in London. He returned to his native land to enjoy the fruits of his labor, but very soon after was drowned in Salem harbor. He left a daughter, of unusual talents, and great strength and beauty of character. She wrote admirably, and would have been distinguished had she lived and chosen to make literature a profession, but she did not long survive her father, whom she mourned with a rare and touching devotion.

The next house on that side of the street, the one now owned by David Coolidge, Esq., was built by Nathan Winchester, the son of Captain John. It has been added to and altered since his day, but the original house is there, though much disguised, and its low ceiling and quaint architecture mark it unmistakably as one of the few old relics of the past, thoroughly identified with the early history of our country, and too rapidly passing away.

At this house, on the day of the battle of Lexington, a detachment of British troops, marching up Harvard Street, stopped for water and were served by the frightened inmates, who received no harm. Like its neighbor this house came into possession of the Griggs family. The ancient doctor alluded to in our sketch of "the Downer house" in the village, came here to live, in the latter part of his life.

Mr. Joshua Griggs, the father-in-law of the present owner, Mr. Coolidge, also lived and died here.

The Winchester family and the Griggs family are both so numerous, and located in so many parts of the town, that further mention must be made hereafter of the various branches of the families.

There was still another branch of the Griggs family located in Roxbury, near the southwest part of this town. They were all from the same English origin and the family coat of arms has within a few years been procured from England by some member of the family who was interested in Heraldry.

Further toward Brighton, and on the opposite side of the street, near Smelt Brook, there stood formerly a very old house, once owned by Amos Gates. He removed to Worcester, and tradition does not report what befell his house. This brings us to Brighton line or Allston, in this direction, and closes the history of Harvard Street. The north part of the town has various other points of interest, however.

Pleasant Street, until about twenty-five years ago, was only a green lane which served to connect Harvard Street with Brighton Avenue. The sides of the lane were a tangled thicket of wild rose-bushes and raspberry and blackberry vines. There were but two houses on Pleasant Street at that time. On the top of the hill, on the site of Mrs. Adams' late residence, stood a large house painted a light dull green. There was no beauty or cultivation around it and no wonder it changed tenants often, for it was as unattractive as a barrack, and too isolated to be identified with the interests of any neighborhood. It was occupied in the summer, several seasons, by Durivage, of some literary note. The green house took fire one day when a high wind was blowing, and was speedily destroyed.

On the corner of Pleasant Street and Brighton Avenue

was another house, with a blacksmith's shop attached, occupied for years by a thriftless family. We have alluded before to the Francis house, further towards the river, once kept as a public house. This was occupied for many years by William Dearborn, now of Walnut Street, who carried on the extensive farms on that side of Brighton Avenue.

On the right of Brighton Avenue, about half way from Pleasant Street to Fourth Street, stood one more house belonging to either the Sears or Francis purchase, which for several years was occupied by Isaac Dearborn, brother of William Dearborn, and afterwards by Rev. Dr. Hague, now of Chicago.

Far down toward the marsh, on land now belonging to the Lawrence estate, near St. Mary's Street, was a most ancient house, but by whom built is unknown. It was on Judge Sewall's farm and may have been the house of John Hull, the ancient mint master of Boston, whose daughter became the wife of Judge Sewall, as it is well known that he built and occupied a house in that vicinity. This house was occupied by a Mr. Easterbrooks in the early part of the present century, and afterwards by Martin Morse. After Mr. Amos Lawrence purchased the place, the old house was taken down. While the work of demolition was going on, the workmen found behind the great old chimney a number of pine-tree shillings and ancient English copper money. They had used it nearly all to pay their toll from day to day over the Mill-dam, before it was known by any one who appreciated the true value of the coin, and but a few pieces were recovered.

This house was accessible originally by a road which skirted the uplands at the verge of the marsh, and of which Sewall Avenue was a part. On Sewall Avenue, stood the old house of Col. Thomas Aspinwall, who commanded Fort Sewall a part of the time during the Revolution, and which was burned some twenty years ago.

These houses were all which then stood upon the whole territory now known as Longwood, except a small house on Sewall Avenue, which was once a cider mill and was altered into a dwelling house by the late Marshall Stearns. It is a matter of regret that the whole farm on the north side of Brighton Avenue, commanding as it does a beautiful and extensive prospect both up and down the river, and with the greatest variety of surface and noble old shade trees, could not have fallen into the hands of gentlemen of taste and wealth, and become a fitting precinct of beautiful Longwood.*

Until within thirty years the whole of that part of the town was quite wild and picturesque. Within three miles of the State House and closely bordering on one of the great thoroughfares leading to Boston, it seems strange that the dream of the founders of the Mill-dam should have so long remained unfulfilled; but could they see it in its present wealth of cultivated beauty and select population, it would seem that they must find that the reality had exceeded their anticipations.

* By an Act of the Legislature of 1873-74, all the territory north of the southerly line of Brighton Avenue became a part of Boston.

CHAPTER VII.

WASHINGTON STREET. — HOLDEN'S HILL. — LEED'S PLACE.—
DANA PLACE.

RETURNING to Harvard Square, it will be recollected by those who have read the early pages of this volume, that the old Dana Tavern, though it fronted upon the Square, extended somewhat toward Washington Street. In the rear of the old tavern, in what is now the easterly part of Mr. Panter's yard, was situated in the latter part of the last century a wheelwright's shop, occupied by Mr. James Holden, the owner and occupant also of the house, which has been within a few years rebuilt entirely by Mr. Panter.

We have not been able to ascertain any facts respecting this ground before Mr. Holden's day, and probably his was the first house built upon that site, as the whole hill, including all the ground from Harvard Street to Washington and thence to School Street, was once a part of the Davis estate.

Mr. Holden, having married the widow of the third Ebenezer Davis, who owned, besides a large part of the hill, all that is now Linden Place and a large tract of marsh below it, found the pursuits of agriculture more profitable than the making of wheels, and thenceforward devoted himself to the farm.

After the old tavern was burnt, if not sooner, the shop was removed and the yard in front of the house was filled with peach and cherry trees. Close to the sidewalk stood an immensely large and high buttonwood tree, perfectly straight and symmetrical, and a little east of it a fine graceful elm, also of large size. The lowering of the road to its present level made it necessary to cut these trees down. The buttonwood, like most of its kind, suffered from an epidemic about that time and was apparently in a dying condition. It was over a hundred feet high. Behind the house, and extending up the slope of the hill, was a small apple orchard, covering the ground now east of Holden Street as far back as the Baptist church and a part of what is in Holden Street, only it was higher than the roofs of the houses now situated there.

There are many persons who remember Mr. Holden and his wife perfectly well, and the great flat boxes of cherries containing a bushel or two apiece which used to stand along his yard, ready to be loaded upon his wagon for Boston market, and later in the season the peaches which loaded his trees and blushed in crimson and gold from the great baskets and boxes.

The aged couple preserved their old fashioned customs after many of their neighbors had discontinued them, and the bright andirons and red bricks made the sitting-room cheerful, as the wood fire burned on the hearth in winter, and the old kitchen retained its wooden settle alongside the wide fire-place long after every neighboring kitchen was warmed by a cooking stove. Mr. Holden became a Baptist late in life, and was baptized by Rev. Dr. Shailer when over seventy years of age.

The next house also belonged to this estate, and has been entirely rebuilt and much enlarged since the death of the old people.

On the opposite side of the street the ground lay open as a pasture, belonging to the Davis estate until 1833, when two brothers, Seth and Isaac Thayer, came to Brookline, and bought a large tract of ground, and settled here.

Mr. Seth Thayer had married into the Davis family, however, and his house-lot came in that way. He built the house now occupied by Mr. Eastman, lately by Mrs. Fitz as a boarding school, and his brother Isaac built and occupied the house now owned by Mr. Beck, fronting on Davis Avenue, formerly Washington Place.

The two brothers laid out the grounds with taste and elegance, terraced the sloping parts, and set out beautiful shade and fruit trees.

For a dozen or twenty years these were the finest houses and grounds in that vicinity. There were no other buildings on the grounds, the store on the corner not being built till the latter part of Mr. Seth Thayer's life.

From the time the front corner was taken for that purpose the beauty of the place had departed, and a few years after, Mr. Edwin Field bought another lot next it and built the store now occupied by M. Kingman. The more recent changes thereabouts are familiar to all. Mr. and Mrs. Thayer both died in the house and their large family of children are scattered. The second son, John Gorham, was a fine, manly boy, very popular among his schoolmates; his handsome face and deep, strong voice are well remembered by all who knew him. He had left Brookline before the War of the Rebellion, but he enlisted in the service and did brave duty as a cavalry officer till his health was sacrificed and he retired from the army to die. He was brought home to Brookline cemetery, where he sleeps in an honored soldier's grave.

Theodore A. Thayer, sixth son of Seth T. Thayer, was Captain of Company G, Massachusetts Forty-first

Regiment. Clarence H. Thayer, the seventh son, was promoted from Company A, First Massachusetts Regiment, to rank of Captain in a colored Regiment. He died in South Africa in 1873.

Mr. Isaac Thayer, it will be remembered, bought and took down the old Punch Bowl tavern and built ten houses in the village. He also at one time owned the land now belonging to the town between Holden, Prospect, and Pierce streets, which was very high and without trees or buildings. On the summit of this hill he intended to build an academy. He terraced the southerly slope of it and ground was broken for the cellar of the proposed building, when his enterprises met sudden reverses and he left town. The whole of the ground now owned by the town in that vicinity, was at one time purchased by Mr. Samuel C. Davis for four hundred and fifty dollars.

After the town purchased the hill, and began to dig into it for gravel, it remained for twenty years or more an unsightly gravel bank. The top was often used on holidays as a sort of public ground, and for years a cannon was fired from there on the morning of the Fourth of July, greatly to the excitement and delight of the boys. It was a favorite spot also for kite-flying, and many a favorite kite has soared from its youthful owner's grasp on Holden's Hill, and been wafted away into the unknown, a fitting emblem of later losses of what seemed more substantial treasures.

In 1845, enough of the original hill was leveled and graded to admit of building thereon the wooden townhouse now known as the Police Station on Prospect Street. There was a great celebration at the "Dedication," which took place on the 14th of October. Dr. Pierce, of the First Church, was the orator, and his address "bristled with figures," for he was eminently a man of statistics and much valuable information was preserved to future generations by his careful compilation for that occasion.* Two apartments in this building were fitted up for school-rooms and were thus used until the erection of the Pierce Grammar School-house.

The gravel-bank in the rear slowly diminished as the town had occasion to use the gravel, but it was an unsightly place for several years. The wooden building was removed in the spring of 1871, to make room for the new Town House. The Brookline Public Library, which began in the old Town House, is said to have been the first instituted under the general statute authorizing towns and cities to raise and appropriate money for founding and maintaining public libraries. It was established by a vote of the town, March 30, 1857. The sum of $934, being $1 for each ratable poll the preceding year, was appropriated for its foundation; and an additional sum of $233, being 25 cents for each ratable poll, was voted for its increase and maintenance during the then current year.

These were the extreme sums which could be legally raised by taxation for the purpose.

The Library was opened in an apartment on the first floor of the old Town House, December 2, 1857. It then contained 900 volumes, and here it remained until the completion of the new and commodious building in 1869. The Library during the first thirteen years of its existence was under the care of Mr. John E. Hoar as Librarian. It increased, by donations and appropriations, to 11,000 volumes, when the new building was ready to

---

* The author of this work is greatly indebted to the valuable information in the appendix to this address, as to location of ancient houses, and other matters of interest.

receive it, and since 1870, when the generous fund of $10,000 was presented by John L. Gardiner, Esq., the number of books has been increased to 16,000.

The ground on the south side of the street, including both sides of Thayer Place, and the site of the Engine House, was pasture land and belonged for many years to the Thayer estate. It extended southward to Dr. Shurtleff's line, and included the whole space which has been so highly improved by Mr. E. C. Emerson. The rocky nook, with the brook winding about it, was known for years as "Brignal Banks" by many who delighted in its picturesque beauty.

On the north side of Washington Street, from the corner of Prospect Street to the grounds of the Public Library (and including a small strip of that ground), and on the south side of the street, from the Engine House to the house of William Heath, was the "Leeds place," so called for fifty years or more, prior to 1868.

In the latter part of the last century and the early part of the present one, this place was occupied by a mechanic named King, though the ground on the south side of the street was then a part of Benjamin Davis's farm. For many years Mr. King was the only wheelwright in Brookline. The two taverns brought much business of this kind into town, and this man, an excellent workman, had a monopoly of his particular line of work.

He had a large family of children and could have maintained them all comfortably and brought them up, an addition to the wealth and prosperity of the town, but for the excessive use of liquors, in which he not only indulged himself, but to which he brought up his children. From the time the little ones left the cradle they were accustomed to the free use of rum and molasses, both of which were kept standing upon the kitchen table, and to which they early learned to help themselves. The result was as might be expected. The whole family grew up worthless in mind and body, and one by one became town paupers.

The parents died, but the children were numerous, and though they scattered in different places they surely came back, in what might have been the prime of life, helpless and worthless, for the town to support, till it became a question with the selectmen whether Brookline would ever see the last of the Kings. The race has been extinct now for several years and it were better their memory should perish with them, only for the lesson it bears for those similarly tempted. Brookline could furnish material for more than one temperance lecture, from more than one class in society.

More than fifty years ago, the place, of which the Kings had been the thriftless occupants, was purchased by Mr. James Leeds. In his early manhood Mr. Leeds was a boot and shoe manufacturer, and was the only person in that business in the place, for several years. Later in life he invested his capital in a more extensive and profitable business of another sort, in Boston, and having acquired a handsome property retired to enjoy the fruits of economy and enterprise, and employ his leisure in making his surroundings attractive.

The house, which had been thoroughly refitted and ever after kept in repair, was the house a few years since removed from the site of the houses of Messrs. Collins and Chase. On the site of the Express stable was the barn and what was once the shoe-store of Mr. Leeds.

Mr. Leeds made his place a marvel of cultivation and neatness. Choice fruit trees and grape vines were planted in every available spot, and the very grass was rich and wavy under successful fertilization. Near the shop door, just east of the pump which stood close to the sidewalk, overhung by a cherry tree, were two poplar trees which shaded the shop from the glare of the sun, and from one to the other a ladder extended horizontally some twenty feet from the ground.

Along this ladder a grape-vine which crept up the cherry tree extended its length and let down its tempting purple clusters between the green leaves and among the rounds of the ladder. Many were the school-children who stopped at the pump, and gazed up at the grapes like the fox in the fable, but never thought of calling them "sour," for the September rains beat down the ripest, and those who picked them up well knew how sweet they were.

Behind the house, the hill rose steep and green and well covered with fruit trees, among which was one white mulberry. Here, too, was a cluster of three trees from one root, in which was placed a small platform with seats and a railing around it, a few feet from the ground, and very happy were the young people who were so fortunate as to be invited to play there. At the foot of the hill, behind the house, extended a long trellis of grape vines, and on the sunny side of it, above the gravel walk, bloomed a gay display of flowers, from the blue and white fleur-de-lis of May, and the dark red peony of June, to the gorgeous and towering dahlias of late autumn.

Two great boxes of hydrangeas bloomed in the front yard, half shaded by the cherry trees, and under the parlor-windows blossomed, early in spring, the quaint, old-fashioned crown-imperial. Mrs. Leeds was one of those people for whom plants always blossom, like Aaron's rod, because they cannot help it.

The very walks from the door to the street, though paved with bricks, which always had the appearance of being newly scoured and carefully wiped, were gay in all their chinks with the bright little pansy, or ladies' delight, and not a weed was suffered to show its head. The Missouri currant and the yellow rock roses grew on either side of the gate, and the crab-apple tree hung its pretty little fruit west of the parlor window.

For years, as closely identified with the place as its master and mistress, was their good-natured yellow dog, Diamond.

As long as the daughter of Mr. Leeds remained unmarried and at home this house was a favorite resort for a circle of young people on whose memories every detail of this charming old place is minutely photographed.

On the hill between Mr. Leeds' house and Prospect Street, fronting Washington Street, stood a cottage which he also owned, and which he rented from time to time to various tenants. It must be remembered that the hill extended from the old Baptist church to School Street, behind the row of houses on Washington Street, and neither Holden Street or Prospect or Pierce Street was then dreamed of. The Leeds cottage was high up on the hillside, and approached by three flights of steps in the terraces in front. From the southerly windows was a delightful prospect. In the rear was a garden. For several years this place was occupied by Mrs. William Sturgis of Boston, a lady of much taste, who kept it attractive with flowers.

Prospect Street, when first laid out, went only to the top of the hill, and was merely a rough cart-road, which when the hill was dug down enough to admit the building of the Town House, was left high and impassable, leading nowhere.

The digging of this down to its present level, necessitated the removal of the whole hill west of it, and the lowering of the Leeds cottage, which was set back, altered into a two-story house, and is now occupied by C. W. Bachelder, next the Police Station.

The land belonging to the Leeds place, on the south side of Washington Street, was till so recently a green field covered with apple trees that it needs no description. No part of the town has altered so essentially or so rapidly as this street from Harvard Square to School Street within a few years, and it would be difficult for a former resident who had been ten years away to identify it.

The grading of the street to its present level, has produced a corresponding change on either side. Formerly there was a deep depression in the "road" in front of the present Library grounds, so that in sleighing time scarcely a day passed but some rapid riders came to a sudden halt and total discomfiture in going through it.

The Leeds house was on a bank, and reached by a flight of stone steps, while in the field opposite, the hollow was so deep as to hold quite a skating pond in winter, and late in spring small boys resorted to it to paddle about on rafts.

Not much more than twenty-five years ago there was not a house from the Thayer house to the Tolman house, corner of Cypress Street. Now there are some forty buildings on the south side of the street between those two points.

CHAPTER VIII.

THE FIRE DEPARTMENT.* — THE DANA PLACE. — MRS. TOLMAN.

THE next place of interest, upon the south side of Washington Street, is the lot occupied by the Engine and Hook and Ladder Houses, and on which the town has lately erected a commodious brick building, which it is expected will meet the wants of this part of the town in the accommodation of adequate fire-apparatus, for years to come.

Before further mention is made of recent buildings there, it will be necessary to go back a little, as the history of the fire department properly belongs to "the village," that is, below the bridge. The first engine-house was situated for several years at the point of junction between Walnut Street and what was till lately called "Village Lane." It was a little building ten feet by fifteen, and when Mr. Oliver Whyte was about to improve his front yard, was easily transported to the lot between Walnut and Boylston streets, where Quinlan's building now stands. About when this transfer took place it does not appear. However, it was certainly located on the last mentioned spot in 1820, and for some time after, as the last surviving member of the company of that date remembered, that a tree which stood upon that lot was blown over, and the roots upturning, broke

* Rewritten March, 1873.

a hole through the side of the house, which remained unmended as long as the old building stood.

It will be remembered that about half the old Punch Bowl Village was then a part of Roxbury, so the engine was owned by both towns, and the men, fifteen in number, were chosen nearly or quite equally from the two towns. The members " took turns in being Captain," like a boy's military company, believing evidently in "rotation in office." It would be charitable to hope that the system worked more successfully in cases of fire, than it sometimes does in politics.

A list of the old " Vigilant " company of 1820, presents names familiar to all old residents of this town : —

Jeremiah Lyon, Captain ; Isaac Davis, Lemuel Foster, Wm. H. Brown, Jerathmiel Davenport, James Leeds, Reuben Hunting, Reuben Smith, Silas Snow, Robert S. Davis, senior, Caleb Clark, Moses Jones, Edward Hall, Samuel Slack, —— Whiting.

To those of us who remember these individuals only as corpulent, or lame, or asthmatic old gentlemen, the very idea of any of them *running* is sufficiently ludicrous, to say nothing of working the brakes of an engine, climbing ladders, etc. But they were all young and vigorous then, incredible as it seems.

It was a fashion they had in those times for each new Captain as he came into office, to give a supper to the whole company, either at his own house or the " Punch Bowl," for in the engine-house there was only room for a single row of men to stand around the engine, and those suppers were hugely enjoyed by the company. The Captain's wife may have had opinions of her own about these festivities.

There came a time at last when the old engine was — we hope it is allowable to say it of an engine — " played out," and a new one was to be bought. It was an event. The town was astir. The purchase of three new " steamers " would not create such a sensation now as did this affair.

A committee was chosen to make preliminary examination; and Thayer of Boston, and Hunneman of Roxbury, two rival engine-builders, were both conferred with.

Suction, if then invented, was not aspired to by the " Vigilant " Company, and having but few men it was thought best to secure an engine that would work easily. All the Roxbury engines were built by Hunneman, but the " Vigilants " decided to take Thayer's, a tub engine. All the water was brought in buckets by hand and turned into this kind of engine. It was bought, and named " Norfolk;" the new engine-house, over the brook where Mahoney's building is, next the depot, a small one-story building, was already built some time before.

All were pleased with the purchase; but Mr. Hunneman's son came up from Roxbury to see it experimented upon, and pronounced it a poor affair, and disparaged it generally, — which perhaps might have been expected from a man whose business it was "to throw cold water," and whose father didn't build the engine, as he had hoped to.

The Brookline Company were as sensitive to censure of their "tub" as sailors about their favorite ship, and the affront rankled.

Shortly after there came a challenge from Roxbury, for the " Norfolk " to meet them at " Hog Bridge," for a trial. The challenge was accepted, and the men drilled for practice. There was such an excitement about it that many supernumeraries drilled, so as to be ready to take the place of any who might fail from exhaustion. Among these was a Mr. Hill, an elderly man, whose son was a confectioner in the village. He was a very stout and powerful man, and went into the contest with a will. The five engines from Roxbury were all present.

The contest began in the forenoon, and continued all day, the "Norfolks" being reinforced by fresh men from time to time. Night found them exhausted, but conquerors. Roxbury had done its best and could not "wash the tub," as firemen express it; and they took up their homeward march with the proud steps of victors. Village pride was gratified, and the engine always maintained its well-earned reputation. Mr. Hill, however, was too old a man for such a strain of muscle and nerve, and he never saw a well day afterwards.

Under date of April 25, 1829, the engine company petitioned the towns of Roxbury and Brookline " for six additional members, making twenty-one in all, taken from the militia roll." This was granted. It was also " Voted, that on cloudy days when the sun at its setting cannot be seen, that its setting be determined by time as given by J. Davenport's clock and the ' Farmer's Almanac.' " Also " Voted, that the custom heretofore in practice, of the members giving entertainments, be abolished."

About the year 1838 a new suction engine was purchased, which was called " Brookline No. 1." The old company had all been superseded by younger men, and some difficulty occurred about the choice of a foreman or captain, and for some little time there was no organized company.

During this interval, in the autumn of 1843, the engine-house was fired one night by some miscreant, who secured the engine so that there was great delay about moving it. The house was entirely destroyed, and the engine damaged.

Before there was time to have the engine thoroughly repaired, the great fire in Church Street, Boston, occurred, and the blackened machine with its name burnt off, went to the fire with its name chalked on the back of the tub, and did good service.

Soon after, the town contracted with Edward Hall, Jr., a carpenter, who lived on the corner of Washington and School streets, to build a new, two-story engine-house, and purchased a lot of land just about where the railroad goes under the bridge, the old lot being very small, and only over the brook.

But the owner was unable to give a satisfactory title to it, and the bargain was not concluded. Meantime, the timber was already prepared and waiting to be put up, and the builder was desirous to fulfill his contract; and Mr. Thayer offered the site of the present brick enginehouse on Washington Street, for one hundred dollars, provided it should never be used for any other purpose. In case of violation of this restriction the land should revert to the heirs. As no other lot so near the village was available, it was accepted with the restrictions upon it. The lot for the Hook and Ladder house was not purchased till several years afterwards.

The engine company reorganized, with the engine thoroughly repaired, took possession of the new house in September, 1844.

The same engine is in the service of the town now, and like its predecessors has always been the pride of the company, and is not now surpassed by any engine of its kind and size in the vicinity of Boston.

There was no regularly organized hook and ladder company until February, 1871, though the town owned a second-hand apparatus purchased of the city of Roxbury. The name "George H. Stone," was appropriated by this company in honor of a deceased comrade who had been a very efficient fireman, and was exceedingly popular among his associates. He had also been a gallant soldier during the late war. He was a son of Elisha Stone, before mentioned, as for many years the principal sexton, undertaker, and constable of the town. The town purchased a modern hook and ladder truck at an expense of about twelve hundred dollars. The present elegant buildings of the Fire Department, said not to be exceeded by any in the State, were built in 1872, and the first steam fire-engine was purchased in 1873. The "Good Intent Hose Company" was organized more recently, and does efficient duty with engine, steamer, or hydrant, as the case may be, when its services are needed. The buildings occupied by the steam fire-engine "Thomas Parsons," and by the "Good Intent Hose Company" are within a few feet of the spot occupied fifty-five years ago by the first engine-house in town.

THE DANA PLACE.

Next west of the Leeds place on the north side of the street, was formerly the Dana place.

This included all that is now the town land about the Public Library except a strip a few feet in width, next Mr. Collins' residence, all that is in Mr. John Gibbs' lot, except a few feet on the west side, and on School Street the house lot of Mr. Matthews. There were two acres and a half in the place, a part of it the highest and steepest part of the hill so often before mentioned.

On this place stood, until about twenty-two years ago, an ancient house dating back to the earlier part of the last century. It stood about twenty feet from the sidewalk, and the southeast corner of it was directly in the rear of the elm tree on the Library grounds, that being the corner of the front yard of the old house.

It was two stories high, three rooms long, on the front, with two front doors. The kitchen was in the centre between the two front doors. An immense chimney, or "stack of chimneys," belonged to this kitchen, and the east room. The wide and deep fire-place would accommodate wood of cord length, and an enormous crane with hooks and trammels was suspended within it. Looking up from below one could see the open sky, and snow was sometimes in the fire-place, of a winter morning.

Two brick ovens, one in the chimney back and the other at the side, furnished ample baking facilities, and old fashioned " dressers " along the wall served instead of closets. Here, too, were " the whitewashed wall and sagging beam," and the small, old-fashioned windows, half sash, through which the light came dimly. In front of the house were peach trees, lilac bushes, and two very large locust trees, the great roots of which coiled about on the sidewalk like huge snakes. Behind the house was an open well with curb, windlass, and bucket. It was never known to fail in the dryest seasons, and the water was of the best quality. The two back doors of the house opened out upon a green orchard and garden, from which the hill rose steeply; and the fence along the highest ridge, which separated it from Mr. Holden's hill-pasture where the coasting ground used to be, was nearly concealed from view by a natural hedge of barberry bushes and wild vines.

The same house stood west of it which stands now west of Mr. Gibbs' house.

As long ago as 1740 the place was occupied by Nathaniel Shepard, who afterwards removed to Needham.

After this the house was owned by a man named Jackson, who in the War of the Revolution was on the side of the royal cause, and made himself distasteful, as a Tory.

The house was taken as barracks for the colonial troops during the siege of Boston, at which the unpatriotic Mr. Jackson was so disgusted that he sold it as speedily as possible to Mr. Daniel Dana, then living at Brighton and engaged in supplying the British troops in Boston and the harbor with meat.

Mr. Dana came to live in the house we are describing, during the war, after the evacuation of Boston; and from that time until 1848 the house was in possession of his family and known by his name.

"Othello's occupation" being gone, when the British troops left, it became necessary to look about for new business; and as Mr. Dana had but one hand, he began to keep a store on the corner of School Street, and kept it as long as he lived. There is one person still living in town who can remember going to this store to buy slate-pencils as long ago as 1795.

Mr. Dana had married for his second wife, a sister of the Rev. Cotton Brown, the second minister of Brookline.

A son of Mr. Dana was taken prisoner during the Revolution, by the British, carried to England, escaped to France, took passage in a ship to return to America, and was lost at sea. There was no one left of the family after 1803, but the only daughter, Miss Anna, who lived till 1847, when she died at the age of ninety-two, and it is with her that our story is chiefly concerned.

After the death of her father, Miss Dana kept a few small wares for sale for a while, using the east room of the house for a shop; but she soon discontinued it, and reserving the two easterly apartments for herself she let the rest of the house for her maintenance. In this house the writer of these sketches spent ten years of her childhood.

Miss Anna Dana was one of the marked characters of Brookline during her long life, and her eccentricities were so frequently spoken of and dwelt upon, that by many persons the finer qualities of her mind and heart were either unknown or overlooked.

She had been an indulged and petted only daughter, and prided herself upon always having had her own way. Her proclivities were strongly in favor of everything English, and her admiration for the royal family was intense. She was an eye-witness of the battle of Bunker Hill, from a house-top in Boston, where she was staying, she being then twenty years of age, and more than half a Tory probably.

She used to exhibit with great pride an ancient china bowl within which was inscribed, " Success to the British Arms," and tell how they were obliged to keep it hidden during the war. All events, social or political, which met her disapproval, she attributed to two causes, Sunday-schools and a republican form of government. Not that her dislike to Sunday-schools arose from want of respect for religious teachings, but they were an innovation ; and she would not allow that anything modern was an improvement or an advantage over the ancient, except in the construction of shoes and boots, which were then worn without raised heels. Had she lived to see in these days the revival of the ancient fashion which she so detested, she would have thought modern people had lost their last and only grain of common sense.

It was her pride and boast that she had no occasion for the services of a doctor, as she never had a day's illness sufficient to keep her in bed, or need to consult a physician for seventy years. She rose and retired early, lived plainly, had plenty of fresh air, and ripe fruit; and though she never failed to warm her bed with a long-handled pan of wood coals every night in winter, she kept her attic window open summer and winter, for forty years.

A carpenter who repaired the roof, had once told her that if she kept that window open she would live to be a hundred years old. Her room was thus kept supplied with fresh air, from the attic, as the stairway opened into it; and whether the carpenter's advice was the cause of it or not, she possessed vigorous health and unimpaired faculties till she was nearly ninety years of age.

At that time there was sickness in the house, and the rains of a chilly autumn made it necessary for the family occupying the house to have it closed. No persuasion or entreaty could induce the old lady to close the window or allow any one else to do so. No one had seen the inside of her chamber or the attic for half a century but herself, except a child, and she was determined that no one should. Those who knew her only by report imagined she had money or valuables stored away there, and that this was the cause of her reluctance to admit any one, for she said that she could not close the window herself, it had been so long open, which very likely was true, it being then swollen by the rain.

The doctor, however, said the window must be closed at any risk of offense, and an energetic neighbor came to the rescue. Armed with hammer and nails she very decidedly informed the enraged old lady that she was about to do the audacious deed, and up stairs she went, and through the secret chamber, into the forbidden attic, shut the window and nailed it down, and for once the discomfited maiden did not have her own way.

The peculiarities which characterized Miss Anna Dana, made it very difficult for her to retain tenants in her house; and until the last ten years of her life scarcely a family stayed two years on the premises. She was frequently alone during an entire winter, even after she became very aged, but her wonderful pride and independence carried her through what most women would have shrunk from as severe hardship.

There was a standing feud between her and all boys. She seemed to hate them with all the energy of her nature. She "did not see where all the children came from," she said; "they were thicker than oak leaves," — and if she saw two boys passing by peaceably she went to the door and called to them sharply not to shake her fence, or throw stones at her house. Of course, boy-nature could not stand that, and the consequence was that her fence was shaken till it would scarcely stand alone, her windows were occasionally broken, her doors were tied up on the outside in nights, her bucket would be taken from the well, and her cats were persecuted. For, hard as her nature seemed toward children, she was very tender and loving towards her feline pets, of which she had at one time more than a dozen.

Her seeming harshness was probably the result chiefly of her solitary and single-handed grapple with the world for so many years. In the latter part of her life, when there was a permanent tenant to protect her property, and stand between her and the boys, she softened into a much more pliable mood to all around her. There was one boy, we should have said, now a Professor at Cambridge, whom she not only tolerated, but for whom she had a real affection, though not of the sort which manifests itself in caresses. Her test of a child's good manners was its ability to enter her room and leave it without laying a hand upon her highly polished, round, mahogany table.

There are many persons who remember that east room, with its white floor, well-sanded, the old-fashioned desk with its piles of books, the long mirror, the round table in the centre before the fire-place, the brass andirons, and the two ancient chairs on either side of the fire, covered with tapestry work, imported from England, which had belonged to Governor Hutchinson of colonial times, but in each of which now sat a cat. The old lady herself always sat in a straight, high-backed chair beside the round table, on which she never laid anything but her spectacles or a newspaper.

She could be very entertaining when she chose, for her memory was wonderful and her perceptions very clear; and to talk with one who remembered events before the Revolutionary War, and could tell of what was done in the Colony of Massachusetts Bay under King George's governors, was no small privilege.

About two years before her death, when she was ninety years of age, she grew sick; but true to her old prejudice she would not allow a doctor to be sent for, nor resort to any remedies, nor even allow herself to be in a room where there was a fire. This course she persisted in till she became helpless and others assumed the responsibility and controlled her, though with great show of resistance on her part. Her iron constitution was slow in breaking down, but after being confined to her bed about two years she died in February, 1847, aged ninety-two years and one month, the last of her race.

There was not a human being of even the most distant kin surviving, to follow her to the grave or drop a tear to her memory, or even claim the poor trifles left behind.

The forbidden attic, which had caused so much curious conjecture, contained only chests and boxes of old books and papers, an old sword and cutlass, and a few articles unsold in the stock of Mr. Dana's store, such as pointed-toed shoes, cards of queer buttons and buckles, some bonnets, either of which would have made six of the present fashion, and other odds and ends, but nothing of any intrinsic value.

After the death of Miss Dana the place reverted to Peter C. Brooks of Boston, to whom it had been mortgaged during her father's lifetime. By him it was sold to Timothy Leeds, son of James Leeds, and the house was purchased by Mr. Nathaniel Lyford, who took it down.

The elm tree, by the west gate of the Library grounds, and which was in the front yard of the Dana house, was Miss Dana's especial pride and delight. It came up in the east corner of the yard about sixty years ago, and Miss Dana protected it the first summer from the scythe of the mower, by turning a tub over it. She watered it and tended it with care, and lived to sit for years in its shadow. For several years past it has made scarcely any growth, and many elms much younger now far exceed it in size.

CHAPTER IX.

THE HALL HOUSE. — THE TOLMAN HOUSE. — THE CROFT HOUSES. — "BLACK SUSY." — MISS HANNAH ADAMS. — DR. WILD. — THE BLAKE PLACE. — THE ASPINWALL PLACE.

THE next house west of the Dana place and now standing on the corner of School and Washington streets, though built some time before the Revolution, has been modernized from time to time so that only its low walls indicate its age. It was occupied some years after the Revolutionary War by a Major Thompson of Revolutionary service. It is said of the Major that he had a horse which had served in cavalry during the war, and when old and stiff, no longer in use as a working animal, the sound of a bugle would so inspirit him that he would leap the fence and prance along the street wholly unmindful of his infirmities, going through the various evolutions with perfect precision. It was during the Major's residence here that Mr. Dana kept his shop in the west part of the house.

In the year 1796, the house was occupied by Zephion Thayer, who was the son of Captain Jedediah Thayer, a Revolutionary officer.

Zephion Thayer died in this town in 1803. The distinguished founder of Chauncy Hall School in Boston, and for twenty-five years its principal, was his son. Gideon F. Thayer was not born in Brookline, but he spent his childhood here, and so great was his love for Brookline that he used to say he would have been born here if he could.

After the death of Mr. Thayer, a man named Leverett, a wheelwright, occupied the house for a few years.

About the year 1805 or 1806, Mr. Benjamin Davis, who till that time had owned all the land on the south side of the street (excepting the corner lot, which had been sold years before), had a public sale of lots, and one nearly opposite the Dana place, where Mr. William Heath now lives, was purchased for the site of a blacksmith's shop. Mr. Edward Hall, either then or soon after, became the owner of the house of which we are writing, and also of the shop where he carried on the blacksmith's business for many years. After his death the shop was let for the same purpose till about the year 1850, when it was taken down.

Mr. Hall had a large family, but only three of his children now survive, and of these not one is settled in Brookline.

The part of the house projecting towards the west, was built in modern times, and covers what was formerly a pretty corner yard, where flowers and trees relieved the plainness of the house. In front was a row of tall fir trees.

The opposite corner, formerly called the Tolman place, was thickly covered with barberry bushes; and at the time Mr. Jonas Tolman purchased, was offered at one hundred dollars for the lot, about an acre in extent. Mr. Tolman said he would never give one hundred dollars for it; but he wanted the place very much, and finally a compromise was made, and he paid *ninety-nine* dollars.

Next the blacksmith shop, on the same side of the street, was the house of Mr. Tolman, who was a shoemaker. This house, like the Hall house, is still in good preservation, although built in the last century. Mr. Tolman had a one-story shop, painted red, behind his house, and during his lifetime was the principal shoemaker of Brookline.

After his death his son Charles carried on the business, and built the shop now on the corner of Cypress Street. The land belonging to this corner lot was much more extensive formerly than at present, as two sales have been made from it much reducing its dimensions.

The grade of the street has been materially changed between the two houses above mentioned and about the corner of Cypress Street. The Hall house formerly stood but one step higher than the sidewalk, while the Tolman house was reached by three steps in a wall at the edge of the front yard next the sidewalk.

The front yard of this house was so filled with clumps of lilac and syringa as nearly to conceal the lower front of the house. In one of the west rooms a small select school was kept for many years by Miss Rachael Cushing; it enjoyed an excellent reputation, and many persons look back with pleasure to pleasant years of school-life spent there. The Misses Elizabeth and Mary Peabody (the latter afterwards became Mrs. Horace Mann), also taught at one time a select school in this house.

Mrs. Tolman, the widow of Jonas Tolman, lived to a great age, and her long life was nearly all one of active usefulness. She was one of those "mothers in Israel" who could find room in her heart and home for almost everybody, though her life had many and great sorrows. If a friendless teacher needed a boarding-place, or a wandering student a home, if a widow had a child whom she must board out, if a family by some domestic emergency needed apartments for a week or a month, Mrs. Tolman would find room somewhere in her house. If a female prayer meeting, or a maternal society, or sewing society, or anything else with a good object in view, wanted accommodations, Mrs. Tolman's parlor was open. In her old age this good woman became wholly blind, but she bore her privation with wonderful patience and cheerful fortitude till released by death from darkness and pain.

The opposite corner of School Street was a part of the Craft farm. It was separated from the streets by a low stone wall and within it were two or three apple trees. It sloped steeply down to the brook at the bottom of the meadow, and was a good coasting place in winter for children not venturesome enough to try the steep north side of Holden's Hill.

Until the year 1844 there were but two churches in Brookline, the Unitarian and Baptist. The families of Orthodox Congregationalists either worshipped with the Baptists or were united with the more distant societies of Brighton and Roxbury.

In 1843 steps were taken to unite these various interests in one society, and secure a place to build a church. The corner lot, then owned by the late Samuel Crafts, was secured for that purpose, and in 1844 the present church edifice was built. It was dedicated August 20 the same year, and a church of twenty-eight persons was formed. In May of the following year Rev. R. S. Storrs, Jr., was invited to become the pastor. He was installed the following October. In a little more than a year Mr. Storrs was called to Brooklyn, N. Y., where he has ever since labored as pastor of the Church of the Pilgrims. Since then the church has had five pastors: Rev. Joseph Haven, Rev. M. M. Smith, Rev. J. L. Diman, Rev. C. C. Carpenter, and Rev. C. M. Wines.

The material prosperity of this society is sufficiently indicated by its enterprise in building the elegant stone edifice on the corner of Harvard and Marion streets, and the subsequent sale of the old building to the Methodists in the spring of 1873.

THE CROFT HOUSES.

Nearly opposite the Methodist Church, on the corner of Washington and Cypress streets, stands now the ancient gambrel-roofed house which was occupied in 1740 by Captain Samuel Croft. How long it had then been built we have not ascertained, but afterwards it was the property of Dr. Aspinwall. The house has been occupied during the last hundred years by successive families, till they would form quite a host in the aggregate. In 1805 or 1806, it took fire in the roof and narrowly escaped destruction.

Captain Croft was born in 1700. The land, it will be recollected by those who have read these historical papers thus far, on both sides of the street in this locality, was very early in the town's history a part of the Cotton estate.

From the Cottons a part of it came into possession of the Sharps, and from them to the Crofts.

The elder Captain Samuel Croft built in 1765 a large house on the north side of the street, in what is now the garden of T. P. Chandler, Esq., a rod or two west of the house.

At the time of his death in 1771 it was owned by his son, Captain Samuel Croft, Jr., who married into the Sharp family. With this house was included as the Croft farm all that part of the Sharp farm from the corner of School Street to a point nearly up to the present residence of Thomas Griggs, Jr., and extending back to Stephen Sharps' part of the farm.

Captain Croft's house was a large, square, two-story house, with a spacious front yard, well filled with trees and shrubbery. Behind the house was a deep ravine, and here was a spring of cold and excellent water, overshadowed by two very large buttonwood trees.

An old barn stood opposite the house on the site of Mrs. Crafts' present residence, and there for some time was kept the hearse, until a permanent place was provided for it near the Unitarian Church. In more recent times a large barn stood east of the house on the same side of the street.

The old couple had no children, and they adopted a member of the Davis family, a lovely girl, whose name was Sarah. She had a fine voice, and her singing at the dedication of Brookline meeting-house * in 1806 was the occasion of much commendation.

This young lady died in 1808. It was during the fatal illness of Miss Sarah, that the hearse was brought, to be kept in the barn opposite; and Mrs. Croft, almost superstitious in the matter of signs and omens, feared that her adopted daughter should know it. It might perhaps have been unpleasantly suggestive, but the young lady is said to have been "a lovely Christian," who had no fears or weak dread of a change which to such as she would bring only release and joy.

The energy of three or four generations of Sharps concentrated in Mrs. or Madame Croft, as she was often called, and she carried sway with a high hand. If the Scriptural doctrine that "it is good for a man that he bear the yoke in his youth," is to be understood literally, there were and are those who derived great good from a residence in this household. At least they bore "the yoke" there, according to unquestionable testimony.

Perhaps the most distinctly remembered personage of this household, inasmuch as she lived the longest, and was a marked character, was an old colored woman named Susy Backus. We say *old* because she called herself fifty, for about forty years, and neither she nor any

* Then the only one in town.

one else knew her age; but she was a young girl when taken into the Croft house as servant, and here for board and clothes she rendered such service as money cannot buy, during the lifetime of her master and mistress.

It has often been said by Brookline people that Susy was a slave, but this was not the case. Her father was a kidnapped African who served a blacksmith in Dorchester, and was called by his name, Backus. After the death of the blacksmith, the negro kept on with the business in the same shop, but assumed the more aristocratic and imposing title of "Mr. Cleveland."

There was a poor Indian woman living in Brookline by the name of Molly Hill, and "Mr. Cleveland" relieved his solitude and perhaps added to his importance by marrying her.

Susy was the child of this marriage, but somehow the name of Cleveland would not stick to her, and she was always known as Susy Backus.

Susy was cook, chambermaid, milkmaid, hostler, and gardener for the Croft family. In fact her service was only limited by the fact that there are but twenty-four hours in the day, and that poor humanity must sleep sometime. She shoveled snow in winter and gathered vegetables in summer which her own hands had planted in spring.

The Captain had a white horse and an old-fashioned, square, standing-top chaise, a most cumbrous "one-hoss shay," which had done duty from time immemorial; — also it came to pass that in later years he possessed a new and most respectable vehicle for those times.

So when there had been a rain on Saturday, Susy was sent out on Sunday morning to run the length of "the new lane," as Cypress Street was then called, to see if the mud was deep enough to imperil the respectability of the new chaise, and on her report, to the one vehicle or the other the white horse was harnessed to convey master and mistress to "Brookline meeting-house."

Susy's seat was in "the negro pew," a high and narrow place above the singer's gallery in the old meeting-house where Dr. Pierce preached. She was the last person who occupied that place.

Captain Croft died in 1814. In 1818 Dr. Charles Wild, then a young beginner in the practice of medicine, came to Brookline and took up his abode with Madame Croft. He became quite a favorite with the old lady, and at her death a few years later, she gave him two acres of land on the opposite side of the street.

To Susy she left two hundred dollars; and the money was placed in the hands of Dr. Pierce as her guardian.

Mr. Croft also left provision in his will "for supporting and maintaining in sickness and in health but not in idleness, except when past labor, my faithful servant Susanna Backus during her life."

The old Croft house was let for several years, and then sold to Mr. John Kendrick, who lived in it a short time. He then left town, and when the estate was sold to Mr. Chandler, the old house was moved to Thayer Place, where it still serves the purpose of a tenement house.

The farm became the property of Mr. Samuel Crafts, who was Mrs. Croft's nephew. From the Croft family Susy went to Mrs. Downer, formerly a Wyman, who was a daughter-in-law of the Dr. Downer in the Punch Bowl Village, and in this family she lived thirty-nine years, rendering devoted service.

With the intense loyalty of her race she identified herself with them and theirs, and no labor was too hard or sacrifice too great for her to make for them. And her fidelity was appreciated. Though her voice was rough, and harsher than that of men in general, and her physiognomy would have delighted the heart of Darwin, though for years and years she was bent almost double, so that it was a marvel how she could walk at all, she never looked repulsive or even unlovable to the children and grand-children of the household.

Yet there was a picturesqueness about her as she walked to church on a Sunday morning in her white dress with a bright flower pinned upon the bosom, her handkerchief carefully folded outside her book and a large fan in her hand. She made regular visits in some of the most respectable old families of Brookline; those at some little distance, like Deacon Clark's, for instance, she called her *foreign* visits, and at certain houses she was always invited to tea with the family.

When she grew too old and infirm to walk to Dr. Pierce's church she went to the Baptist, and in both churches she was treated with marked courtesy and consideration. Indeed no one was ever disrespectful to Susy, except rude boys in the village, who sometimes called after her, or occasionally threw a stone, because she was old, and black, and crooked.

But a beautiful soul dwelt in the uncomely body. Truth, and justice, and kindly charity were her characteristics; and the singing of the earliest bird and the blooming of the first daffy in spring called out her innocent delight. She had been taught to read, and her well worn and much used Testament gave evidence of faithful perusal.

At last the time came when the provision made for her in the Croft will was needed, and the money was paid semi-annually as long as she lived.

For several years before her death Susy was entirely blind, cataracts having grown over both eyes. She still lived on, in the family of Mrs. Hancock (the daughter of Mrs. Downer), her efforts to help often a hindrance, and the infirmities of her great age making her a ceaseless care; but she was not disposed of in hospital or poorhouse, as was suggested by some advisers, for her love and devotion in her better days forbade the thought of such a requital. So she felt her way about the familiar house, and was indulged in her pet whims, which were few, a handful of peppermints and a glass of rum once a day being her luxuries.

After a four weeks' illness she died in 1863, probably eighty-four years of age, if not older, judging from her recollection of ancient events. To the very last her hearing was acute and her love of life strong. The old Croft tomb in Brookline cemetery, which had not been unclosed for nearly forty years, was opened to receive the body, worn out with a long life of toil for others,—and then closed up forever.

Who shall doubt that her white soul was welcomed in the better land with a " Well done, thou good and faithful servant."

After the death of Mrs. Croft, the house was occupied by Mrs. Walley, formerly of Walnut Street, and with her, boarded in the latter part of her life, Miss Hannah Adams, a literary lady of much celebrity at that time, who is well remembered by many persons now living, and whose memory deserves to be kept green.

Miss Adams was a native of Medfield in this State, but spent most of her life in Boston and vicinity. In her childhood her father was in comfortable if not affluent circumstances, but his failure and loss of property and the early death of her mother, threw Miss Hannah upon her own resources.

She was of a sensitive and delicate organization, and apparently little calculated by nature to grapple with the world, but like many others of her sex who do not care to battle for rights, and desire no right but that of filling some domestic niche peacefully and honorably, she was forced to an energy not natural to her and developed talents and resources of which her friends would have scarcely supposed her to be the possessor.

In her childhood she had few advantages. She was too feeble in health to attend school, but she learned to read at home, and devoured volumes of poetry and novels, which she said in after years, made her keenly sensitive to the evils of life, but gave her no strength and vigor of mind to rise above them or overcome them.

When it became necessary for her to maintain herself, or partly do so, she learned to weave bobbin lace. This was in the Revolution, and as soon as the war was over all demand for such a home-made fabric ceased. She tried straw-braiding, and other feminine employments, but the profits were but slight, and wholly inadequate for support.

She taught a country school a few summers, but her health could not bear such a strain upon her vital powers, and she relinquished this employment. In the mean time, however, some literary gentlemen who boarded at her father's, taught her at her own request Latin and Greek, which it was then considered the height of folly for a woman to spend her time in learning.

About this time she became accidentally interested in the points of difference between different forms of religious belief, and was led to read all the works treating of various denominations, which were available. The result of this was her writing a book called " View of Religion." Speaking of her reading, preparatory to writing this work, she says she soon became disgusted with the want of candor in the authors consulted, " in giving the most unfavorable descriptions of the denominations they disliked, and applying to them the names of heretics, fanatics, bigots, enthusiasts, etc." It is one of the cheering signs of progress in society that the bitter hatred once existing between rival sects is now modified to kindly tolerance, which offers ground for hope that some future day may find many of them uniting upon one common ground of faith and hope.

Miss Adams' work went through several editions and brought her a moderate compensation. In the hope of larger pecuniary success she wrote after this, a " History of New England," there being at that time only two works of the kind extant, Mather's " Magnalia " and Neale's " History," neither of which came down to the American Revolution. It was a laborious task, involving much perusal of old manuscripts and other close investigation, and some journeyings. Before the work was completed her eyes failed, and for two years she was totally debarred from all use of them in reading, writing, or any close application, and it appeared that all literary work must be abandoned forever. She however so far recovered the use of them, under skillful medical treatment by Dr. Jeffries of Boston, that she could make a moderate use of them and completed her work.

As there was no history of our country at that time adapted to schools, Miss Adams intended to abridge her work and adapt it to school uses. But in this she was anticipated by a clergyman who stepped between her and her prosperity and reaped the benefits.

In the mean time her History was well received and met with a large sale. But through some unfortunate circumstances connected with the printing and publishing she received but little profit for all this labor.

Her next work was a " History of the Jews," a carefully prepared work which occupied several years, and afterwards she wrote a little volume entitled "Letters on the Gospels." It was so unusual a thing in those days for an American woman to read the dead languages or attempt authorship that Miss Adams was looked upon by uneducated persons as a sort of human phenomenon, a curiosity to be gazed at and criticized. Her works were of solid worth, yet the compensation she received for them all was trifling, compared probably to what a modern novel-writer receives for a sensation story.

She would have suffered in old age from want, but for the kindly thoughtfulness and generosity of a few gentlemen and ladies, who admired her talents and loved her for her personal worth. These settled an annuity upon her which made her declining years comfortable, and filled her warm heart with the liveliest gratitude.

The Hon. Josiah Quincy, Stephen Higginson, and William Shaw, were the principal movers in this generous deed.

The Rev. Joseph Buckminster, his successor Rev. Mr. Thacher, and other eminent clergymen and authors were her personal friends, and her correspondents both in this country and abroad were people of eminence. The elder President Adams in writing to her once said: —

"You and I are undoubtedly related by birth; and although we were both born in obscurity, yet I presume neither of us have any occasion to regret that circumstance. If I could ever suppose that family pride was in any case excusable, I should think a descent from a line of virtuous, independent, New England farmers, for one hundred and sixty years, was a better foundation for it than a descent through royal or titled scoundrels ever since the flood."

There are various anecdotes extant respecting Miss Adams' little peculiarities, most of which rose from extreme sensitiveness and diffidence or underrating of herself. Some however grew out of her lack of knowledge of most common things, her attention having been always so absorbed by books, and some from a singular absence of mind, or concentration on one subject to the exclusion of all others.

Dr. Pierce used to relate an incident of her which was characteristic. She stayed all night in a friend's house and slept in a room where in the morning for the first time she saw a knob instead of a latch upon the chamber door. Having made her toilet she tried to open the door, but the knob refused to pull out or push in, or lift up or go down. It never occurred to her to try to *turn* it, so she labored at the refractory thing, till finding it all in vain she sat down and waited till a maid-servant finally came and let her out.

The anecdote of her forgetfulness about her baggage in travelling is perhaps too familiar to be repeated here, yet it may be new to young readers. A gentleman was very desirous of making her acquaintance, having heard that her conversation was highly interesting. Learning that she was to ride in a stage-coach on a certain day, he also took passage in the same. But in vain he tried to draw her into conversation. She seemed oblivious to everything about her, but kept repeating to herself, "Great trunk, little trunk, band-box, and bundle," a formula with which her friends had charged her memory, because she was so apt to be wholly unmindful of her possessions.

A hack was called to take her home from some place in Boston, where she had been visiting for the day. She was at that time boarding with a Mr. Perkins in Leverett Street, but she told the driver to carry her to Mr. Leverett's in Perkins Street. The man drove about Boston till eleven o'clock in the evening trying to find Perkins Street. He could get no further information from his absent-minded passenger, and at last drove back to the stable to ask his employer what was the next thing to be done. The stable-keeper went out and looked into the carriage. "Oh, that's Miss Hannah Adams," said he, "carry her to Mr. Perkins' in Leverett Street," and so at last the estray was deposited in safe quarters.

The librarian at the Athenæum often found it impossible to get her away from the library when it was to be locked up at the dinner hour, and so was obliged to lock her in, and leave her there during his absence. On his return he found her so absorbed with her reading that she did not even know that he had been out.

She was considered by some as eccentric, and by many as a sort of walking Greek dictionary, or an animated History of the Jews, yet she was as simple-hearted and affectionate as a child, and was dearly beloved by those who cultivated her acquaintance enough to overcome her natural diffidence.

She wrote her last letter from one of the large, sunny front chambers in the old Croft house, in November, 1831. In it she says to her friend, "I need not inform you, and I am unable to express, how much pleasure it would give me to see you in Brookline. The lady with whom I board is all goodness."

She perfectly delighted in the sunshine and the beautiful prospect from the pleasant apartment, so in contrast to the closeness and limited range of a Boston house. "How can any one be tired of such a beautiful world?" she said to a friend who called upon her, as she pointed out the beauties of the scenery.

She died the same winter, at Mrs. Walley's, at the age of seventy-six. A portrait of her in her close white cap, and lawn handkerchief, not unlike a Quaker's garb, can be seen in the Boston Athenæum.

Miss Adams was one of the first persons buried in Mount Auburn Cemetery. Her memoir, begun by herself, but finished after her death by a friend, is in our Public Library.

Opposite the residence of Mr. Chandler, on the site of the barn before mentioned as belonging to the Croft place, Mr. Samuel Crafts built the house, which is still standing, somewhat more than thirty years ago.

Mr. Crafts was a native of Brookline, and lived in the southwest part of the town in his early years, then resided several years in the house formerly owned and occupied by his uncle, Stephen Sharp, and finally built the one above alluded to, in which he resided till his death in 1856. Mr. Crafts was very active in establishing the Congregational Society in this town, and was an influential man in the church.

The next place west was the house-lot of two acres which was given to Dr. Charles Wild. Dr. Wild was so thoroughly identified with Brookline for over forty years that his name is a household word. It is hardly possible to prepare a satisfactory sketch of a man whose biography should be fully written by some able pen, or to describe him as he was known among his patients so that those who never saw him can have any adequate idea of him.

Dr. Wild was born in Boston in January, 1795. He was a graduate of Harvard College of the class of 1814. Dr. Walker, late President of Harvard, Judge (Pliny) Merrick, W. H. Prescott, the historian, and other eminent men were his classmates.

In the year 1818, when Dr. Charles Wild came to Brookline, Dr. Aspinwall, the skillful and beloved physician of the town and vicinity for many years, was in the decline of life, and his son the young doctor had just been removed by death. A good field for practice was open, and the Doctor began business under favorable circumstances, and soon made for himself a name and reputation. He built his house, married young, and reared a large family of children.

The Doctor was of course in those days a practitioner of the old school. People thought they had not their money's worth of service from a doctor unless they swallowed physic in fearful doses, and were blistered and bled within a small fraction of their lives, and Dr. Wild was "equal to the occasion."

Those who can remember the Doctor in his prime, can well recall his tall, well-formed figure, his firm tread, his deep voice which seemed to come from cavernous depths, and the eyes which seemed to look from behind his spectacles into and through one.

If there was occasion to send for him, unless the case was represented as a matter of life and death, the chances were even that he might not appear till the patient either died or recovered, unless the call were repeated two or three times. Not that the Doctor was intentionally heedless or neglectful of his patients when he found them very severely sick, but the difficulty was to find him, and get the impression made that he was actually needed. In serious cases he was devotedly attentive, and so great was the public confidence in him that in ordinary illnesses people would wait his tardy attention rather than send for another physician. It was quite as likely to be a successful hunt for him, to go through the streets and look for "old Sal," his sorrel mare, and the familiar old buggy before some house door, as to go to his house for him, for he had a way of going from one patient to another for a day and a night or more, without going home, getting a lunch at one house and a nap in another, particularly if there was much sickness.

He had a breezy way of entering a house, stamping off the snow or dust with noise enough for three men, throwing off his overcoat, untying a huge muffler that he wore about his neck, and letting down his black leather pouch with emphasis. There was an indescribable noise he made sometimes with that deep gruff voice of his which cannot be represented in type. It must have been heard to be understood, and the first salutation was quite likely to be (if the patient were an acquaintance), "Well! well! well! what kind of a kick-up have you got now?" If the patient was an infant it might be "How's Nicodemus to-day?" or, "Well! is Ichabod's tooth ready for the lance this morning?" His fancy for nicknames was proverbial. He usually called a friend's child whose name was Florence, either " Rome," " Milan," or some other Italian city. A charge upon his books of a visit to " Don Sebastian," rather nonplussed the member of his family who was to make out the bills. On inquiry it proved his nickname for a member of the Cabot family.

And who that ever saw the solemn deliberation with which he stirred thick yellow powders into molasses in a table spoon, silently, with an ominous glance occasionally at the hapless victim who lay waiting for the order to open his mouth, will think of them without a recoil? When one thinks, in the light of modern science, of the fearful potions of calomel, rhubarb, and jalap, picra, ipecac, and antimony, and countless other abominations, swallowed by hopeless humanity in former times, the chief wonder is that any lived to tell the tale.

When the business was transacted, and there was no special anxiety, then the Doctor settled himself to be sociable, and there he stayed often for two or three hours at a time, telling the drollest stories, with comical grimaces and hectoring the children, who never could keep away from him though they knew he would surely torment them. But if the case was serious or doubtful, the Doctor was grave and silent, and sat catching flies with the rapidity and precision of a terrier, if there were any to catch, — or walked back and forth cutting tobacco and chewing it with an avidity that was marvelous.

In the great and solemn crises of birth and death, in the great domestic trials through which all families must pass somewhere between the cradle and the grave, the Doctor was the calm counsellor and the sympathizing friend. His quaint brusque speeches and ways were seldom an offense to any one, and his hearty cheerfulness was better than medicine to dispel the blues. He enjoyed the ludicrous side of life to the full, and when anything occurred that he considered " too good to lose," he would give everybody the benefit of a hearty laugh over it.

An incident that suited the Doctor exactly, occurred in a farmer's family. The farmer was sick from a strain or something that required an external application, and the Doctor ordered a large slice of brown bread to be soaked in brandy and laid upon his stomach. The next day when the Doctor called, the wife met him at the head of the stairs. " Doctor," said she, " that brown bread hasn't done any good. I couldn't make him eat more than half of it, and he 's dreadful sick." " *Eat* it! good gracious, woman! *Eat* it?" growled the astonished Doctor, " I didn't tell you he was to *eat* it! It was to go on outside."

" Will it kill him, Doctor ? "

" Kill him! No, he'll live through it!" and he did, and soon got well.

The Doctor's salutations at his departure were unique, as well as those which marked his entrance to a sick room, " Now if you can't sleep well and don't know what to do you can amuse yourself with taking an emetic."

There was no end to the odd conceits, the quizzical expressions, the grotesque turns of thought which were constantly occurring to him. And he was wonderfully kindhearted withal, and as prompt about doing a favor, as if it was a matter of course, and never afterward appeared to remember it.

He was consulted upon all sorts of matters, from choosing a matrimonial companion to building a porch or a hen-coop, and his opinion was authority, for his shrewd good sense was seldom at fault.

In the year 1839 the attention of Dr. Wild was turned to homœopathy, which was then new in this part of the country. He was convinced that there was something more than mere theory in the matter, and by trying it in a chronic case where other means had failed, the happy result confirmed his previous opinion.

In the language of another, " From this time he pursued the investigation and trial of the system until he became a firm believer in its truth and efficiency. He was a man of quick observation, of an investigating mind, and disliked to leave a subject until he had mastered it. He had great intellectual candor, looking at a new subject, thought, or creed with interest, not casting it aside as humbug or charlatanism till he was convinced from investigation that it was such."

While the Doctor was in what might be called a transition state, between the old practice and the new, there was a trying time both for him and his patients, for he had new difficulties and old prejudices to encounter, but he carried along with him to a wonderful degree the confidence of his patrons and met with marked success in his practice.

The second meeting held in New England by physicians who were pioneers in the new practice was held at Dr. Wild's house February 16, 1841, and the Massachusetts Homœopathic Fraternity was organized, and a constitution and by-laws adopted. The present chartered society is a continuation of this original institution.

He carried his books with him from house to house and studied by the bedside of the patient, comparing and observing, and referring to the best authorities then extant for the wisest methods of procedure.

Miss Amanda M. Corey, afterwards the wife of Mr. James Edmond, was then a school girl, very bright and original, but often under the Doctor's care, and was a great favorite of his. Soon after he began practicing the new treatment she wrote the following lines, which greatly amused and delighted the Doctor.

ILLI, CUI CARMINA APPLICENT.*

A son of Esculapius comes,
 I hear his chariot wheels;
The very sound my soul benumbs,
 A shiver o'er me steals.
Ye muses, aid me if you can,
 Ye sundry settled bills,
In self-defense to sing the man
 Of gallipots and pills!

Ye classic bards of olden days,
 My vacant soul inspire;
Ye smiling ghosts of comic lays,
 Awake my sleeping lyre.
Desert your graves in winding-sheets,
 Diseases fierce and grim;
Ye aches and pains your dark retreats
 Forsake and sing of him.

Ye memories of departed pills,
 Of bitter powders too,
Support my shrinking soul that fills
 With horror at the view.

* "Him to whom the song applies."

POEM ON DR. WILD.

Ye spirits all of tuneful rhyme,
  Where'er ye chance to be,
Come mount Parnassus' heights sublime,
  And sweep the lyre for me.

Come, sing the *Homœopathic knight;*
  Describe him, as he comes
To kindly give the aching wight
  A dose of *sugar-plums!*
Who banishes disease and woe,
  And contradicts the song,
"Man wants but little here below,
  Nor wants that little long."

Come, sing capacious pockets crammed
  With roots the fields supply,
That in the sounding mortar jammed,
  Diseases stern defy.
The names that on his vials wrote,
  In goodly rows appear,
That choke the rude, contracted throat,
  And stun the vulgar ear.

But most of all, his awful *eyes,*
  That pierce my very soul;
That scan my feelings as they rise,
  And penetrate the whole
For eyes and "*specs*" together, strike
  The very seat of life;
And scare my timid spirit, like
  A ——— keen-edged carving-knife!

But, lo! his steed is at the gate,
  And *he* is at the door;
Be steady now, my whirling pate,
  Ye shaking nerves give o'er.
He doffs the frightful rubber coat,
  That dark'y shrouds his form,
And, fastened tight beneath his throat,
  Defies and scares the storm.

He leaves his cap and gloves below,
  Arise my longest hairs!
For now, with solemn step and slow,
  I hear him on the stairs.
Two ponderous volumes in his hands,
  This second Galen brings,
And by the couch of sickness stands,
  A man of mighty things.

And now he reads those mystic books,
  Enlighteners of disease,
And grasps his patient's wrist, and looks
  Profound as Socrates.
Prescribes a dose, then lifts his eyes
  And fastens them on me;
My blood runs cold, my spirit dies,
  So terrible is he!

Ye pitying Muses, one and all,
  That e'er on mortals smiled,
O teach me how to break the thrall,
  The spell of ——— ———.
And if the task of serving you
  Apollo e'er assigns,
It shall be hers, life's journey through,
  Who perpetrates these lines.

Dr. Wild was a public-spirited man, interested in whatever promoted the welfare of the community. For many years he was an attendant upon the ministry of Dr. Pierce, at the Unitarian Church, and was a member of the choir connected with it. Before the days of the organ the Doctor played the flute.

As his health began to fail with advancing years, he relinquished by degrees his practice, to his son, Dr. Edward A. Wild.

He had now more leisure for reading and thought, and became interested in the theology of the New Jerusalem Church. He considered it with candor and patient investigation, and was satisfied that here at last he had found the two great books of nature and revelation in harmonious agreement instead of seeming antagonism.

He heartily embraced the doctrines of the Church and was baptized in the High Street Church in Brookline. He spent some months in a curative institution in Boston without any manifest improvement to his health, and returned to Providence whither his wife had already gone, and in that city he died on the 3d of May, 1864, aged seventy-one years.

His son, Dr. Edward A. Wild, had gained an extensive practice in his father's stead, in this town, previous to the War of the Rebellion. He had spent some time abroad during the great war between Russia and the allied armies, and gained much knowledge in the hospitals of the Crimea. At home he was a public-spirited citizen as well as a popular and successful physician.

When the Rebellion began he gave up his profession to enter the service of his country, and gathered and drilled in this town, Company A, of the First Massachusetts regiment.

From the office of Captain which he held at the opening of the war, he rose, as is well known, to the rank of Brigadier-general. Of what he did and what he suffered for his country his empty sleeve is but a partial testimonial. He is too well known to need any tribute from our pen, and we share the regrets of a large community that not one of this respected family remain in the town where the two doctors were so long useful, and where they were and are still held in grateful and affectionate remembrance.

Captain Walter Wild, the Doctor's youngest son, also was in the service of the United States during the late war.

THE BLAKE AND ASPINWALL PLACES.

The whole hill extending westward from the first rising ground west of Cypress Street to Beacon Street, and from Washington Street on the north to the railroad in the valley on the south, is one of the most beautiful hills in our town to look at or to look from. Though of less height than Corey's Hill, it commands a wide and varied prospect which never tires the eye, and its undulating surface is very beautiful in detail.

The part of it now comprising Mr. Blake's estate, ex

cept the orchard on the southeast, was purchased off the Croft farm about fifty years ago, by Mr. Lewis Tappan, who built the stone house which is still standing, and occupied it a few years. The place extended a little further west than at present, and included a strip of land now on the Aspinwall place.

After the removal of Mr. Tappan to New York the house was occupied by Mr. Nathaniel R. Cobb, and subsequently by Henry Robinson, an English gentleman, who resided there a number of years. All its owners have been gentlemen of wealth and taste, but no one has brought the place to such elegance and perfection as its present owner.

About forty acres of land, including the higher part of the hill and the woods that crown it, were purchased by Dr. Aspinwall in 1788 of Mr. Benjamin White. The Doctor's fine taste is evinced in the selection of the site for his house, commanding as it does an unbroken view of Boston and Charles River, with all the towns along the north side of the river for miles, while the most beautiful part of Brookline lies directly in the foreground. When the house was built in 1803, there were not more than six houses in view in Brookline from the front of it.

There was an old house standing on the lower slope of the lawn, near the street, whose owner, a Mr. Blanchard, was the first sexton of " Brookline meeting-house," but this was removed about the beginning of the present century.

The late Augustus Aspinwall, a son of the Doctor, continued to occupy and improve the place after the death of his venerable father; a sister of his remaining unmarried being his housekeeper, and the companion of years of loneliness which followed the early death of his much-loved wife. Mr. Aspinwall made his garden and greenhouse his recreation after business hours, and they became famous for the most exquisite roses that money and choice cultivation could procure.

His love for them was almost a passion, and it seemed as if the affection which might otherwise have been lavished upon the dearest of kindred, found occupation and solace among his beloved roses. There were hundreds of varieties, and they bloomed successively through all the seasons, and their admiring owner shared them with such of his friends as were appreciative of their rare beauty. Choice vines and fruit trees were also an attraction of this fine garden and farm.

On this place, as on the adjoining one of Mr. Blake, the fine native forest trees have been allowed to grow and expand, and choice evergreens, on the Blake place particularly, planted in groups and trimmed into symmetry, contrast exquisitely in autumn with the brilliant hues of the abundant maples.

The road-side trees along both these places are a perpetual blessing, and make Washington Street for a half mile like a woodland avenue.

We have heard strangers remark upon the richness and beauty of the grass in many parts of Brookline, comparing it with English lawns so famous for their beauty. It has often been said that a New Englander must go south and remain for a time before he can appreciate the luxuriance and greenness of the grass of his native soil; but we think the dullest eye could not look upon the closely trimmed lawns, without a sense of their beauty, or the waving wealth of cultivated grass upon many of the finely kept places in our town, without a glow of appreciation which will reveal to him that though there may be "a great crop of hay," there is something more and finer than that.

On the opposite side of the street, a long stretch of land, once the Cottons', then the Sharps', then the Crofts', and afterwards the Crafts', has been divided and subdivided among many owners, and separated by beautiful avenues which it is a matter of public regret were laid out so narrow that their widening now begun, involves the destruction of the beautiful trees which have so long been their chief charm and attraction.

From Park Street west on this side of Washington Street the changes have been so slight during many years, that the returning native of the town who might wander perplexed and bewildered in the lower part of the town like an awakened Rip Van Winkle, would here find himself at home again, and the finely cultivated farm of the Griggs family and the familiar sight of the tannery beyond, assure him that he was still in Brookline and following the windings of the Brighton road.

CHAPTER X.

THE ROBINSON, WITHINGTON, AND COREY PLACES. — CYPRESS STREET. — BOYLSTON STREET. — GIDEON THAYER. — DR. SHURTLEFF. — BRADLEY'S HILL.

AMONG the earliest annals of the town of Dorchester appear the names of Robinson and Withington, and from 1636 downwards they constantly reappear as "Elders" in the church, or selectmen of the town. In 1690 we find "Captain John Withington" leading the Dorchester soldiers on the "Canada Expedition;" and in the Revolutionary War, the young men of both families seem to have been numerous and active in the service of the country.

During Shays' Rebellion in 1787, we find "Captain James Robinson" of Dorchester, in command of a company of men from that place who were employed to assist in putting down the insurrection. In this company appear the names of John and David Withington, corporals. In an old diary kept by Colonel Samuel Pierce of Dorchester, appears a curious incident under date of December 30, 1773. On December 15th he notes the destruction of the tea in Boston harbor. It seems that some chests of it not wholly broken up or emptied, were carried out by the tide, and about a half chest had drifted ashore at "the Point," doubtless now South Boston or City Point. An old gentleman of the Withington family had fished it out and carried it home, not because of any Tory leanings, but probably because he liked a good cup of tea and could not bear to see it wasted. Colonel Pierce's diary reads, —

"*December* 15. There was the destruction of the Tee; they supposed there to be about 340 chests destroyed, all thrown into the dock in one nite."

"*December* 30. There was a number of men came from Boston in disguise, about 40; they came to Mr. Eben Withington's house down in town, and demanded his Tee from him which he had taken up, and carried it off and burnt it at Boston."

It was publicly burnt on the Common.

Henry Withington from whom the Brookline families descended was a " Ruling Elder " twenty-nine years.

Deacon John Robinson, afterwards of this town, was born in Dorchester in 1763. He was therefore too young for military service in the Revolution, but being often sent by his father with milk to the British troops, then occupying " the Castle," he was justly indignant at their boastful threats of the ability of the King's troops to overrun the country and conquer the rebel colonies, and desired very much to enter the service as a fifer, but to this his father would not consent, on account of his tender years. His memory of the fortifying of Dorchester Heights, the evacuation of Boston, and all the prominent events of the times was very distinct.

About the year 1790 the two young men, now only remembered as venerable, white-haired fathers of the town, John Robinson and Enos Withington, who had been brought up to the trade of tanners, sought a suitable spot to locate themselves and commence business. Their attention was drawn to Brookline at that time, chiefly because of its minister, the Rev. Joseph Jackson, whom they and others of the Dorchester people occasionally walked all the long distance from that town to this on Sundays to hear, he being "a mighty man " in the pulpit in those days. He did not confine the force of his logic, or the power of his eloquence to the sins of ancient Jews or Philistines, or labor vigorously to overthrow a man of straw of his own construction, but rather directed his efforts toward the sins, or what he considered sins of his own people. Deacon Robinson used to mention a sermon of Mr. Jackson's, which he heard one Sunday morning when he had walked from Dorchester, in which there was something of what might be called personal preaching. Some of the good man's parishioners had been rather gay and frisky, and kept late hours, which called down upon them the thunders of the pulpit, in which the pastor seemed to be making vigorous exertions to pound the Bible to pieces.

Whether this particular sermon decided the young men to come to Brookline, does not appear, but they came in 1790, and purchased land of the last Robert Sharp.

All the land at that time from the Croft house to the one lately owned by Mr. Bartlett, on the north side of the street, was then a dark and tangled swamp, full of rocks, and thick with alder bushes all along the roadside. The site for the tannery was selected (where the work is still continued by Samuel A. Robinson), and the work of clearing up and preparing to build was soon in successful progress, much to the satisfaction of market-men and others who had to frequent this lonely road at unseasonable hours.

Mr. Robinson built his house in 1791, married Mr. Withington's sister, and settled to his business. Mr. Withington built his house within three years after, and married Patience Leeds of Dorchester, a sister of the James Leeds of whom we gave an account previously. Both houses were alike originally, and the land about them, by the industry of these energetic young men, was reclaimed from its wildness, and orchards and mowing lands took the places of rocky pastures and alder thickets.

During the earlier years of Mr. Withington's married life, having more house room than was necessary, he let a part of his house in summer to Boston families, who then found fewer places of summer resort than at present. Among these families were Governor Gore's, the Hubbards, Clevelands, and other prominent people of Boston, who enjoyed the fine situation and the grand prospect from the top of the hill.

During the second war with England, when Boston was threatened by British vessels, every available spot of unoccupied room in this house was at one time packed full of duck, which was removed thither by some merchants who were apprehensive of losing it in case of an invasion.

Mr. Withington did not continue a tanner all his life, but devoted the principal part of his life to farming. He died when about seventy-four years of age. The late Deacon Otis Withington of Harvard Church, and our present Town Treasurer,* are his sons.

Mr. Robinson was also an active man in the First Church, of which he and his wife early became members. In this church he was a deacon fifty-seven years, and won the reputation of being a man of untiring benevolence.

Dr. Pierce, who succeeded Mr. Jackson in 1796, speaks more than once after a fifty years' pastorate, of Deacon Robinson and his wife, and Mr. Withington and his wife, as living with the marriage tie unbroken, longer than any other couples whom he found residing in the town when he came here.

When Mr. Robinson had held the office of deacon fifty-seven years, and the infirmities of age had already unfitted

---

[1] Moses Withington, Esq.

him for further active duties, he was presented with a heavy and beautiful silver goblet, with the following inscription: —

To DEACON JOHN ROBINSON,
From the First Church in Brookline.
RECALLING HIS LONG AND FAITHFUL SERVICES AND GRATEFUL FOR HIS
CONSISTENT EXAMPLE OF LOVE TOWARD GOD AND MAN. PRESENTED
MAY 14TH, 1854.
THE 57TH ANNIVERSARY OF HIS APPOINTMENT TO OFFICE.

Deacon Robinson was confined to his bed during the last two years of his life, and it has been said that " it was truly delightful to see him lying so humble and submissive, patiently awaiting his departure. Those in attendance upon him, often heard him quoting from Scripture and verse such passages as best suited his feelings, and which were of comfort and delight." His last utterance upon earth was the Doxology, —

"To God the Father, God the Son,
And God the Spirit, Three in One,
Be honor, praise, and glory given,
By all on earth, and all in heaven."

He died January 13, 1855, aged ninety-one years and six months.

An appreciative memorial of him was published in one of the religious papers soon after his death. The widow and the fatherless often had occasion to bless his memory as one of the Lord's faithful stewards, and none who knew him will fail to recall to memory, his venerable figure and countenance, with feelings of the highest respect and esteem.

Deacon Robinson was overseer of the poor and a selectman for thirty years. He also was a representative in the State Legislature twelve years. The house which he built has since his death been modernized and greatly improved by his son, so that to appearance it has almost lost its identity. The Withington house, which has not been occupied by any of the family for many years, remains as built by its original owner. The large gasometer lately built almost in front of it alters the appearance of the neighborhood, which had remained so many years unchanged. The first tannery buildings were destroyed by fire several years ago, and rebuilt in an improved manner. The second tannery with the house near it were built by Deacon Robinson for his son James, who has since removed from Brookline.

An incident has recently been mentioned to us which indicates Dr. Pierce's estimate of Deacon Robinson. A remark was made in his hearing respecting an ideal character of which one of the family was reading, and it was thought to be overdrawn, and to represent impossible goodness. "Now, where in real life," it was asked, "will you find such a character as that of Lord Orville?" when Dr. Pierce promptly replied that he "*did not believe he was any better man than Deacon Robinson.*"

The anecdote is as good to illustrate Dr. Pierce's beautiful faith and charity, as to indicate the esteem in which the Deacon was held. Dr. Pierce was several years younger than Deacon Robinson, and much more vigorous, and he used to say that he had selected his text for the Deacon's funeral sermon in case he should outlive him, "Mark the perfect man and behold the upright, for the end of that man is peace." But when the time came for Deacon Robinson's funeral sermon to be preached, the grass had long been green above the grave of his old friend and pastor.

THE COREY PLACES.

The next house of ancient standing on Washington Street, was built and occupied by Major Edward Whyte, who died in 1769, aged seventy-six. In this house was born his son Oliver, who was the postmaster and town clerk for many years, and whose house on Walnut Street has recently been taken down by his heirs.

The house of Major Whyte, for a long time the property of the Coreys, is the one now owned and occupied until recently by the family of the late James Bartlett.

On the site of the stone house, nearly opposite the one above mentioned, there stood formerly a two-story house, unpainted and black with age. This was the house of Isaac Winchester, son of Captain John Winchester, one of the old proprietors on Harvard Street. Isaac Winchester died in 1771.

There seems to be very little known respecting this branch of the Winchester family; but there is an old bill of Dr. Aspinwall's, against the town in the year 1780, for "attendance upon Exeter, a Negro Servant, belonging to the estate of Isaac Winchester, deceased." Poor Exeter probably had a hard time of it, as the Doctor charged for one hundred and sixty-six visits, besides " rum and dressings."

Shortly after Isaac Winchester died, the house and a tract of land lying upon that side of the street, and land on the Whyte place on the opposite side, were purchased by Captain Timothy Corey who had married Elizabeth Griggs of Brookline. He was the son of Isaac Corey of Weston. Captain Corey was in active service in the Revolutionary War, and was one of three who were all that were left of an entire company who died of wounds, sickness, and imprisonment. He and his two comrades returned, footsore, ragged, and forlorn, from their terrible exposure and hardships. At the time of the battle of Lexington, his young wife with her two little children left the house, as did many other women of Brookline, and carrying some blankets and provisions with them, sought shelter in the woods, till the fright and danger, from the enemy passing through the town, were over.

Captain Corey is remembered as an old gentleman who dressed in the costume of the last century, as long as he lived, wearing a "three-cornered cocked hat." An anecdote is told of his wife, which indicates her opinion of her husband's appearance. Some one, a stranger, called at his house one day when he was away from home, desiring to see him. Mrs. Corey told him to go down the road and if he met "a fine-looking, portly man on horseback, he might know it was *her husband*." Captain Corey joined the Freemasons in his old age, because his son Elijah did so; and he is said to have given as a reason for doing this, that " no son of his should know more than he did." Captain Corey died in 1811, aged sixty-nine. He was buried from the First Church with Masonic honors. His widow lived to be ninety-two years of age, and retained her faculties to the last.

In this ancient house there was often preaching by various ministers, who were called "New Lights." An old colored Baptist preacher, known as "Black Paul," and quite a local celebrity fifty years ago, frequently preached there. "Father Grafton" also preached there many times. All the family had been members of the First Church, or attendants upon worship there, but the "New Lights," who were a sort of revivalists, caused a secession of many of the people, some of whom joined the Baptists and some the Congregationalists.

The two sons of Captain Corey, afterwards known as "Deacon Elijah," and "Deacon Timothy," joined the Baptists.

Deacon Timothy in his young manhood was a militia captain in this town and in the second war with Eng-

AN ANCIENT WEDDING. 183

land, on the muster roll for 1813 and 1814, his name appears as Captain, Robert S. Davis as Lieutenant, and Thomas Griggs as Ensign.

Moses Jones and Daniel Pierce, with two or three other less familiar names, were " Music Serjeants." It was during the year 1814 that a detachment from the Brookline company consisting of thirty men, was ordered to Fort Independence, by Colonel Dudley, for three months' duty.

Deacon Timothy Corey built the house now occupied by his son of the same name, early in the present century. He married Mary, daughter of Caleb Gardner of this town. After the death of his mother he had the old black house torn down, and subsequently built the present stone house upon the site of it. He was a man who was much beloved and respected in his life, and sincerely mourned in his death. He died in August, 1844, aged 62.

Elijah Corey, afterwards the deacon, married, when quite young, Polly Leeds of Dorchester, from the same Leeds family previously mentioned. This was in November, 1797. The " wedding visit " * was a gay affair for those times, and a quiet farming place, as Brookline was then. Almost everybody in the town was invited, and there was the inspiriting music of a fife and drum. There was not much finery in those days, but what there was, was conspicuous on this occasion. An old citizen tells us that his mother, then young and fair, wore a new white silk hat, with white feathers, almost exactly in the style of those worn by young ladies the present season.

Mr. William Ackers, the former owner of the Fisher place on the corner of Boylston Street, used to relate an incident of his own participation in this ancient wedding. He was a stylish young man in those days, and had had

* The old time name for a " Reception."

black satin "small-clothes," ordered for the occasion, but as he was leaving his own house, a sudden slip in the muddy yard brought his satin finery to utter discomfiture, and he was forced to go back and make his toilet anew, in plainer garb. The old house (lately the Bartlett house) was crowded with merry guests and the cheerful occasion was an event long talked of afterwards. In 1821, when his son Elijah was married, the father built the house on the hill on the south side of the street, and the son occupied the old house during the remainder of his life.

Deacon Elijah Corey was left a widower in 1827, and in 1829 married the widow of Captain Robert S. Davis.

The causeway across the valley from Washington Street to the steep hillside was built by Deacon Corey about fifty years ago. At the entrance of it stood a barn, underneath which was a cider-mill. This barn was destroyed by fire several years since.

All the Coreys of three generations have been farmers and have been considered shrewd, practical men. The two brothers, Elijah and Timothy, were among the first projectors of the Baptist Church enterprise in this town, and to that purpose devoted time, labor, and money.

None who were familiar with the old Baptist vestry will ever forget Deacon Elijah Corey's voice and manner in his old age. If the meeting flagged and there was an awful silence, Deacon Corey would strike out in a high key, " Come Holy Spirit, Heavenly Dove," to the tune of Turner, or St. Martin's, or " Life is the time to serve the Lord," to the tune of Wells, or some other familiar old hymn, and by the time he had sung a line or two, other voices joined in and the solo became, not lost in, but a part of, a chorus.

His exhortations abounded in striking metaphors and strong language, frequently beginning with, " Brethren, a thought struck me," and he usually made the thought strike his hearers before he finished. He often ended an exhortation with the desire that the Lord would " make our souls like the chariots of Amminadib" (Song of Solomon vi. 12). But in what respect this would have been desirable, was not apparent to the listeners; and we often wondered what the good deacon's idea of such a condition of soul might be. There is no question, however, but that all through his life he had at heart not only the building up of his church here but of the denomination to which he belonged, not only here but abroad.

He was one of the Trustees of Newton Theological Institution, and many a lack in finance both there and at the Missionary Rooms, was filled out from Deacon Corey's purse.

He died in May, 1859, aged eighty-six, and was buried from the Baptist Church. A bunch of apple-blossoms, a fit tribute to one who had been all his life a farmer, was the only floral offering laid upon his breast.

CYPRESS STREET.

On the 11th of May, 1719, it was ordered that a new town way should be opened, " from Watertown road between the farms of Mr. Rowland Cotton and Mr. Thomas Cotton, all the way in the said Thomas Cotton's land, and so into the land belonging to the heirs of Caleb Gardner, into Sherburne road, for the convenience of the people in the north part of the town in going to meeting."

This was the origin of Cypress Street, which was called the " New Lane " for more than one hundred and twenty years. It was only a narrow lane through woods and bushes, and much of it so low as to be very wet, and at some seasons quite covered with water.

The "Sherburne road," was what is now Walnut Street, and "the land belonging to the heirs of Caleb Gardner," was the present Bird place.

Before Cypress Street was opened, as early as 1706, it was "Voted, that there should be a burying-place, on the south side of the hill on Mr. Cotton's farm, between the two roads, if it can be obtained."

But it could not be "obtained," and for eleven years afterwards people were obliged to carry their dead out of town for burial, as many of their descendants are obliged to do at present.*

The two corner houses at the entrance of this street, have been previously described.

The land in the street in front of the corner house, now owned by Dr. Salisbury, was originally part of the yard to that house, and included the great elm tree. When it became necessary to have the corner rounded on that side of the street, the way was carried through the yard, but the triangular piece, including the great elm and the other elm, not long since cut down, still belonged to the old house, and was at one time inclosed for a short time by a slight railing to prevent forfeiture. The right to so inclose it held good until within the last quarter century.

The place long known as the Searle place, was bought in 1817 by a Mr. Hubbard, a carpenter, who built the church on Roxbury Hill, known as the "Eliot Church," opposite the Norfolk House. Mr. Hubbard altered and added to his shop the next year and made a house of it in which he lived. Directly opposite, there was placed soon after an old barn which was removed from opposite the old Croft house on Washington Street. This was on

* Since this was written, a lot, upon Grove St., has been purchased for a Cemetery.

the Crafts place. Mr. Hubbard did not much admire the addition to his neighborhood and left Mr. Crafts no peace, and after several years the barn was disposed of.

Mr. Hubbard was succeeded in the ownership of his house by Mr. George Searle, who altered and enlarged, and at last built the additional house nearest the street, thus making two houses, though so joined as to appear as one.

The various changes and additions which have been made in these houses have produced some most original specimens of architecture, such as would hardly be found in any volume on the subject, ancient or modern. They must be seen to be appreciated. The garden was formerly a very fine one of the old fashioned type. A large butternut tree near the centre was surrounded by a circular seat. Gravel walks, profusely bordered with pinks, separated beds of tulips, roses, and other flowers, while rustic arbors were overrun with honeysuckle, woodbine, and other vines. Choice fruit trees, and many grafts on natural stocks, two or three on the same, gave great variety in this line, and ornamental trees and flowering shrubs filled up the intervening spaces.

In the eastern house, there was kept for many years a boarding-school for young ladies, under the charge of Miss Lucy Searle, a lady of much culture and taste; and at various times there were pupils here from distant States, even as far as Georgia. The western part of the house was at one time occupied by Hon. Ellis Gray Loring. Many distinguished visitors have at various times been entertained within these houses. Among these were Judge Story, Dr. and Mrs. Follen, Mrs. Lydia Maria Child, Professor Norton, William Page and Gambadelli, artists, Mrs. Caroline Gilman, and many others more or less known to the literary world.

The house now owned by Mr. Sturtevant, was built
for the late Amos Atkinson of this town, was afterwards
occupied by Deacon Lambert, who after several years'
residence here went to New York, and from that time
till it came into possession of its present owner, it was
the property of Samuel A. Walker, the well-known
auctioneer. Mr. Walker at one time owned a great deal
of real estate in Brookline, and took quite a conspicuous
part in local affairs. On the opposite side of the street
about forty years ago, quite a tract of land was owned
by Mr. John Gorham, — the new avenue on that side
bears his name.

Mr. Moses Jones, the father of the present citizen of
that name, built his house about forty years ago, and
settled there, and made his farm on both sides of the
street one of the finest and most productive of fruit and
vegetables of any in the vicinity.

On the west side of the street much of the land, as we
have said, was low and swampy, and some of it was
heavily timbered. Mr. Jones bought twenty-seven acres
of this land for *four thousand* dollars, and proceeded to
clear and drain and improve it. He sold a great deal of
heavy white oak timber off it to Boston ship-builders.
The one great oak at the entrance to Tappan Street is a
specimen of what the place produced in the way of trees.

The road was so low at this point not many years ago
that the land on which the tree stands was walled up
some three feet above the level of the road. There was
probably, at some distant period, a pond covering all the
level ground on both sides of Cypress Street, from the
Blake place to the rising ground west of Mr. Beck's
place in Davis Avenue, and from near Washington Street
on the north to the rising ground near Boylston Street
on the south, since, within the memory of persons now

living at an advanced age, there was a great deal of standing water on this territory during most of the year. In digging to drain it some sixty or seventy years ago, large tree stumps, and beds of clam and other shells, were found from six to ten feet below the surface.

The fine orchard on the southerly slope of the hill, in the sheltered angle between the woods on the Aspinwall and Blake places, was set out by Farmer Jones. He planted alternate rows of apple and peach trees, and while the former were coming to maturity, the latter lived a short and prolific life, and then gave place to the sturdy and beautiful trees that have been admired by every passer-by for many years.

Boylston Street was not laid out when the "New Lane," was made, nor for some time afterwards, so that there was no intersecting street the whole length of the lane. After Boylston Street was laid out there was a school-house built on the corner of what is now Mr. Bird's land, and a private school was kept there for several years by a Miss Stebbins. The name of Cypress Street was given in 1840.

BOYLSTON STREET.

Boylston Street, that is, that part of it from its entrance at the village to the gate-house of the old reservoir, and from the beginning of Heath Street to the Newton line, was a part of the old Worcester Turnpike, and its construction was entered upon in 1806.

An arch over the road at the village indicated the point from which toll-rates were to be reckoned, and the first toll-gate was established at the upper part of the town near what was known for many years as Richards' Tavern. Turnpike roads were constructed so as to be as nearly straight as possible, and with this end in view went over hills and through valleys, when a short detour would have saved time and wear of travel. The road was carried over the summit of Bradley's Hill, and was consequently so very steep that loaded teams almost invariably were obliged to go round by the old road, by the Unitarian Church.

The two old houses belonging to Major White, on the present site of Guild's Block, have been described in a former chapter. From these, to the houses on the estate of the late Benjamin Goddard, there was not a house on either side of the street, for many years.

The first house built was the small one, now the second east of Dr. Shurtleff's and at present standing endways to the street. It formerly stood fronting the street, and was built by a man named Rafter, an English or Scotch gardener, who at that time was employed by Richard Sullivan, Esq., who lived on the place now occupied by Mrs. Bowditch, next the reservoir.

After Mr. Rafter, the house was bought by John Pierce, a tanner, who carried on the business there for several years. He was a worthy man, and in his early years was in the employ of Deacon Robinson, who afterwards aided him in establishing himself in business.

About the year 1820 or 1822, Mr. Richard Sullivan, General Dearborn, and several other gentlemen, formed a company or corporation for the purpose of establishing a classical school in Brookline, for boys, and bought a part of the ground now included in Dr. Shurtleff's place, and built for a school-room the present southerly wing or projection of the house. It was considered at that time the finest piece of architecture in the vicinity, and was looked upon with great interest as a valuable addition to the town.

Afterwards the house was built, as a boarding-house

for the pupils, and thus the school-building lost its distinctive character. The first teacher was a Mr. Barlow. A Mr. Hubbard was for some time owner of the house and school-house. In the year 1830 Mr. Gideon Thayer, the founder of Chauncey Hall School, purchased the place of Mr. Hubbard, and removed here with his family, bringing with him a number of delicate boys whose parents were anxious to have them enjoy the purer air and freedom of the country. Mr. Thayer employed a sub-master for the Brookline branch of his school, and continued his Boston school as before. Mr. Thayer had been a resident of Brookline in his childhood, and his parents died here, in the house on the corner of School and Washington streets. When he returned to Brookline he at once connected himself with the First Parish, and during the five years of his residence here he worked as superintendent of the Sunday-school with all the vigor and personal interest which he infused into everything he undertook. The memoir of this excellent man, while it gives his traits as a teacher admirably, does not treat of that other side of his character, which made him eminently the friend of the poor and the struggling. Many a poor boy he taught gratuitously, and many more he set up in business. Poor women came to him as their friend and counsellor, and wherever he lived or worked he left his mark upon the community. He evidently felt himself but a steward for the Great Master, an almoner of his Lord's bounty. He might have been a rich man, but he preferred to be an unselfish one, and as such he has gone to the reward of the faithful.

After several years Mr. Thayer returned to Boston, having sold the place to George B. Emerson of Boston, the well-known educator. The Classical School was continued in various private houses for a few years longer with varying success, and was finally abandoned. Mr. Emerson lived in the stone house two years, and during that time spent a winter in Boston, having leased his house to William Ware, the author of " Last Days of Aurelian," " Zenobia," and various other works. " Zenobia " was written in the north parlor of that house. It being before the days of furnaces or double windows, the shivering author had a difficult time in keeping his ink and his blood in a circulating condition. The book was published in 1838.

About this time Dr. Shurtleff, the late owner, purchased the place of Mr. Emerson, adding to the land by a purchase of half an acre on the west, from the property of Moses Jones, to whom it came by way of the Clarks, who were owners on the east side of Cypress Street.

There are still standing on the Shurtleff place, an old pear tree and two apple trees, which were set out by Thomas Cotton who built the old Davis house, and owned all the land which has been previously mentioned as the Cotton property. From the Cottons, it will be remembered, it came to the Davises, and was finally sold off in small lots to one purchaser after another, and this place was a part of it.

In this house was born, June 18, 1840, Carlton Atwood, youngest son of Dr. S. A. Shurtleff. He was educated in the Brookline schools, fitted for Harvard College under Mr. J. E. Hoar at our High School, and graduated in the class of 1861. He was greatly interested in botany and entomology, and after graduating, studied with Professor Agassiz for a year. He then studied medicine at the Harvard Medical School, and with his father and Dr. T. E. Francis of this town. During the War of the Rebellion he entered the United States army as a medical cadet, and served first on a floating hospital on the Mississippi River during the siege of Vicksburg. He there contracted chills and fever, and received a short furlough. He came home, but as soon as his health would admit returned to the army, and was assigned to the Cotton Factory Hospital in Harrisburg, immediately after the battle of Gettysburg, where he labored three months, and afterwards was on duty in the hospitals of Philadelphia. His health was impaired by the chills which he contracted in front of Vicksburg, and after a short and sudden illness he died at his home in Brookline, June 26, 1864, aged twenty-four years. He was a member of the Boston Society of Natural History and the Numismatic Society, and in his favorite studies he had made close and valuable investigations, and left ably prepared papers upon various scientific topics.

But it was chiefly for his blameless life and beautiful traits of character that this young man was beloved and mourned. He was a member of the New Church (High Street) in Brookline, and was one of the most active among the young people of the society in all good works. As one of his college classmates expressed it after his death, "he was thoughtful, religious, yet ever happy through infinite faith. He was not afraid to die." Though he did not fall in field or camp, there is no doubt that his precious young life must be added to the fatal list of those which the Rebellion cost.

Dr. Samuel A. Shurtleff, long an eminent physician in Boston, has been identified with Brookline for the past thirty years. He died March 11, 1873. From an obituary which was published in the " Brookline Transcript " soon after his death, the following is copied: —

" He came of the old Puritan stock, being the sixth in descent from his ancestor who came over in the *Mayflower*, and who was still living in 1699.

"His boyhood was spent on the ancestral farm which had descended from father to son from the time that it was bought from the Indians, and which he possessed at the time of his death. He studied medicine with his brother, the late Dr. Benjamin Shurtleff, and taking his medical degree at Brown University he commenced the practice of his profession in Boston, in which he continued until the year 1838, when the destruction of his pleasant garden, by the demolition of Pemberton Hill, combined with serious attacks of ill health, induced by the cares and exposure of a large practice, determined him to remove from the city. In that year he removed to his late residence on Boylston Street in this town, where he has since led a life of comparative retirement.

"He had a great fondness for the study of natural history, especially conchology. He discovered a number of new varieties of shells, hitherto unknown, and left one of the finest and most complete collections in New England.

"He was also a devoted horticulturist, and succeeded in adding to the list of known pears, a large number of new kinds, some of them of great value. In middle life he was a member, and for some time vice-president, of the Horticultural Society, and took an active part in the proceedings.

"His life in later years has been uneventful, but he had a mind full of resources, and intelligent to the last, and his time was always usefully and pleasantly occupied.

"His final illness was of short duration, and after a few restless hours he quietly passed to that better life, for which he has long been prepared, and to which he looked forward in perfect confidence and peace."

BRADLEY'S HILL.

Bradley's Hill, formerly called Walley's Hill, was bought of Mr. Thomas Walley, who lived on the present Bird place, about the year 1820, by Benjamin Bradley.

This individual was as much a part of Brookline as Dr. Pierce, or the old stone school-house; and no account of the town could reproduce it "as it was," without Ben. Bradley in it.

Mr. Bradley came to this town in his youth, and learned his trade (a carpenter) of Mr. Nathaniel Murdock. He was soon hired as sexton of the Unitarian Church, and served in that capacity for thirty years. For several years he held the office of town constable. He was also captain of the Brookline militia about ten years, and was thenceforth known as Captain Bradley.

We think it was Sydney Smith, who once said that if a woman were obliged to give a military company the order to "Halt!" she would do it on this wise, "Now soldiers, what I want of you is, that you should all stop, and stand still right where you are and not stir another step till I tell you to." One of Captain Bradley's first military orders was about as verbose, "Now fellow soldiers, let's all see if we can't form a straight line;"— quite a necessary arrangement, one would suppose from descriptions, given by witnesses, of the company that marched behind him to the music of the drum and fife.

Soon after Mr. Bradley bought the hill, he purchased a very old gambrel-roofed one-story house of Mr. John Warren on Warren Street, and moved it to the west side of the hill. This was the beginning of the settlement which became so notorious. From time to time other houses were built, or bought and moved to the hill, till it was covered. For many years it was a cheap and comfortable place for poor but respectable American mechanics and laborers to live. Mr. Bradley is said to have been a kind landlord, very reasonable in his charges for rent, and lenient with those who through sickness or misfortune were unable to pay, and had a friendly way of leaving a turkey at every tenant's door the night before Thanksgiving.

What animosities and small revenges he chose to show toward those whom he had occasion, or thought he had, to dislike, generally embodied themselves in little mean-looking houses stuck up on the nearest piece of land, to the object of his aversion, which he could obtain. Several such remain to keep his memory green.

The most conspicuous building upon his hill will long be remembered as " Ben Bradley's Meeting-house." This was a caricature of a church produced by the transfer of a large old barn to the top of the hill. A gothic or arched window, such as usually is placed in the end of a church building, was placed conspicuously in the middle of the side, a belfry and tower surmounted by a painted weathercock graced the front, and the old and time-honored pulpit, once almost hallowed by the prayers and sermons of the venerable Father Grafton of Newton, adorned the inside.

A part of this structure he finished off for tenements and let them to Irish families ; the rest he used for a carpenter's shop. In this shop, by way of keeping life cheerful, he had a coffin which he used to try occasionally, to see if it fitted him, but growing too corpulent, long before he needed such an indispensable article, he had a larger one made. He made the old coffin serviceable for some time by placing it on end, putting in one or two shelves and using it as a closet for his liquors. It was finally sold to one of his tenants.

On Sundays he sometimes gathered around him a crowd of " the baser sort," and mounting the old pulpit, he held forth in harangues more profane and ludicrous than wise or useful, ending with a treat to his audience.

The old building surrounded by little houses was so conspicuous an object that strangers coming to town almost invariably asked what denomination occupied that hill.

The principal part of the settlement near Jamaica Pond, known as "Grub Village," "Dublin," "New Ireland," etc., was built by Mr. Bradley. He purchased the land and put up a little red house in full view of Mr. Thomas Lee's residence, and then went to Mr. Lee and desired him to buy it at a great price. Mr. Lee would do no such thing; whereupon Mr. Bradley proceeded to cover it with little houses. Mr. Lee set out shade trees along his own lawn, on the edge of the hill, and serenely sat down in their shadow, too independent to be annoyed by so small dealing a neighbor.

The two little houses opposite the Philbrick place on Walnut Street are specimens of his handiwork in a good neighborhood; and there was a time when he owned or held mortgages upon considerable property in the village. Though not dependent upon his trade he went about with a tool-box on his arm, in garments that made him look poorer than his poorest tenant. Mr. Bradley was married twice if not more, but left no heirs nearer than cousins. The hill was sold before his death to Mr. Hart.

Captain Bradley died July 31, 1856.

In his will he left five hundred dollars for the poor of the town, but it could not be made available. There were strange contradictions in the character of this singular man. He was genial and kindly with the poor, and old people and little children; and with all his faults he had many redeeming qualities. His keen sense of the ludicrous and his innate lack of reverence, made him turn to ridicule much that others held sacred; yet there were times when the better impulses in his nature seemed struggling for the mastery; and there are people still living to whom he frankly confessed his faults, and owned his struggles after a better life. He had an opportunity to make himself a beloved and respected landlord; and the hill, so beautiful for its prospect and fine air, might be to-day covered with the neat and well-kept dwellings of a respectable class of mechanics and laborers, had he used his means as he might have done, and left a memory to be honored.

Perhaps a slight difference in the training of his boyhood might have prevented the moral kink which twisted his finer traits awry; and might have made him a blessing to the community instead of what he was.

Let us leave him with "Him who seeth not as man seeth," and who alone knows the heart.[*]

[*] The hill was sold again in 1871 to the Goddard heirs, and the houses moved to Sewall Street, a locality which has since been known as "Hart's Content."

CHAPTER XI.

BOYLSTON AND BRIGHTON STREETS. — WALNUT STREET. — HOUSES ALONG THE LOWER PART. — THE WALLEY OR BIRD HOUSES — THE CLARK HOUSE. — THE CEMETERY.

PERHAPS we owe our readers an apology for detaining them so long on Bradley's Hill, but the summer winds have swept over its now houseless summit, and the winter snows have spread their purest mantle over it. Moreover, the prospect from it is very beautiful, so we will take a look and pass on. All the interesting old places from Bradley's Hill to the points of divergence, at Brighton Street and Heath Street, are properly a part of the history of "the old road," and as such we shall leave them till we write of that. Above this point the Worcester Turnpike begins again; and consequently there are no houses upon it which date back to a very early period. Most of the land through which this section of the turnpike passes, has been for the last fifty years the property of the Pennimans, Heaths, Sandersons, and Lymans.

Brighton Street was laid out as a road-way from the "old Sherburne road" to Brighton, more than a hundred and fifty years ago.

The first house on this street stood on the east side, nearly opposite the present residence of Mr. J. Loring. In it lived Addington Gardner, once a prominent citizen of the town, and whose signature, not unlike John Hancock's of Revolutionary fame, in its appearance, is familiar to those who have seen many old legal documents of the town. He married a sister of Rev. Mr. Allen, the first minister of this town, and removed to Sherborn. He was a justice of the peace.

The next house was that of Isaac Gardner, first deacon of the First Church in the town. He died in 1767, aged eighty-three years.

His son Isaac inherited the house, and was in little more than a year after his father's death rendered homeless by fire. The family was very large, consisting of eighteen persons, and nearly all their household goods were destroyed. The loss was estimated, as appears by the "Massachusetts Gazette" of September 8, 1768, at from four to five thousand pounds, O. T. The people of the town met on the following Monday (the fire was on Friday), and though there were at that time but fifty families in the town, they contributed one hundred pounds, toward helping Mr. Gardner to rebuild his house. When it is remembered that this was when the country was comparatively new, that the people of Brookline were nearly all farmers, and that it was also at the time when the colonies were groaning and impoverished under British taxation, it will be seen that the Brookline of those days was generous and prompt to relieve distress as well as the richer and more prosperous Brookline of the present.

The new house was built upon the old site. Mr. Isaac Gardner was educated at Harvard College, but he chose to follow the agricultural pursuit of his father. He was a justice of the peace, and in every capacity, civil, social, and religious, was a popular and much beloved citizen.

The slowly-brewing troubles of the coming Revolution fired his patriotic blood, and the people of the town made him captain of their militia.

On the morning of the battle of Lexington the minute-men of Brookline assembled in front of the church. Their captain, always before so bright and cheerful, was under the shadow of a great oppression. As he took leave of his wife and his eight children, his impression that it was his final leave-taking so overpowered him that he could not conceal it, and he told his wife that he should never return to her alive. Before he reached the church he met the wife of Deacon Davis, who with her little children in a chaise, was hastening for safety to the upper part of the town. He stopped and spoke to her, asking her to call on her way and try to console his wife whom he had left weeping at the gate.

The brave and handsome captain was in the prime of life and "every inch a soldier," but his war-record was brief indeed. Before night he fell, pierced by six British bullets while drinking at a well in Cambridge, about a mile above the College on the Lexington road.

Dr. Aspinwall and Mr. Ebenezer Davis cared for the body as well as they could that night. The sad news was brought home to Brookline, and the next morning Mr. Heath, his neighbor, went to Cambridge with his wagon and brought home to the afflicted family all that remained of the beloved husband and father. The whole town was plunged into grief at the loss of so beloved and respected a citizen.

His age was forty-nine years. His son, General Isaac Sparhawk Gardner, was the next owner of the house. He was an unusually fine singer, and for many years was leader of the choir of the First Church. Dr. Pierce in his Jubilee Address speaks of him as "the sweet singer of our Israel." He died in 1818.

General Gardner had ten children. At the birth of each he planted a tree within his land beside the road.

The whole row had grown to ample size and beauty, but were destroyed at the recent widening of the street.* The descendants of the Gardners, bearing other names, still live in our community.

The house was at one time owned by Mr. Elisha Penniman, and afterwards by Deacon Daniel Sanderson. Mr. Sanderson, though not a native of Brookline, lived here many years, held various town offices, and was a prominent member of the Baptist Church. He built two houses on the west side of Brighton Street.

On the east side of the street, there formerly stood north of the Gardner house, a house owned and occupied by John Seaver, who died before the Revolutionary war. His house was torn down on account of its great age, early in the present century.

WALNUT STREET.

This street, known for years as "the old Sherburne road," is the oldest in the town, and was probably one of the first roads in the colony of Massachusetts Bay. When it was extended as far as Framingham, then the outmost frontier of civilization, it was considered the *ne plus ultra* of Colonial necessity in that direction, as it was not probable that white people would *ever penetrate further west into the wilderness.* And it was little better at first than an Indian trail, winding as it did from the humble abode of one settler to another, between high, thick forests, out of which might echo at any moment the cry of the prowling wolf or the more dreaded war whoop of the red man.

* There is a local tradition that at the time of the battle of Lexington, Isaac Gardner's family was living in the ancient Gardner house now occupied by George W. Stearns, but his descendants have no evidence that he ever lived there, and Dr. Pierce, who received his information from persons who remembered all the circumstances, locates him at the Brighton Street house, where his son set out the trees. See Appendix, house 26, *Town Hall Address.*

Yet less than twenty years had passed after William Blackstone had settled in Shawmut, and called it Trimountain, before Muddy River Hamlet had three highways leading through it, and our Walnut Street began to be called "the old road."

The land from the lower end, or entrance of the street, on the right side as far up as the alley now known as "Cat Alley," and on the left or south side, nearly or quite to Sewall Street, was probably "the great lott," which was granted to Thomas Leverett, and was afterwards for many years the property of Governor Leverett and was used by him for pasture lots for his cattle and sheep. Northward it was bounded by the lands of the Cottons. How far southward this "great lott" extended we cannot learn, but there were one hundred and seventy-five acres of it and somewhere upon it stood a house. The Governor, John Leverett, inherited it from his father, Thomas. He was Governor from 1671 to 1673.

Sometime, but at what date we cannot learn, a part of this land came into possession of the Whites. It is so often necessary to allude to this once numerous family that perhaps it is proper to explain that the common ancestor of the Brookline families of this name, whichever way it is spelled, was John White, born in England and who is traced to Dorchester, to Watertown, and thence to Brookline. From him descended Major Edward White, and all the rest, some of the family having gone back to the original spelling of the name as ascertained in English records to be Whyte.

All the early settlements on this road were from about the head of Cypress Street and so on westward, for many years. The whole history of the lower part of the road is comparatively modern. The garrison-house for the settlement, when it was so small and so exposed as to need a garrison-house, was just behind the present house of the Clark family on the left of the entrance to Chestnut Street.

As some of our younger readers may not have met with a description of this sort of house we will briefly describe it in passing. It was a log-house, with one door but no windows in the lower story. The upper story projected over the lower, three or four feet on all sides. This was fort and storehouse for the whole settlement, and into it were huddled the women and children in all cases of alarm from the Indians. In the projecting floor of the upper story were loop-holes, from which the boards could be taken up, and through which the women could pour down boiling water upon the savages in case they came close to the building to set it on fire.

Whether the Brookline garrison-house was ever thus attacked and defended, we have unfortunately no historical records in existence to tell us. Of the wild animals which made personal defense necessary, there is sufficient evidence, in the fact that a premium of twenty shillings was paid to Philip Curtis for killing a wolf, in November, 1657.

It needs therefore no great stretch of imagination to picture to the mind one of the ancient Whites, Goddards, Aspinwalls, or Griggses, riding on horseback on a Sunday morning, with his wife on a pillion behind, and his musket strapped across his shoulders, winding along the narrow and thickly wooded road to Roxbury meeting-house to hear the Apostle Eliot preach; or returning at nightfall along the same way, with a furtive glance toward the darkening shades of the stone-quarries then unbroken by the hammer, lest the sly panther in the boughs of some overhanging oak might pounce upon him from its dusky retreat; or a pack of wolves baying with hunger in the wilds of Parker's Hill, or the Ward farm, should scent human prey and come out upon its trail.

But though, as we have said, the lower end of Walnut Street was not built upon till many years later than the upper part of it, there are some houses which have acquired age enough to need mention and we therefore return to the beginning of the street.

The house now used as the Infant Asylum was built early in the present century for a man named Eliphalet Spurr, who owned the line of coaches which in those days made daily trips to Boston.

The coaches ran from the " Punch Bowl." Mr. Spurr sold out to Azariah Fuller after a while, but whether Mr. Fuller ever occupied the house or not we are not informed, nor of anything further in its history till it became the property of Thomas and Elizabeth Aspinwall, children of Colonel Thomas Aspinwall who lived in the house on Sewall Avenue which was at last burnt, and who was commander at the fort on Sewall's Point.

" Mr. Thomas and Miss Eliza," as they were commonly called, lived for many years in the house on Walnut Street. Mr. Thomas was deaf and dumb, but like many others thus afflicted, his other faculties seemed sharpened to unusual acuteness. He was for years thoroughly identified with the village and its surroundings, learned all the news, and every morning walked up to the house of his elder sister, Mrs. Holden (who lived where Mr. Panter now lives), and told her upon his fingers all the items of interest which he had collected.

Mr. Aspinwall loved his garden and cultivated it with his own hands with much success, and evident enjoyment of flowers, fruits, and vegetables. He had quite a genius for mechanical employments and was very skillful in the use of tools. Mr. Aspinwall inherited from his father some land where Longwood Station now stands. About the time the Brookline Branch Railroad was projected, this land was purchased for one hundred and fifty dollars an acre. It has since been sold for seventy-five cents a foot.

He was already quite far advanced in life when the Hartford Institution for such unfortunates was founded, yet having heard of it he desired to receive its benefits. He stayed but a little while and then returned, and when met by a look of inquiry from any of his friends, he shook his head sorrowfully and touched the wrinkles upon his forehead. Yet he was a cheerful man, and always especially kind to children and interested in them; "Uncle Thomas," many of them called him, and so indeed did many who were past childhood. New inventions and improvements awakened his keen interest. The writer remembers in her childhood meeting "Uncle Thomas," near the door of Lyceum Hall building, which was then nearly finished; the stairway at that time went up through a commodious entry which has since been turned into a shop. The old gentleman instantly began to gesticulate with delight; he had discovered something new to him, and he would have us share his pleasure. He took us into the entry and pointed out the hole in the floor, at which the furnace pipe was to come through, and with all the animation of a boy, described with his nimble fingers the fire that was to burn in the unseen depths below, and the heat that was to come up and be diffused through the building.

He saw that he was understood, and with a gesture of satisfaction put back the board that covered the hole, and bowing, walked away with his hands behind him.

He was very religious, and greatly interested in all the missionary and other benevolent enterprises of the church.

He had one spot where he knelt to pray, year after year, two or three times every day, till the floor was worn thin where the toes of his shoes rested. What secret wrestlings with sorrow and pain, what humble confessions or heaven-born aspirations were wafted upwards in those silent communings none ever knew or will know; but that they were heard in "the secret places of the Most High," while many a sounding and wordy prayer falls baffled by the way, none but the irreverent can doubt.

Miss Eliza, his constant companion, sank in consumption and died in the year 1842, aged 64. Her silent brother survived her but little more than a year, and died of the same disease in December, 1843, aged 74. His benevolent face and affable manners had won for him a niche in the tender memories of all who knew him. Since the Aspinwalls passed away, the house has had many different occupants, and has been modernized and greatly improved within a few years.

The old-fashioned, white English roses, with their peculiar fragrance, are somehow always associated in our memory with Mr. Thomas Aspinwall and his sister, and the same bushes which he trained beside the door were very recently growing there and may be still.

The next house standing upon the lower part of Walnut Street was upon the Philbrick place. It was built by John Tappan in 1821, and was the one hundredth house built in Brookline. Mr. Tappan was not long a resident here, and was succeeded by Mr. William Ropes who lived here eight or ten years, and was succeeded by Mr. Samuel Philbrick, who identified himself with the interests of the town. He held various offices at different times, being an Assessor, a member of the Board of Selectmen, and also of the School Committee.

The next house upon the same side of the street,

though built a year earlier, was that now occupied by
Mr. Cobb. It was built by Rev. Henry Colman, who
studied theology with Dr. Pierce, was afterwards settled
for several years over a church in Hingham, and then
returned to Brookline.

During several years of his residence here, he was
principal of a select school for young ladies in Boston.
He was afterwards pastor of the Barton Square Church
in Salem, and died there.

After Mr. Colman it was occupied by Captain Oxnard,
Henry J. Oliver, Hezekiah Kendall (a son of Deacon
Thomas Kendall), and since then by various others.

The large stone house next beyond it, was built by
Joseph Sewall, a descendant of Judge Sewall, whose
history was given earlier in the course of these sketches.
The grounds belonging to this place were quite extensive. Mr. Sewall lived here ten or twelve years, and his
wife and three daughters died here.

Sewall Street, as the upper part of Cypress Street was
called, until the recent widening and extension, was but
a narrow lane leading from Walnut Street to the back
part of the Sewall place, and the wooded lands in the
rear, and did not become a public way until within the
last quarter of a century. It was a part of the "great
lott of land" assigned to Governor Leverett, and afterwards became the property of a branch of the White
family. Mr. Thomas White's heirs were the last of this
family who owned any portion of it. It was accessible
(within the memory of middle aged persons) by one of
the most picturesque and beautiful of lanes, which led
into a wild and tangled woodland. There was a path
leading up the hill from where the lane ended, to the
fence on the boundary of the estate of the late Thomas
Lee. Through this there was an opening of which many

availed themselves for convenience of access to Jamaica Pond. A large tract of land now under cultivation or covered with the houses of Hart's Irish settlement, transferred thither from Bradley's Hill, was a thicket of alders, dogwood, and wild rose-bushes. Chestnut Street was not constructed at that time, and the whole area of scores of acres was untraversed except by the single cart path we have mentioned, leading from Walnut Street to the log bridge, and thence by a footpath to the Lee place.

The brook wandered at its own will, overflowing the surface except in the dry midsummer; a rude bridge of three or four logs was the only means of crossing it, and often this was not accessible from either side on account of the deep, black mud.

This wooded tract was a secure harbor for innumerable snakes, of whose size and numbers, as reported by frequenters of the location, we shall give no account lest we be suspected of Munchausenism.

Before Chestnut Street was opened, this region had been partially cleared and drained, and the making of that street and the continuation of the lane, or Sewall Street, through to connect with it, altered the whole face of the country.

There are many men in town, not yet old, who will recall delightful nutting excursions and rustic adventures in this wild and woody region. About thirty years ago a camp meeting of four days' continuance was held in the only piece of "clearing" in these woods. It was accessible only through Sewall's lane. Of the success of the affair we think there could not be much to boast, as the nearness to Boston made it altogether too convenient for a class of persons not drawn there by any religious proclivities.

The widening and extension of the lane made this beautiful rural region accessible for carriages, but it has had its day as a quiet and shady drive. The widening and the class of houses established upon the upper part of it have changed its whole character, and this part of Brookline will with the present generation cease to be remembered "as it was," and be no pleasure to contemplate as it is.

The Sewall house was occupied after the Sewalls' removal by John Tilson, who resided for some years in the stone house near the corner of Sewall and Walnut streets. This family will be remembered by all who knew the three sons, John, Charles, and Robert, in the Brookline schools. John Tilson held a colonel's commission during the late war, and was under General Sherman in his famous march through Georgia. Colonel Tilson bore an honorable record during the war, and at its close was retained in the service with the rank of major. He subsequently resigned. Mr. Tilson, senior, sold the woodland above mentioned, and Hugh R. Kendall, a later owner, began the first improvements, in clearing and opening this retired region to the public.

Deacon Lambert was at one time a resident in the stone house. The heirs of the late Nathan Hale also resided here for some time previous to Mr. Fisher, the present occupant.

The opposite corner of Sewall and Walnut streets was for many years, within the memory of present inhabitants, the property of Jerathmeel Davenport. On this lot, near the street, stood the house of the first minister of Brookline, the Rev. James Allen. He was a native of Roxbury, but came here to live and to preach in 1718, and continued here till his death in 1748.

His house, which was a very old one, was torn down

before the close of the last century, but some roses and sweet-briers which he set out continued to grow from the old roots beside the stone wall, until within a few years. This ground is now in the middle of the street.

THE WALLEY PLACE.

The estate known for many years as "the Walley place," comprised all that is now owned by the heirs of the late Jesse Bird, and extended westward nearly to the boundary of the place now occupied by N. G. Chapin, and across Boylston Street which was not then built, including all that has since been known as Bradley's Hill.

The house, which stood on the site of the one now occupied by the family of the late William Bird, was built in 1750. It was designed to be the residence of the Rev. Cotton Brown, the second minister of Brookline.

Mr. Brown was a brother of the mother of Peter C. Brooks of Boston. Another of his sisters was the second wife of Daniel Dana, who lived where the Public Library now stands.

Mr. Brown was the successor of Rev. James Allen, and was engaged to marry his daughter Mary, a very lovely and beautiful young lady.

Mr. Allen owned, besides the house which he occupied, (before mentioned) an old house which stood west of the present Bird house, in what is now the garden of that place.

It was occupied by John Hammond. After the death of Mr. Allen this house was taken down, and the solid oaken timbers being of enormous size and in excellent preservation, were used in building the new house for the young couple.

But they were destined never to occupy it. A singular fatality seemed to follow the family.

Mr. Allen died in 1747, his wife in 1748, their only son in 1749, and the daughter, the last of her family, in 1750.

The young minister to whom she was engaged died in 1751, at the age of twenty-five, and the house which was to have been the parsonage, and had been the centre of so many bright hopes, passed into other hands.

It became the property of Henry Sewall, a grandson of Chief Justice Sewall, of this town, but whether he ever occupied it or not we have no means of knowing. It was occupied for several years by Dea. Elisha Gardner of the first church. After Mr. Sewall's death it was inherited by Mrs. Walcott, another of the Sewalls.

In the year 1796, the house was still the property of Mrs. Walcott, but before 1800 it was sold.

Toward the close of the last century the house was purchased by Thomas Walley, a merchant of Boston, with ample wealth and cultivated tastes. The grounds west of the house were covered with a beautiful growth of chestnut and walnut trees. Back of the parsonage on the rising ground near the site of the house of M. P. Kennard, Mr. Walley had a summer-house built. The brook wound its way through the grounds uncurbed by walls, and the wild flowers of every season grew in native luxuriance. The place was a delightful resort for the few children of the neighborhood.

The house stood upon the same raised bank which is there at present, and had a broad piazza on two sides. On the west end the front room had a projecting alcove with two or three windows in it. Mrs. Walley was a French lady from Martinique, of Catholic faith. There was no Catholic church at that time nearer than Federal Street in Boston, and the large west room was fitted as a private chapel for the family according to the forms of the Catholic church. There was an agreement between the parents that the sons should be educated in the religious faith of their father and the daughters in that of their mother. But before many years Mr. Walley also embraced the religion of his children. Of the two children who still survive one is a Catholic and the other an Episcopalian.

Bishop Chevereux was a frequent visitor at the house and the Oratory was his appropriate apartment.

There were several children in the family, and for the convenience of his own daughters and those of his neighbors Mr. Walley built a school-house on his own grounds, fronting on Cypress Street near the corner of Boylston Street.

This school was taught by Miss Stebbins for many years. Several branches were taught here which were not then taught in the public schools, embroidery and sampler working included.

The fine arts also received a due share of attention in the elaboration of certain melancholy pictures, such as may occasionally be found in a country farm-house chamber, or perhaps even now stored away among the lumber of some Brookline attic. A church-front with a path leading up to it, on either side of which stands a white monument surmounted by an urn and overhung by a very green, heavy, weeping willow. Two wretched females in trailing dresses, stand one by each monument weeping, in identical attitudes. In families already broken by death, pathos was added to the painted scene by an inscription of the name and date of the sad event.

In families still in the joy of a full circle the artist left a blank under "*In Memory of*" — and as the dismal reminder hung upon the parlor walls, the thought must sometimes have intruded unbidden upon hours of pleasure, of whose name should stand first on the waiting monument over which the black-robed females were apparently weeping in advance.

It would seem as if the pathetic and the ridiculous could hardly ever be found in closer proximity than in these absurd pictures.

One can only guess at the moods induced in the young artists by their laborious application to these tasks. A lady teacher of painting was hired, after several years, who brought a higher taste and better practice into the artistic culture of her pupils. Miss Stebbins was a good woman, of the severely pious order, and read her pupils moral lectures of amazing length and dryness.

After several years Miss Stebbins went to Georgia where she taught school, first in Powelton and then in Mt. Zion. She finally removed to Washington, D. C., where she died several years ago at an advanced age. She was a teacher more than forty years.

After Miss Stebbins' removal Miss Mary Downer continued the girls' school for some time.

The school-house was for some years occupied by a preparatory department, for the Classical School, before mentioned, taught by Miss Louisa Reed. The very building in which so many young ladies of that period received their book-knowledge, worked their samplers, and painted their mourning pieces, is still in existence, and doing service as a *hen-house* on Dr. Shurtleff's place.

After Mr. Walley removed to Boston the place was occupied by Reuben Hunting, who purchased it. Mr. Hunting was a butcher and he added a section to the large barn behind the house and there carried on his business for several years.

He sold the fine trees which formed the grove in the westerly part of his grounds, and they were soon all cut down. The summer-house was bought by Captain Bradley, who already had an embryo village, on the hill which he had bought of Mr. Walley, and having moved it to the highest part of the hill he added a little room to it and made a house of it. This was the last habitation left on the hill after the sale and removal which took place there in the spring of 1870.

Mr. Hunting lived in the house ten years or more and sold it to Mr. Jabez Fisher. During his residence there the large old barn and slaughter-house building was bought by Captain Bradley and this he added to the other adornments of his hill. This was the building which he surmounted with a steeple, and which was known as "Bradley's meeting-house."

Mr. Fisher's successor was the late Jesse Bird.

After he had occupied the house a short time he had it torn down, and built the present house upon the same site. The old timbers which had formed a part of the frame of the Allen house, which was so old in 1750 that it had to be taken down, and were used in building the house for Rev. Cotton Brown, had served over one hundred years in the latter house. The old mortises made by the Muddy River workmen of two hundred years ago, were laid bare to the light; the beams were in good preservation, and for aught we know are in existence yet. The fir trees in front, probably as old as the house, but never ornamental, were cut down and gave place to the present graceful shade-trees now higher than the house.

The grounds were improved and the place soon became once more one of the pleasantest upon Walnut Street.

THE CLARK FAMILY AND HOUSE.

The first ancestors of this old family traceable in Muddy River are James Clark and his wife Elinor. From them in a direct line are descended the families of the late Deacon Joshua Clark, Caleb Clark, and Moses Jones.

The will left by this ancient citizen of Muddy River is still in good preservation, and is chiefly interesting for bearing upon it the names of Governor Leverett, Simon Bradstreet, William Stoughton, and Major Thomas Clark, perhaps a brother of James. He was a prominent citizen in those days. John Sharp, who fell the next year, 1675, at Sudbury fight, was also one of the witnesses.

James Clark had a son, Samuel, and there has ever since been a Samuel Clark in the town from this ancestry. The first of this name was born in 1654. The paternal estate lay on both sides of Cambridge road, now Harvard Street, the house being near the site of the one afterwards built by Stephen Sharp.

There were also marsh lands joining the possessions of the Sewalls and Aspinwalls, as well as woodlands and pasture lands in other parts of the town. All the Clark property in the vicinity of Harvard Street eventually became the property of the Sharps.

The first Samuel Clark was a wheelwright. He died in 1727, aged seventy-three years. This is probably the person of whom Judge Sewall speaks in his diary under date of March 12, 1684. "Watched, with Isaac Goose and Samuel Clark. Pleasant night." This was a time when the Indians were particularly troublesome, and probably the *watching* referred to was on their account.

This Samuel Clark was the father of Samuel, John, and Mary. An old receipt of John's, given to Samuel, shows that their father was one of the Muddy River Company in the Canada Expedition in 1690. He was a near neighbor of the Robert Sharp who went forth in that Expedition and perished in the wilderness. Samuel Clark it would seem returned.

The receipt reads as follows: —

May ye 29. 1738.

Received of my brother Samuel Clark of brookline the full and just sum of thre pound six shillings and eight pence being the full of what came or fell to me of the wright that befell us by the coloy (colony) by varty (virtue) of our father's going in the exspodition to canady i the year 1690 i say Receeived by me
JOHN CLARK.

This second Samuel Clark was a carpenter, and built the first meeting-house in Brookline. He was the first person who was published in the church. He was a deacon of the church and was very highly respected in Brookline. He lived to the age of eighty-one years. Died in 1766.

The Clark house on Walnut Street at the corner of Chestnut, was built by this Deacon Clark. He was married the year after the church was first gathered in Brookline, and no doubt built his house about that time, as it is known to have been standing and occupied by him a few years later, and is therefore probably not far from one hundred and fifty years old. Directly behind it, stood the house used for a garrison-house. This was probably used as a dwelling-house afterward, as in an indenture made to Nehemiah Davis in 1765, Deacon Clark reserves to himself the use and profit of "the two houses," but allows Davis the " privilidge of keeping sauce in the cellar of the new house yearly."

His son Samuel, who died at the age of thirty-nine, six years before his father, left a widow who married a Nichols and went to Ward, Mass., to reside. There was a Samuel in this family, the fourth of the name, as the widow writes to her son of that name, who it seems was living in Brookline, under date of November 17, 1778, (probably), the date is partly obliterated. We copy it for its quaintness, and the bit of family history it contains.

"Loving Child, these lines come from your affectionate mother, almost overwhelmed In trouble, by a sore and awful, yet just dispensation of Providence. It has pleased God to take from ous our Sun Joshua by a sudden and suprisen Death, on the 13th of this Instent as he was a riden in the cart suposed to faul out and the wheal run over him, and within about half a nouer Expired, and has left us to mourn the absence of his delitesum coumpeny, but believing that God who orders all things knows what is best would therefore Desire to acquiesce in his Will.

"I would therefore as a mother in duty to a child remind you the sartainty of Death, and the unsartenty of the time when, and that now in time we may Be prepared for Death, and that we may have an Intrest in him that has tuck a way the sting of death which is sin.

"So I Remain Your Dutifull Parent till Death.
DEBORAH NICKELS."

The Joshua whose death is here recorded was no doubt a child of the second marriage, and must have been less than ten years of age, if the date is correct.

The Samuel to whom this letter was written, became, like his grandfather, a deacon of the church. He married Mary, daughter of Robert Sharp, 4th. He lived to be sixty-one years of age and died in 1814, leaving his son Caleb possessor of the homestead.

The fifth Samuel, son of the deacon last mentioned, was born in 1782, and was a graduate of Harvard University in 1805. He taught in Brookline during his college vacations, in the old brick school-house, of which an account will be given hereafter. He was ordained as a Unitarian minister in Burlington, Vt., in 1810, but resigned in consequence of ill-health, and died in that town in 1827, aged forty-five years.

Another son of Deacon Samuel Clark, was the late Deacon Joshua C. Clark of Warren Street in this town, a man who was universally beloved through a long and useful life.

An incident is related of the late Deacon Clark in his youth, which shows the unselfish disposition which characterized him through life. The information did not come from his own family. When he was seventeen years of age, Dr. Pierce, his minister, then in the prime of life, was stricken down with rheumatic fever which rendered him perfectly helpless. For six weeks the young man went of his own accord, with cheerful devotion, three or four times every day, to assist in turning the helpless sufferer. Besides this he rendered other efficient service. The same spirit was manifested throughout his long and useful life. He literally obeyed the Apostolic injunction, " Do good as ye have opportunity " — and he did it without ostentation, or hope of reward.

Deacon Joshua C. Clark, died July 22, 1861, aged eighty years.

An infant born in the old Walnut Street house, in the spring of 1873, child of William and Helen (Clark) Cutler, is the sixth generation of one family, born within its walls.

WALNUT STREET CEMETERY.

On the 26th of March, 1706, " it was voted that there should be a burying-place on the south side of the hill, on Mr. Cotton's farm, between the two roads, if it can be obtained."

This was the southerly slope of the hill near the head

of Cypress Place. But it was not purchased, for some reason now unknown, and the matter lay over for about eleven years.* In December, 1713, it was "voted that Mr. Samuel Sewall, Jr., and Peter Boylston should procure a pall, or 'burying cloth' at the town's charge," and six pounds were appropriated in addition to the usual annual appropriation, " to cover the charge of said cloth."

In April, 1717, half an acre of the ground now comprised in Walnut Street Cemetery was purchased of Samuel Clark, the carpenter who built the first meeting-house, and was afterward deacon of the church. This was all the ground thus appropriated for more than a hundred and thirty years.

The entrance, by a wooden gate, was in the centre, just at that part of the wall where the monument of Dr. Pierce stands. The driveway went in but a short distance and turned to the left, ending between the two ranges of tombs. A procession could not enter, because there was no room for the carriages to turn around.

Rows of gravestones, on the right, of dark slate, embellished with the skull and cross-bones, came close up to the narrow driveway. These bore the names of whole families now extinct among us. On the hill near Chestnut Street, were square, red, brick tombs, two or three feet high, with a slate slab on the top of each. In the wall next the street, the backs of tombs were built up high and narrow, above the level of the rest of the wall. Rank grass, white-weed, and blackberry vines, overran the ground, and everything conspired to give the place that neglected look that characterized country cemeteries in former times.

* It is somewhat remarkable, how the experience and practice of the forefathers, in such matters, seems to have descended to the present generation.

It would seem as if the spirit of Puritanism, admirable as it was in many respects, deemed it a virtue to invest death with all the external horrors that could be gathered about it. No wonder that superstition was rife. The hearse, a shabby old vehicle, after being kept in the Croft barn for years, was removed to the corner shed of the row back of the old stone school-house, where the very sight of its black doors with their long iron hinges and heavy padlock, struck a chill to the hearts of children at their play.

Within the cemetery, many of the old graves were sunken, and the stones leaning.

The ground beyond the range of tombs which front northward, a narrow strip compared with what is now inclosed, was the "Potter's field," or burying place for the slaves. There were few stones, but one bore the name of "Dinah," an old slave in the Heath family, and another the name of "Ben Boston," another slave of a still more ancient Heath.

More than one Revolutionary hero who died in the Brookline barracks found his last resting-place in Brookline Cemetery. Lieutenant Abell of Rehoboth was one; and he and two soldiers of a Connecticut company, probably the same that was quartered in Mr. Benjamin Davis's house, had their resting places marked by stones. The two latter remain, and have been decorated, on recent Memorial Days, as has been also the tomb of Captain Isaac Gardner and General Gardner.

It will be remembered by those familiar with the early history of Massachusetts, that the widow of Rev. John Cotton, the first minister of Boston, and mother of Seaborn Cotton, born on the voyage, as his name implies, — afterwards married Richard Mather. After his death, — being a widow for the third time, and Thomas and Rowland Cotton, one, if not both, being residents in Brookline, she came here, took the small-pox, of which she died, and was buried in Brookline Cemetery, where her gravestone is still to be seen.*

Here, too, lies buried the first wife of George B. Emerson, a sister of the lamented Joseph S. Buckminster, and daughter of Dr. Buckminster of Portsmouth. She was a person of lovely character and accomplishments, worthy of the distinguished family to which she belonged.

Many of the early inhabitants of Brookline were no doubt buried in the old Roxbury cemetery on "the Neck," as they worshipped in the Eliot Church, and that was the nearest burying-place. But there were graves enough to fill the Brookline cemetery before the present century began, and for several years previous to 1840, some of the ground had been used for the same purpose, over and over again. About this time, Dr. Shurtleff, Mr. Philbrick, and others who were interested in public improvements, saw the necessity of enlarging the area of the ground, a matter attended with almost as much difficulty then as the purchase of a new cemetery lot recently. But after some negotiation the improvement was begun, though hotly contested by many substantial citizens.

The result was, that sometime during the year 1840, the town purchased another half acre, of the Clark heirs. This lay chiefly on the south side.

When the grading of the ground was in progress, a skeleton was exhumed on the Clark land, outside the old boundary of the cemetery. It might not have attracted any special attention, but for the fact that there were

---

* Dr. N. B. Shurtleff in his *History of Boston*, says there is a stone erected to the memory of this lady in the King's Chapel Cemetery. There is something probably to be explained with reference to this circumstance.

good reasons for believing the bones to be those of an Indian, and one of the thigh bones had been broken, but never reset. The fractured parts had over-lapped and grown together in that way, so that the poor victim must have found his mended leg inconveniently short. The bones were interlaced with roots of some shrub which drew its nourishment from them.

If the cattle browsed upon the shrub, and men ate the cattle, a query might be raised as to who owns a future interest in " poor Indian," nearly as interesting as the much discussed question, " Who ate Roger Williams? "

During the progress of the improvements, many old gravestones were dislodged and removed, some being thrown in to fill up the roadway which was being constructed. A stone, bearing the name of one of the earliest Winchesters, — among the first settlers of the town, — was carried to Lyceum Hall and there set up, but without questioning the taste or the motives of the individual who thus distinguished himself, a member of the Board of Selectmen remanded it back to the cemetery forthwith.*

The new ground, being some of it very low, was raised, graded, drained, and fenced. The gateway was removed to its present location and the carriage road through the centre, as a matter of necessity, laid out, irrespective of ancient graves. After a great deal of effort on the part of Dr. Shurtleff, the consent of the owners was obtained, and the hideous brick tombs, resembling old chimney-tops, which had so long disfigured the highest part of the hill, were leveled, shade trees set out, and the place divested of much of its former repulsiveness.

Within its limited area, lie the honored dead of most of the old families of the place, and probably few live

* Deacon Thomas Griggs.

here who have not at some time shed the tears of sore bereavement or keenest sympathy, within its shaded inclosure. Here the patriot dead of three wars have been brought, folded under the flag for which they fought, to slumber in the soil for whose freedom they died.

Who among us has not followed thither some fair-haired and beautiful child, out of whose sunny eyes the light has been quenched forever? Or the friend, of youth or middle age, with whom we took sweet counsel, and whose vanished presence has left an aching void which no other can ever fill? And through that narrow gateway we have followed the slow-grinding wheels, which were bearing from our sight, dear aged faces, out of which death had smoothed the furrows of care and pain, and whose tired hands, life's work being done, were folded, forever at rest.

We cannot be too grateful for the happy faith which will not allow us to believe, that the beloved ones we have seen laid away, are slumbering there in unconscious gloom; or floating as formless ether in some vague unknown, waiting for a day when, perhaps millions of years hence, they shall receive back their worn-out, wasted bodies. We cannot believe that those bodies which are returned to their original elements, and re-incorporated in a thousand forms of animal and vegetable life, will be the resources to which the Creator must turn, that the mortal may be clothed with immortality. We think the Scriptures which seem to warrant this belief, will admit of quite another interpretation.

Rather do we believe with Paul, that " there is a natural body and there is a spiritual body," not " there *will be*, but there *is*," and in that spiritual body we hope to to meet our lost ones, and know and love them again.

CHAPTER XII.

THE OLD BRICK SCHOOL-HOUSE. — MASTER ADAMS. — THE STONE SCHOOL-HOUSE. — THE FIRST CHURCH. — REV. MR. ALLEN. — REV. MR. JACKSON.

ALTHOUGH the old *stone* school-house, near the Unitarian Church, is the next building of any special interest on Walnut Street, there are reasons which will be apparent as we proceed, why the history of the old *brick* school-house should stand first recorded. From the earliest records, and still earlier traditions of the town, it appears that the principal school was always kept until quite modern times at the centre of the town. Not that this location of church and school-house was merely the geographical centre, for it was also the centre of population until after 1820.

As early as 1686, the people of the town, preferring to manage their own school affairs, instead of having them controlled by men in Boston, petitioned to be allowed to direct and maintain these things themselves. In December of that year, it was ordered " that henceforth the said Hamlet be free from Town rates to Boston, they raising a school-house, and maintaining an able reading and writing master." The promptness with which they acted upon the matter, shows that they were glad to get any part of the management of their local interests into their own hands. They called a meeting of the inhabitants, (it is recorded as a *full* meeting), and voted twelve pounds per annum, to pay the school-master and that if more be necessary to defray expenses, a tax " be laid equally upon the scholars' heads, save any persons that are poor, be abated, the whole or in part." Signed, Thomas Boylston.

This is the first town clerk's record, as such, made in the town, though the separation had not then been demanded, from Boston. Many of the old inhabitants, however, were as anxious to get out of Boston then, as some of the modern ones are to get in. Dr. Thomas Boylston was " directed to buy a book, and enter all the proceedings of the settlement therein from time to time." But he died before the vote could be carried into effect, and the record was made in the book by " Josiah Winchester, Clerk."

This first school-house built by the people of the town, unaided by Boston, stood on the hill, on the triangular piece of ground where Warren and Walnut Streets diverge, near the church. It was probably a small wooden school-house, but it must have served for a hundred years or more. An ancient bill presented to the Selectmen for repairs on this building is a curiosity. It reads as follows : —

December ye 6. 1758.

to work don at the Skul hous	
to shinggeling the ruf and finding 15 shingels, and nales and Lime to pint it,	1.1.0
to Laying the harth and finding 60ty bricks and wheling 12 whelborrers of Durt to Ras it.	2.00
Lathing and plastern Severl plases	0.1.0
MOSES SCOTT	4.00

We do not find Mr. Scott's arithmetic or spelling to indicate that he ever spent much time in the "Skul hous," except in the exercise of his calling as carpenter.

The endorsement of the Selectmen, on the back of the bill, orders the Town Treasurer, Jona Winchester, to pay him ten shillings and eight pence, for his work. Another old bill, presented by a female teacher, who probably taught in School Street affords a similar anomaly.

"The Town of Brookline Depttor to Mary Bowen for Keeping School fore months from the seventh of June 1760, at twenty six shillings and Eaight pence per month." 5. 6. 8

On which the endorsement reads : —

"Allowed twenty four shillings pr. month In Consideration of her haveing a great number of Schollers & there being but one school Kept."

We have known of instances where an increase of the number of scholars did not secure a corresponding increase of salary, but hope the above is the only instance on record of an abatement being made for a similar reason. Probably, however, the deficiency was made up by a tax on the pupils.

The next school-house of which we hear, on this spot, was of brick, and was built in 1793. This building was the *Alma Mater* of many, if not most of our present middle aged and elderly towns-people. It was a square, hip-roofed building, fronting eastward, without blinds, porch, or shed, and here school was kept, always by a male teacher, from April till November. Then it was closed, and the winter school for many years was kept by " the master," in the School Street school-house. Another school was also kept during the same time, in a small wooden school-house on Heath Street near the junction of Warren Street.

There were various teachers employed, but one among them seems to have made his mark (in more senses than one), and stamped his memory indelibly upon his pupils and the old brick school-house. This was Master Isaac Adams, who came to Brookline about the year 1815 or 1816. Nothing indicates the growth of a people in intellect and refinement more than the condition of their schools. The history of Master Adams and his methods, is a chapter which will shed much light on the progress of Brookline during the last forty years.

Our knowledge of him has been gathered from verbal testimony, from both male and female residents of this town who were his former pupils. The accounts given are wonderfully uniform. There were usually from thirty to forty pupils, of all ages from four to sixteen or eighteen, and of both sexes. No one seems to retain a very clear idea of the studies pursued or of anything interesting in the teaching. Of the discipline, however, there is a most vivid recollection. Whether whipping was laid down in the programme as a part of the master's necessary duty does not appear, but it seems to have been in accordance with the expectations of the parents and children, that it should form a part of every day's routine, as much as the lesson from "Murray's Grammar" or the spelling-book. School was opened with a long, extemporaneous prayer, by the master. During this prayer, nothing escaped his vigilant ears, eyes, and nose, and the slightest sound or trick was traced at once to the right source. By common consent, the catechism of public opinion would have made answer to the question, "What is the chief end of *boys?*" "To be whipped." At all events Master Adams seems to have acted upon the theory of the old schoolmaster of whom we read, that "a boy cannot be whipped amiss, because if he has not just done a piece of mischief he is *just going to.*" Therefore, after prayers, the next proceeding generally was to punish somebody for something either real or imaginary.

The chief weapon used was called a "clapper," and was made of leather; a circular piece about three quarters of an inch thick and five or six inches in diameter, attached to a stout leather handle some two feet long. In the centre of the circular piece was a round hole. The handle was slightly flexible. This barbarous instrument was kept at the master's boarding-place, and the first culprit on whom it was to be used in the morning was sent to bring it, chewing the cud of bitter reflection, or foreboding, by the way. The clapper was eminently adapted for *spanking*, to which use it was usually applied. There are gentlemen now living in town who have smarted under the infliction scores of times without shedding a tear, and others more sensitive and perhaps less "stuffy," who roared lustily but were none the better able to escape a similar fate next day. For minor offenses, like a whisper or an involuntary giggle, it was common for the master to send out for a branch of a sapling (the woods were near), about four feet long. From this he would trim a part of the twigs and leaves, split the thick end of it far enough to allow the poor little offender's nose to be inserted in the crack, and in this plight he would be obliged to stand as a spectacle before the school. For girls, the split stick was often applied to the ear. Another of his unique inventions was the "*unipod*," perhaps suggested by the Latin *tripod*, — a stool with only one leg and that in the middle. On this the offender was seated where she must balance herself with scrupulous nicety, straining every muscle and nerve to maintain the perpendicular, lest gravitation obtain the mastery, and the performer come to grief in the manner of the inexperienced practitioner on the modern velocipede. There were two of these unipods, one being triangular, with the leg at one corner.

A delicate young girl, who had been a gentle and docile pupil all her life, began to show peculiarities of manner and disposition while at this school, so different from her former appearance and habits, as to attract the notice of the master, who to take the "oddity," or *perversity* as he considered it, out of her, frequently kept her sitting for hours on one of these instruments of torture. The peculiarities however were only the indications of incipient insanity, which soon was broadly developed, and of which she died at the age of twenty-one.

But the elder pupils alone were not the only victims of this man's tyrannical discipline. The front row of desks had a long, low seat in front, and on this sat a row of little ones from four to six years of age. The only break in the monotony of their long, dull session, was in being called up once in the forenoon, and once in the afternoon, and naming the letters of the alphabet through from A to Z. The rest of the time they were expected to "sit up straight, and keep still."

Now " to sit up straight and keep still," is what no bright, healthy child was ever yet able to do, for even one hour, and the parent or teacher who requires it, is either a tyrant, or destitute of common sense. Rampant animal life will squirm, and latent fun will bubble out in an ill-suppressed giggle. If it does not come to hair pulling and fisticuffs, then the children are little short of angels, and fit to — "with the angels stand." But the poor infant class in Master Adams' school was not composed of angels ; only a row of very human babies, most of whom should have been out frolicking on the grass or under the trees with somebody to take care of them and preserve the peace. It happened upon an evil day that the master seized upon one of these little victims and taking him out upon the platform laid him face downwards upon the floor,—another and another were laid beside him, then others piled upon them, till he had made a pyramid of them with the last and perhaps greatest rogue on the top. Then seizing the clapper he proceeded to apply it vigorously to the topmost child of the heap, while groans, and cries, and lamentations, in every key, proceeded from the struggling pile.* Does any reader close the book in disgust, and say, " Of course this ended the man's career in Brookline?" Not at all by any means. The half is not told,—nor shall we tell it. It would not be believed. One instance more of his dealings with the little ones must suffice.

A little boy, between four and five years old, who walked nearly a mile to the school in the care of his two sisters a little older, coming in the early morning and staying till nearly night, was guilty of the gross misdemeanor of falling asleep in school one hot summer afternoon. The sharp-eyed master perceived it. It was a case for discipline. Such a palpable violation of the rules of propriety involved a severe penalty. Stepping lightly to the little sleeper, with his handkerchief he tied the little feet together to a stout umbrella, which he gave to a large school-mate in the row behind, to hold. Then going back to his chair, he stamped upon the floor, and in a stentorian tone, called out, " Daniel! come here!" The poor child sprang up, and of course fell upon his face, crying bitterly. The little sister cried too, and was derided and disgraced by the master, before the school, for her weakness.

If any one thinks this is too much to believe, let him read George MacDonald's book, " Alec Forbes," and in

* Had there been less elasticity in these little martyrs, our town might have been minus its present worthy Treasurer, as well as sundry other good citizens.

the Scotch school-master, Malison, he will think Master Adams sat for his portrait. Such discipline and such a state of heart and mind as could produce it, were extreme instances of the natural outgrowth of the New England Calvinism and asceticism of the two preceding centuries.

Children were not allowed to complain at home, and often if it was found that they had been punished at school, they were punished at home also.

The present public opinion which will scarcely tolerate the moderate punishment of a child for even the most outrageous conduct, is but a vibration of the pendulum to the opposite extreme, and is as weak and foolish as the former practices were cruel and unjust.

After teaching here for seven years, Master Adams left town and taught elsewhere for a while, but was hired back again, returned, and taught here more than thirteen years longer. There was another side, however, to his character, and the old master was not wholly a barbarian.

Master Adams was not, as might be supposed from accounts of his school government, a man of no principle. On the contrary, he was a religious man, who made long prayers; but his religion savored of the law rather than the Gospel, and neither his principles nor his feelings prevented the skillful aiming of his ruler at his pupils' heads, or the practice of any of the methods of punishment already recorded.

Yet all this severity failed of producing order, or commanding the respect which a teacher should have from his pupils. There was no end of devices for circumventing his plans, and setting at naught his authority, although he was feared and hated.

Master Adams was comparatively young, when he

came to Brookline, and single. He continued to live single till past middle life, when he married a young lady of Portsmouth, Miss Martha Washington Hill. Miss Hill was a very lovely girl, with a voice of such unusual melody, that all who heard her were fascinated. The old schoolmaster's devotion to his young wife was perfectly wonderful, but we have not heard that the development of his affections extended to the school-room and its inmates.

A year or so of wedded life was all that was accorded to the singularly mated couple, and then the tie was broken by death, and the devoted husband became the distracted widower. Mrs. Adams was buried in Walnut Street Cemetery, and night after night the half frantic man lay moaning upon her grave. He was like one beside himself. He planned an anagram of his wife's name, Martha Washington, and actually had it incorporated into his own name by act of legislature, on this wise: "Isaac Mahtra Wanshongtri Adams."

It seems marvelous that a man capable of such a passionate and devoted attachment, could also have been capable of such cruelties as he practiced in his school. After a while he gave up teaching the public school, and went to Jamaica Plain, where he taught a school for young ladies for some little time, but was barely tolerated. From thence he went to Newport, R. I., and soon after died. At his own request, his body was brought to Brookline, and buried beside the young wife whom he had so long mourned. His name and epitaph are to be seen by any of his former pupils who may desire to visit his grave. Under the name and the dates on one of the stones are the words, —

"THIS LIFE'S A DREAM."

On the other, —

"WE PART TO MEET AGAIN."

"*Requiescat in pace,*" Master Adams! We trust thou hast found the Great Teacher more lenient with thee, than thou wert to his little ones.

After Master Adams' removal from Brookline, or during the interval in which he was absent, the winter school was taught one season, if not more, by Rev. Thomas Worcester, then a young man. His cousin, Gilman Worcester, was for several winters a teacher in Heath Street School. His brother David also taught in the brick school-house.

A greater contrast in men or methods could scarcely be found than that between Master Adams and the Worcesters. Gentle firmness, and a sympathetic regard for childhood and youth, were the characteristics of their teaching.

The brick school-house was not an important building in town merely for its service in school uses, but it was also used for town meetings, from the time it was built, as long as it remained standing. It was at the brick school-house that the people of the town met to form a procession, on the occasion of the funeral services in honor of George Washington. From thence they marched to the church, then standing in what is now the garden of the parsonage, and listened to the eulogy delivered by Dr. Pierce.

After the close of the second war with England, the town began to grow more rapidly. Several gentlemen came here and built fine houses, and there was a general increase of prosperity. The subject of building a townhouse began to be discussed, but met with considerable opposition from old citizens, who thought the schoolhouse had been good enough for them and their fathers,

ORIGIN OF THE OLD STONE SCHOOL-HOUSE.

and ought to suffice for the coming generation. However, the more enterprising carried their point at last, so far as to get a vote to build a town-house. The next thing to be considered was the place and the material. The brothers, John and Lewis Tappan, and Mr. Joseph Sewall, had built stone houses, and it was proposed to build a stone town-house. This was opposed, of course, as unnecessary extravagance, by the men who thought the old school-house was good enough. But once more enterprise triumphed, and the building was decided upon, as well as the location. This was the origin of the building known as the old stone school-house, still standing next the Unitarian Church.

The contract for building it was let out to mechanics from Roxbury; but the work is said to have been badly done. The building was completed in 1824, and dedicated with appropriate ceremonies, on the first day of January, 1825.

The lower room was fitted for a school-room, and the old brick school-house was taken down the same year. On the spot where the building stood, at the site of the door, an elm tree was planted by Mr. Ebenezer Heath, and it still marks the spot. The old plan of keeping the school a part of the year in that neighborhood, and changing to School Street in winter, continued for a while longer, but the increase of population soon made it necessary to have a school the year round in that part of the town.

For several years the town hall, on the second floor of the building, was a popular place for singing schools, political meetings, and Lyceum lectures. About the year 1832, Mr. Isaac Thayer, who had rushed like a comet into the quiet atmosphere of Brookline, and left his trail along the horizon for some time after his departure, started the idea of a series of Lyceum lectures. A company was organized as the Brookline Lyceum Society, and for several winters the hall was filled with the *élite* of the town on these occasions.

On alternate weeks a debate was held instead of a lecture. A course of lectures on Phrenology, the first season, created much discussion and awakened great interest. An impulse was given to intellectual growth by the Lyceum lectures, which was felt throughout the town. Quiet farmers who scarcely read anything before but the Bible and the Almanac, were roused into new mental life. A premium of ten dollars was offered by the Lyceum Society to the person who should remember and be able to repeat the most of any lecture heard. A daughter of Deacon Joshua C. Clark was the successful competitor.

The first public High School in Brookline was opened in this building in May, 1843, under Mr. Benjamin H. Rhoades, a graduate of Brown University, now librarian of Redwood Library, Newport, R. I.

His assistant teacher, James Pierce, a young man of great promise and much beloved, though a native of Dorchester, was related to Brookline families, and well identified with its interests. He was preparing to enter the Unitarian ministry, when his health failed, and a trip to Europe was advised. On the return voyage he died, and was buried in the sea. Many hearts sincerely mourned his loss, and still tenderly cherish his memory.

Mr. Rhoades was succeeded by Hezekiah Shailer, a brother of Rev. W. H. Shailer, who was then minister of the Baptist Church in this town. He was called a good disciplinarian, as those who experienced the shakings which he gave in a quiet way, after school, were usually reduced to submission, as effectually as if they had been experimented upon with the "clapper" of his ancient predecessor.

Mr. Shailer was succeeded by Professor William P. Atkinson, now of Cambridge, who taught for a year or two. Two others succeeded Professor Atkinson for a short time each; and then Mr. Hoar, the present teacher of the High School, received the appointment in April, 1854, which he has ever since kept.

After the school was removed to its present location, the old stone building continued in use for primary schools, until sold by the town a few years since, when it became private property.

THE FIRST CHURCH.

The act of the Assembly and Council, by which Brookline was incorporated as a separate town in 1705, contained a clause which enjoined the building of a meeting-house and the settling of "an able Orthodox minister" within three years.

But the inhabitants were too few and their means too limited, to enable them to comply with the injunction, and for nine years longer they continued to worship at Roxbury. On the 2d of March, 1713, it was

Voted, "that three men be chosen and appointed to survey the limits of this town, and to find the centre or middle thereof, and to enquire where a convenient place may be procured whereon to build a meeting-house as near the centre of said town as may be."

Voted, "that Samuel Aspinwall, John Druce, and Peter Boylston, be appointed a committee to manage the affair relating to the meeting-house aforesaid."

There were several places proposed, and a Committee of the General Court was called to visit the places.

The record of the next Town Meeting contains the following : —

December 2, 1713. At this meeting Mr. Caleb Gardner, Jr., did offer and bequeath, ratify and confirm unto the town of Brookline a piece of land nigh to his Dwelling House, lying westward therefrom on the left-hand of the roadway leading to Roxbury, whereon to build a Meeting House for the Public Worship of God."

Voted, "that Lieut. Thomas Gardner, Lieut. Samuel Aspinwall, Mr. Joseph White, Mr. Thomas Steadman and John Seaver, be a committee to treat with Mr. Caleb Gardner, above said, about the bounds of said piece of land, and to desire of him a legal conveyance and confirmation thereof to said town."

Voted, "that the Meeting House aforesaid should be of the same dimensions with the Meeting House in the southwest part of Roxbury."

Voted, "that Lieut. Thomas Gardner, Lieut. Samuel Aspinwall, Mr. Erosamond Drew, Mr. Thomas Steadman and Mr. John Seaver, be a committee to manage the concern, or affair of building the above said Meeting House."

The Committee of the General Court decided upon the site above mentioned, and there seems to have been no further opposition.

Mr. Caleb Gardner lived in a house directly opposite what is now the Cemetery, but it must be remembered that the Cemetery had not then been bought or its location decided upon. Mr. John Hammond's old house was standing just about where the entrance to Mr. Kennard's place now is, and Mr. Gardner's between that and the present parsonage.

From Mr. Gardner's, to the house now occupied by Mr. Chapin, there was no building except the old school-house in " the fork of the roads."

THE FIRST MEETING-HOUSE.

All was woods on both sides of the way, and neither Cypress Street nor Boylston Street were thought of. The exact spot given by Mr. Gardner was that now covered by the stable west of the parsonage, and a small piece of the garden of the latter place. Mr. Samuel Clark, as has been previously stated, was the builder. The frame was raised November 10, 1714. The young carpenter and another youth, Mr. Isaac Gardner, when the frame was raised, played at leap-frog on the ridgepole. They lived to be, the one eighty-one years of age, and the other eighty-three, and each came to the same place of worship in his old age supported by two canes or crutches. The meeting-house was forty-four feet long and thirty-five feet wide. It originally contained but fourteen pews, and several long benches. There was a gallery round three sides, and probably long benches therein for the children, who in those days never sat with their parents. Afterward fourteen more pews were added on the floor and four in the gallery. There was no steeple to this house till the town voted in September, 1771, to build one, and accepted thankfully the bell which was presented by Nicholas Boylston, Esq. The pulpit was of oak, and upon it was kept an hour-glass for measuring the time. A clock was a luxury not yet aspired to by the fathers of the town.

The building stood with the side to the road, entrances at each end, and a door in the centre of the front. The steeple was at the west end. The bell presented by Mr. Boylston was a very fine toned one, but was cracked in 1803, much to the regret of the people. The pulpit was overhung by an immense sounding-board, which threatened the minister like a large extinguisher.

The people were arranged by a person appointed in Town Meeting for that purpose, according to dignity, age, standing, etc.

The church was gathered the 26th of October, 1717, by Rev. Mr. Thayer, of the Second Church in Roxbury. There were seventeen male members, and twenty-two females.

The arrangement of the people, after the pews were sold April 29, 1718, was on this wise: —

Samuel Sewall, next the pulpit, west.
John Winchester, Sen., next west.
Capt. Sam. Aspinwall, Northwest corner.
Lieut. Thomas Gardner, between west door and men's gallery stairs.
John Seaver, between west door and men's gallery stairs.
John Druce, left of men's gallery stairs.
Joseph Gardner, left of front door.
Josiah Winchester, Sen., right of front door.
Thomas Stedman, right of women's gallery stairs.
William Sharp, left of east door.
Ensign Benj. White, right of east door.
Peter Boylston, Northeast corner.
Ministerial Pew, right of pulpit stairs.

One of the above mentioned Benjamin Whites, and Lieutenant Thomas Gardner, were the first deacons, and were chosen in 1718.

Deacon White lived in a house which stood on the site of the present residence of Colonel Lyman. This house was purchased by Hon. Jonathan Mason, who had it torn down in 1809. Between the floors of this house was found a carefully folded paper, which contained an account of the manner in which the congregation was seated March 9, 1719. "Whole number of individuals seated, 66, of whom 28 couples were men and wives."

In the men's foreseat, in the body seats, are seated Josiah Winchester, Captain Aspinwall, Joseph Gardner, and Edward Devotion.

SEATING OF THE CONGREGATION. 241

In the second seat, are seated William Story, Joseph Goddard, Thomas Woodward, Daniel Harris, and John Ackers.

In the third seat, are seated James Griggs, Samuel Newell, Abraham Chamberlain, Ebenezer Kendrick, and Robert Harris.

In the fourth seat, are seated Thomas Lee, William Davis, and Joseph Scott.

In the front foreseat in the gallery, are seated Caleb Gardner, Josiah Winchester, Samuel White, Henry Winchester, Joseph Adams, Robert Sharp, Thomas Cotton, and Samuel Clark, Jun.

In the foreseat in the side gallery, are seated Joshua Stedman, William Gleason, Dudley Boylston, Addington Gardner, John Taylor, Stephen Winchester, and Philip Torrey.

In the second seat in the front, are seated Isaac Gleason, John Wedge, Thomas Woodward, Jun., and James Goddard.

In the women's foreseat, in the body seats, are seated the wife of Josiah Winchester, Sen., the widow Ackers, the wife of Joseph Gardner, and the wife of Edward Devotion.

In the second seat, are seated the wife of William Story, the wife of Joseph Goddard, the wife of Thomas Woodward, the wife of Daniel Harris, the wife of John Ackers, and the widow Hannah Stedman.

In the third seat, the wife of James Griggs, the wife of Samuel Newell, the wife of Abraham Chamberlain, the wife of Ebenezer Kenrick, and the wife of Robert Harris.

In the fourth seat, the wife of Thomas Lee, the wife of William Davis, and the wife of Joseph Scott.

In the front foreseat in the gallery, the wife of Samuel White, the wife of Henry Winchester, the wife of Joseph

Adams, the wife of Robert Sharp, and the wife of Samuel Clark, Jun.

In the foreseat in the side gallery, the wife of Joshua Stedman, the wife of William Gleason, the wife of Dudley Boylston, the wife of Addington Gardner, the wife of John Taylor.

In the second seat in the front, the wife of John Wedge and the wife of James Goddard.

A fast day was appointed on the third of July, 1718, " to seek Divine direction in the ordination of a minister."

On the 5th of November the same year, the Rev. James Allen of Roxbury was ordained first minister of the church.

Mr. Allen lived, as we have before mentioned, in a house on the south side of Walnut Street, opposite the head of Cypress Street.

Mr. Allen preached here more than twenty-eight years. He died in February, 1747, aged fifty-six years. His death was caused by a lingering consumption. He was buried in Brookline Cemetery. During his ministry one hundred and fifteen were added to the church, " besides forty-four who owned the Covenant without coming to the Lord's table." The baptisms were two hundred and sixty-one. Mr. Allen was called " a pious and judicious divine." There are seven sermons of his now extant which were published during his lifetime, which have been said to " do equal honor to his head and heart."

The period of Mr. Allen's ministry, however, was not without its troubles. During the time of powerful religious excitement produced by the preaching of Rev. George Whitefield, the Brookline church was much affected by it; and Mr. Allen described this work in a letter to Rev. Wm. Cooper in glowing terms, saying, that " scores of persons have been under awakenings."

It seems, however, that during six years from 1738 to 1744, there were but twenty-two added to the church. The effect of the excitement, however, like similar religious fervors in our own times, was to produce a reaction, and in less than a year from the time Mr. Allen wrote his enthusiastic letter to Mr. Cooper and the Convention of orthodox ministers, he condemned the whole thing as a delusion.

The effect of this revulsion of feeling on his part was to cause six of the leading members of his church to secede with their families. They wrote him a caustic letter in which they say, " Now we desire with humility and meekness to give you the reasons of our withdrawal from you and your church."

We copy from this paper a few of the reasons given by the seceders for their course.

" I. The first reason we shall mention, is Mr. Allen's speaking against that, which we think to be the glorious work of God, but he calls it a delusion.

" II. His speaking against those ministers, which we believe the Lord has sent out to invite sinners to Christ. Mr. Allen warns people not to go to hear them, and said they who go to hear them go upon the Devil's ground.

" III. We cannot join with Mr. Allen in letting in those to preach who we fear are strangers to the life and power of God in their souls; because they preach only the form, as we think. One of which coming into Mr. Allen's house one time, he said he had as lief see the Devil."

There were other similar reasons given, and the paper was signed by Ebenezer Kendrick, Nath'l Shepard, John Seaver, Jr., Elhanan Winchester, Jr., Richard Seaver, Dudley Boylston, Jr.

This secession, from this and other churches, was the

origin of the "New Lights." They began to hold meetings in Mr. Shepard's house, which was where the Public Library now stands, and was afterwards known as the Dana house.

Those who lived in the upper part of the town held meetings at Mr. Winchester's, afterward "the Richards Tavern." The sect finally broke up, and distributed its members among Baptists and Shakers. We shall give a further account of Elhanan Winchester at some future time.

The Rev. Mr. Allen remained firm in the Orthodox faith till his death, notwithstanding his disapproval of itinerant revivalists and the measures they employed. But the effect of the division and unkind feeling among his people was to render Mr. Allen very unhappy, and is said to have been the cause of the consumption which ended his life.

After Mr. Allen's decease the Society gave a call to the Rev. Cotton Brown, son of a minister of Haverhill; he was ordained October 26, 1748. Those who read the account of the Walley house will remember that he was there mentioned as having been engaged to Mr. Allen's daughter, and that the Walley house (so called) was built for him to live in. The young lady, however, died in 1750, and Mr. Brown died in 1751, aged twenty-five years, having been pastor of the church not quite two years and a half.

The eminent Dr. Cooper of Brattle Street Church, spoke thus of his character at the time of his decease : —

"He was a gentleman who, by the happiness of his genius, his application to study, and taste for polite literature, his piety and prudence, his sweetness of temper, and softness of manners, had raised in his friends the fairest hopes, and gave them just reason to expect in him one of the brightest ornaments of society and a peculiar blessing to the church."

EXPENSES OF ORDINATION. 245

Mr. Brown was buried in Brookline Cemetery.

The next clergyman who accepted a call to the Brookline Church was Mr. Nathaniel Potter, of Elizabeth, New Jersey, who was ordained pastor of the church November 19, 1755. He remained in this connection three years and a half. He had been hastily called, from a distant city, without credentials, and was as hastily settled. Of him Dr. Pierce remarked in an anniversary sermon, that " though professedly orthodox in faith, he was destined, during a short ministry, to give woeful emphasis to the apostle's monition, ' Lay hands suddenly on no man.' "

A bill presented to the town by Deacon Elisha Gardner for the expenses of this man's ordination, possesses a curious interest when viewed with modern eyes.

to monney Pad at The ordanation. old tenor £ 6. 0 0 0	
to Rum	£ 1. 1 4. 0
to Shugar	£ 1. 1 0. 6
to spice	
to turces (turkeys?)	3 0. 0. 0.
to fouls	1. 1. 0 0
to pork	3 0 4 6
to crambres	0 0 8 0
to puding pans	0 1 5 0
	£18. 0 2 6

Of this charge the Selectmen ordered the paying of £. 2. s. 8. d. 4. and probably the Society paid the rest. Ordinations in those days evidently involved the consideration of material as well as spiritual wants, for the time being.

REV. JOSEPH JACKSON.

After the removal of Mr. Potter, the church extended a call to the Rev. Joseph Jackson, at that time a tutor at Cambridge. He had occasionally preached for the Brookline society, and was much liked by his hearers.

Mr. Jackson accepted the invitation, and was ordained fourth minister of the church, April 9, 1760. The only relic or memorial of his ordination which we have been able to trace out is the bill for the expenses of the dinner. It is somewhat similar to that of his predecessor.

"Brookline, 1760. Elisha Gardner's accompt to providing at the Ordination of mr Joseph Jackson   old tenor

to cash for Sundries at the ordination	£14. 00. 0
to cash for crambres and Ross water	2. 00. 0
to cash for butter and Eggs and Pickels	2. 15. 0
to cash for to pay the Cakes	6. 00. 0
	£24. 15. 6

Errors Excepted.
Allowed by the Selectmen."

The rum being omitted, perhaps the rosewater served instead.

Evidently some repairs were made on the church-building and things put in order generally, for the coming of the new minister, as we find the following bill, dated two days after the ordination: —

"*April the* 11 *Day* 1760.

for work Brookline Meeting house on the Pulpit Laying a floore in the Same and Raising the Same and Paint and Painting, for weather Boairds and Doore.	£2.-2.-8
caseings for one End of the Meetting hous	0-5-4
for a Lock for the Doore and a Paire of hinges	. 9-4 . 5-9
for three Bolts and three Quarters of a hundred of Board nails.	4-8
for the Doors and Step. Except Arrows.	1.-10-0
	£.4-17-9

EBENEZER THWING.

A year later was the following: —

BROOKLINE *March* 19, 1861.
The Select men of Brookline in Behalf of ye town to Joshua Davis Dr. Decem 16th.

To a Shutter for the Meting-house & a Draw for ye Bible Puting up ye same	£0. 5–4.
To a bench for the School and mending seats	5–4
	10–8

Errors Excepted.
JOSHUA DAVIS.

Mr. Jackson married Hannah, daughter of John Avery, Esq., of Boston. He occupied the house which his predecessors had occupied, during nearly twenty years of his ministry. During his absence one day the house took fire, and though not wholly destroyed, was badly damaged.

Dr. Aspinwall, who was passing, rendered efficient service in saving Mr. Jackson's library. In May, 1781, the ground occupied for now nearly a century for a parsonage lot, was given for that purpose by Mrs. Walcott, a daughter of Judge Sewall, and a house was built the following year, into which Mr. Jackson removed, and there he spent the remainder of his days.

Mr. Jackson was admired by many as a preacher; he seems to have been greatly respected and beloved by his people; but there was an awe amounting almost to fear on the part of the children and young people of the parish. Perhaps the austere manners, the style of dress, and the powdered wig worn by the clergy of those days, may have had something to do with this feeling.

An incident is related of the boys of those days, which illustrates this point. In the old meeting-house the children occupied the gallery. A broad balustrade ran along the front of this, and one Sunday a stray dog having found his way into the gallery, mounted this balustrade and took a survey of the congregation. Either with or without the help of the boys, the dog by a sudden lurch was precipitated into the pew of Mr. Winchester, below, with such violence as to split the seat. What the consequence was to the dog is not reported. But the boys, in spite of minister and tything man, were convulsed with laughter which they could not repress.

The next day, when they were having their recess at the brick school-house, the dignified clergyman was seen walking up the hill. When he reached the school-house not a boy was to be found far or near. Over walls, behind fences, into the woods, anywhere out of sight of the minister, they scattered like frightened partridges, and kept still till he had gone, invisible as Roderick Dhu's men till the whistle was blown.

When he called on his parishioners, the children often hid themselves till his visit was over. Not that he was unkind, or intentionally repellant to the little ones, but the office of minister was held in greater sanctity then than now, and the children were taught to fear him. Many a child used to hide behind the wall when about to meet him on the street, rather than make the bow or courtesy which the custom of the times demanded.

In 1790, Mr. Jackson lost his only son, an affliction from which he never fully recovered.

Like Mr. Allen, he too had some parish troubles, principally arising from the preaching of the "New Lights." Mr. Elhanan Winchester, previously alluded to, had a son of the same name, who was nine years of age when Mr. Jackson came to Brookline. This young man became a Baptist, and afterwards a Universalist, preaching the final restoration of all men, a doctrine which gave Mr. Jackson much trouble. Mr. Jackson's health began to fail after the death of his son, but it was his constant prayer that his life and his usefulness might terminate together. His prayer was answered, for he continued to preach till the last Sabbath of his life, and even made arrangements for the supply of his pulpit for the following Sunday. He died on the 22d of July, 1796, aged sixty-two years, having been pastor of the Brookline Church thirty-six years.

Such was his extreme modesty and diffidence that he never would allow a sermon of his to be published, and he ordered that all his manuscripts should be destroyed at his death.

Mr. Jackson was not buried in Brookline, but his body was carried to Boston, and deposited in his family tomb. He left a daughter, Sarah, who married Atherton Thayer, Esq., of Braintree, and after his death, his brother Stephen. She died in 1809, leaving a son and three daughters. Mrs. Jackson died in 1800.

In the year 1759, Mr. Samuel White gave a wood-lot in Newton, to the First Church, for the perpetual use of the ministry in Brookline.

An old bill in our possession reads as follows: —

"*Augst ye* 3 1763 Deacon this may inform you that I have carted the Revnd mr Jackson four cord & a half of wood & I pray you when you and your brethren the Select men meet you would writ me an ordr for my money & in so doing you will oblige yours to serve
old tenor.
22-10-0.   JOSIAH WOODARD "

Mr. Jackson was a smoker, and when the ministers met at his house, it was customary for him to invite such of his guests as indulged in the same habit, to share in a

17

social smoke. An old tin case for pipes and tobacco, and a pair of tobacco tongs, were long preserved in the family of his successor, not for use, but as curiosities.

The religious views held by Mr. Jackson and his predecessors, were those now held by conservative, or old school, Orthodox churches. The dividing line between Unitarianism and Orthodoxy had not then been so sharply defined as to leave the Brookline Church on the liberal side. Mr. Jackson was much lamented by many friends, not only in his own church, but in other places. Many persons were in the habit of walking a long distance, some even from Dorchester, to hear him preach. With all his diffidence and modesty about preaching on public occasions (which it was his habit to decline), he was fearless in denouncing what he believed to be errors, either in belief or practice, among his own people.

When the people of this country were suffering from impoverishment by the Revolutionary War, and many were content to pay their obligations to their clergymen in depreciated currency, the Brookline people showed their appreciation and regard for Mr. Jackson, by allowing him, from year to year, above his stated salary, as much more, as covered all his annual expenses.

CHAPTER XIII.

REV. DR. PIERCE: BIOGRAPHY. — MR. PHILBRICK AND THE ANTI-SLAVERY MOVEMENT. — POLLY HATCH: ANECDOTES, HER MARRIAGE AND DEATH.

IN writing at the head of this chapter the name of the venerable clergyman so well remembered and so much beloved in our town, we feel that we are only just beginning the story of the First Church, he was so long identified with it, and was so essentially a part of Brookline. In the language of Rev. Dr. Putnam, on a memorable occasion, "As I understand it, Dr. Pierce is Brookline, and Brookline is Dr. Pierce."

He was so truly identified with all our local interests, that Brookline has never seemed the same since his departure, to those who knew him, that it did before.

Dr. Pierce was born in Dorchester, July 14, 1773. He graduated, holding high rank in his class, at Harvard College, in 1793. He was for the two succeeding years assistant preceptor at Leicester Academy. In 1795, he commenced the study of theology with Rev. Thaddeus Mason Harris, of Dorchester.

In 1797, he was invited to fill the vacancy in the Brookline Church, caused by the death of Mr. Jackson. He held at that time a tutorship at Harvard College. The invitation was accepted, and he was ordained pastor of the Brookline Church, March 15, 1797.

In October of the following year, he was married to Miss Lovell of Medway, who had been one of his pupils at the Academy. She died in July, 1800, leaving an infant son, who lived but two years.

In 1802, Dr. Pierce was married to Lucy Tappan of Northampton, a lady beloved for her quiet virtues, and who lived to a venerated old age.

The old church edifice, which had now been standing more than fourscore years, was quite inadequate to accommodate the increased population of the town. The congregation received quite a large accession soon after Dr. Pierce's ordination, of Dorchester people, who removed here, following their fellow townsman, in whom they took a just pride. Among these were the Robinsons, Withingtons, Leedses, Tolmans, and others.

The subject of building a new meeting-house was soon agitated, and some mischievous person, probably desiring to facilitate the matter, set fire to the old one. It was soon discovered, and extinguished after some damage to one of the rear corners.

May 16, 1804, it was voted to build a new meeting-house on the site of the old one. This, however, was found to be impracticable for various reasons, and the vote was reconsidered. On the 5th of September of the same year, it was voted to build the meeting-house on the spot occupied by the present house.

In April, 1805, the corner-stone was laid. The frame was raised by the help of machinery in a few days. The architect and master-builder was Mr. Peter Banner, an Englishman. This man settled in Brookline, and for many years after his death his widow occupied the house in Aspinwall Avenue, now owned by Mr. Melcher.

The new meeting-house stood fronting the street, with a grass plat in front of it. It was sixty-eight feet long, and sixty-four feet wide, with a porch nineteen feet long and thirty-eight feet wide. There were lobbies or anterooms each side of the porch, eleven feet square. There was no cellar under the building, it being a rocky foundation, and the house was raised up a little from the ground, and openings on either side in the under-pinning afforded space for ventilation. The height of the house was thirty-five feet and six inches from the foundation to the eaves. The spire measured one hundred and thirty-seven feet from the ground.

There were seventy-four pews on the floor and fourteen in the gallery. Afterwards, during Dr. Pierce's ministry, some improvements were added. No provision was ever made for warming the old church, and the women carried foot-stoves with them. The new church was warmed by two square box stoves, in which wood was burned.

The pulpit and the caps of the pews were made of southern cherry-wood, contributed by Stephen Higginson, Jr. The bell, which was cast in London, and weighed one thousand pounds, was given by Hon. Stephen Higginson, father of the above.

Mr. John Lucas, who lived nearly opposite the Reservoir, gave four hundred dollars, out of which was purchased a clock, which served faithfully as long as the old meeting-house stood, and still does duty in the old Town Hall.

Richard Sullivan, Esq., who lived on the place now owned by Mrs. Bowditch, gave a hundred and fifty dollars, for the stone steps. Mr. Thomas Walley gave an elegant pulpit Bible, valued at thirty-six dollars. Mr. David Hyslop gave a baptismal basin, which cost forty-seven dollars.

The whole cost of the house was $18,083. Some additional expenses, of furnishing, probably, brought the amount up to $20,193, and the whole was apportioned on the pews, which were sold at auction.

No pew on the first floor was prized at less than one hundred and sixty dollars, and none in the gallery at less than one hundred and ten dollars. The highest cost of a pew, including a bonus paid for a choice, was five hundred and twenty-five dollars.

Dr. Pierce preached a valedictory sermon on leaving the old house, June 8, 1806, from the text, " Lord I have loved the habitation of thy house and the place where thine honor dwelleth."

The dedication sermon was from the words, " In all places where I record my name, I will come unto thee and I will bless thee."

The next day, the work of demolishing the old church commenced. The ancient pulpit which had been faithfully pounded and belabored by the fists of the energetic Mr. Jackson, was denuded of its upholstery, and carried into the parsonage attic, where it served as a playhouse for the pastor's children for many years. It has since been tastefully remodeled as a bookcase, and still graces the parsonage. The hour-glass, whose sands had run through many a tedious hour for the unfed souls in the old house, or had needed turning only too quickly for the more devotional, now served its time in fleeting minutes among the attic treasures of the little ones. The ancient pewter christening basin, from which Mr. Jackson had bathed the infant brow of many a now gray-haired father and mother of the town, was turned to domestic uses in the pastor's house. After many vicissitudes it came into possession of the writer, with the ancient tin tobacco case, previously mentioned as belonging to Mr. Jackson, after the death of the late David R. Griggs, to whom they had been given as curiosities.

It seems that the ancient church for many years, instead of having a sexton, was taken care of by a slave belonging to the Sewall family, as Henry Sewall's bill against the town for the services of his "slave Felix," in that capacity, is still in existence.

The first white sexton of whom we can gather any account, was a man named Blanchard, who lived in a little house on the Aspinwall estate, close to Washington Street. He was succeeded, if we are correctly informed, by Captain Benjamin Bradley, who served for many years in that capacity, after the second meeting-house was built.

Very little information has come down to us respecting the singing in the First Church, in the early times. A brief note written by Mr. Jackson lets a ray of light on the forgotten history of those days. It is addressed to Mr. Isaac Gardner, who was afterwards killed at Lexington.

"BROOKLIN Aug. 8, 1763.

"Sir,

"I perceived it was not agreeable to you to lead in the singing yesterday — If Mr. Aspinwall does not return before ye Thanksgiving I will speak to Mr. Bowles,

Yrs.
J. JACKSON."

What Mr. Aspinwall this was, we have no means of knowing, but it is certain that Mr. Isaac Gardner was a fine singer, and did "lead in the singing," as did his son Isaac S. Gardner, after him. The bass-viol and trombone were the principal instruments used. When Dr. Pierce came, a new impulse was given to the music, as he had a clear, strong voice, and sang with great energy.

After Dr. Pierce had been for some time settled in Brookline, a board of trustees was organized to take charge of all matters concerning the church music. Mr. Ebenezer Heath was president and secretary, and Dr. Charles Wild, vice-president.

By request of Mr. Heath, on behalf of the board, Mr. Benjamin B. Davis was requested to take charge of the singing, as chorister, in the year 1818. Of the faithful devotion with which for thirty-eight years he led the choir, any attendant upon Dr. Pierce's ministry for that length of time will bear witness.

The choir consisted of thirty members, many of the names being still familiar to the people of the town. Prominent among these at that time, or a little later, were Deacon Pierce, James Pierce, John Woodward, Jabez Hunting, Lewis Withington, James Leeds, Samuel Barry, Jeremiah Lyon, E. W. Stone, Eben Heath, Charles Heath, Jona Jackson, Capt. Charles Stearns, Marshall Stearns, James Robinson, the daughters of Mr. James Pierce, Eunice Ford, Ann Dunn, two daughters of Mr. Celfe, three daughters of Dr. Pierce, and some years later, Susan, the eldest daughter of Mr. Benjamin B. Davis. This young lady was not only a sweet singer, but lovely in mind and person, deservedly a favorite with all who knew her. But her fair young life, only just unfolding its charms to a loving circle of friends, was like a spring flower, the joy of but a brief season; and the voice which had given such pleasure on earth, was called to join the choirs who praise in "the house not made with hands." Several years afterwards, the other daughter of Mr. Davis, who was also a member of the choir, died young, leaving a childless father to sing sorrowfully without them.

Mr. James Pierce, who also played the bass-viol, as well as sung, took his little daughters into "the singers' seats," when they were so small that they were obliged to stand on crickets to bring their heads above the balustrade. One of them, who was afterwards the wife of Charles Stearns, Jr., was for years the leader of the female voices.

The instrumental music, as there was no organ, was subject to variations at different times, but several performers were for years identified with the society. Among these were William H. Brown, who played the bassoon, John H. Pierce, Dr. Charles Wild, and Charles Lyon, the flute, George Murdock, bass-viol, Artemas Newell, bombadoon, Job Grush, clarionet, and somewhat later, Mr. Flagg, who for several years was hired, also played the clarionet.

Dr. Pierce attended nearly all the meetings of the choir, for practice, and his affable and courteous manners, and the intense interest which he took in sacred music, no doubt had much influence in preserving harmony among the members, and keeping up their interest. He usually stood in the pulpit and joined with great fervor in the singing. He frequently attended the Oratorios of the Handel and Haydn Society, and enjoyed them exceedingly. Dr. Pierce and Dr. Bates of Dedham called a meeting of the singers of Norfolk County, to improve church music, from the use of newly published books. On one occasion when there was an unusually severe snow-storm, there were but thirteen persons at church, but Dr. Pierce went through the services as usual, and he and Mr. Davis were the choir.

Among the Doctor's parishioners was Mr. David Hyslop, an estimable citizen, but who could not tell one tune from another. One Sunday, a stranger who was preaching instead of Dr. Pierce, took occasion to quote in his sermon,

"The man who has no music in his soul,
Is fit for treason, stratagem, and spoil."

Mr. Hyslop felt himself severely reflected upon, and rising from his seat near the pulpit he walked deliberately out.

It was customary to open the services with an anthem. One Sabbath morning a dog, which had ventured into the church in search of his master, had reached the broad stair near the pulpit, when suddenly, the preliminary scrape of the instruments being given, the choir burst forth in a jubilant anthem. The terrified dog, having no ear for music, set up a tumultuous barking, which accompaniment not having a tendency to promote devotional feelings on the part of the congregation, the sexton appeared and assisted him in retiring promptly from the scene.

Great attention was given to rehearsing suitable music for Thanksgiving Days. Sometimes a sum was raised by subscription to secure the services of some extra musicians from Boston, so that there was quite an orchestra.

In the year 1800, there were but six hundred and five inhabitants in Brookline, but it will be recollected that no other church was formed until 1828. Most of the church-going people, therefore, were attendants upon Dr. Pierce's ministry. He knew personally every man, woman, and child, who thus attended, and remembered the name and age of every child whom he baptized, and none were beneath his notice or ever forgotten.

For many years, Dr. Pierce's salary was but four hundred dollars, besides the rent of the parsonage and a supply of firewood annually. This, however, was generously supplemented by his people by gifts of every sort, and neither he nor his large family knew any lack. This, however, was greatly owing to remarkable domestic economy.

The church was thrifty but not wealthy, as the people were chiefly plain farmers or mechanics. There was however a gradual increase of merchants either active or retired, among the tax-payers, and an increase of wealth in the society, and also of culture.

One upholstered pew in the church was looked upon as a most aristocratic institution. This was the property of Mr. David Hyslop, who also indulged in the luxury of red morocco covered books with his family coat of arms upon them, and a drawer in the pew to hold them, greatly to the admiration or envy of the children of the less favored.

Any attempt at display in dress or manners was noticed fifty years ago in Brookline, as the same things are now in obscure country villages. There were eccentric individuals, curious oddities, intermingled with the general average of the people, any one of whom might be the subject of an entertaining sketch. Among these were Black Susy, of whom we have already written, who always sat in the high narrow pew above the singers' seats, known as "the negro pew," — and Miss Prudy Heath, a quaint character, who was never seen in the street without a large green cotton umbrella, yet who remembered her minister with many generous gifts. Many anecdotes are told of these persons.

There was also at one time an Englishman, employed as a shoemaker, who appeared on Sundays at church in the afternoon in small-clothes and a generous expanse of highly ruffled shirt-bosom, always with a rose in his button-hole as long as roses lasted. He was a subject for much amusement and comment, and just such a character as to call out the quizzing propensities of such a wag as the late well-remembered Jerry Davenport, who sat conveniently near him in church. The hero of the ruffles and roses was usually asleep soon after the sermon began, and on waking had a habit of smelling at the rose he carried with great energy.

One Sunday the irrepressible Jerry, quietly reaching over the sleeper, filled the rose in his button-hole with pungent snuff, which he carried for the purpose. After a while the sleeper woke, and as usual drew out the rose and took a vigorous smell at it. Such a sneezing as followed! Sneeze upon sneeze, which could not be held back or smothered, and the discomfited dandy made the best of his way out of church sneezing till he was out of hearing. The joke was better than a good dinner to the waggish perpetrator, who chuckled over it long afterwards with great delight.

In 1829 or 1830, Mr. Elisha Stone succeeded Captain Bradley as sexton of the church, which office he filled for thirty years. He was a plodding but faithful citizen in the duties not only of his office as sexton, but was the only undertaker and constable in the town for many years. He lived to lay away all but two of his own large family in the cemetery whither he had carried so many of our townspeople, and where at last he was borne, worn out with the infirmities of age.

Previous to Dr. Pierce's time there had been presented at various times to the First Church four silver tankards. One was the gift of Edward Devotion in 1744, one the gift of Miss Mary Allen, daughter of the first minister, in 1750; one was given by Miss Ann White, and one by Mrs. Susanna Sharp in 1770. In the same year two silver cups were presented by Thomas and Mary Woodward, and two more were given by William Hyslop in 1792. This ancient silver is still the property of the church just as it was presented.

In addition to these, two silver cups were presented by Miss Prudence Heath in 1818, and two by Deacon Robinson and wife the same year. In the year 1805 Dr. Pierce preached a sermon on the anniversary of the completion of a century from the incorporation of the town. In 1837, when he had been settled forty years, he delivered an address called "Reminiscences of Forty Years," filled with interesting local history and rich in valuable statistics. In 1845, when the second Town Hall was dedicated, he delivered an address which exceeded the previous one in historical value, and created a great interest. It was printed and freely circulated. A valuable appendix to this document has been a mine of information, from which much material for these sketches has been drawn.

The Doctor called himself a matter-of-fact man, and he was eminently so. Not an incident of local or public interest but was treasured up in his memory; not a birth, death, or house-raising in the town but he recorded and remembered it; not a circumstance connected with the schools or teachers, that did not enlist his interest. "There was," it has been said, almost "as much truth as wit in the remark of the late Judge Davis, when — all other attempts to find out having failed, and Dr. Pierce could not tell the birth-place of a certain person — he said, that it was no use to make further inquiries; for if *the Doctor* did not know where the man was born, *he was not born anywhere.*" *

A strong friendship existed between Dr. Pierce and Rev. Wm. H. Shailer, the third minister of the Baptist Church. In 1840 when the Baptist Church was enlarged and remodeled, a cordial invitation was given the people of that society to worship in the First Church while the repairs were going on. This was gratefully accepted, and Dr. Pierce and Mr. Shailer occupied the pulpit together, one preaching in the forenoon and the other in the afternoon.

* A conundrum had local circulation at one time, to this effect: "Why is Dr. Pierce like a palm-tree?" but the dullest could scarcely fail of giving the only possible answer: "Because he bears dates."

When a half century from his ordination had elapsed, Dr. Pierce had a jubilee, which was one of the pleasantest local affairs which ever occurred in the town. Scattered natives of the town came home from distant places to participate in it, and hosts of friends of the good old minister, from far and near, joined in the celebration to which he and they had long looked forward. Dr. Pierce's discourse was from the text, "I have been young and now am old." It was like the other addresses alluded to, full of historical interest, and is invaluable for the statistics it contains. In the evening there was a collation at the Town Hall, and a presentation of silver-plate, money, and flowers to the venerable man who was the centre of interest. It was on this occasion that Rev. Dr. Putnam made the remark, previously quoted, that "Dr. Pierce is Brookline and Brookline is Dr. Pierce."

At this time, March 15, 1847, Dr. Pierce was in vigorous health, and as full of energy as at any time during his life. He however consented to the appointment of a colleague, Rev. Frederic N. Knapp, who was ordained October 6, of the same year, but he continued to preach, and to take part in various meetings, both in Brookline and in various other places.

The meeting-house and the minister grew old together. There would have been something incongruous in the building of a modern church, with stained-glass windows and new and fashionable appointments, while Dr. Pierce was the only minister. The house and the minister were in perfect adaptation to each other. Many regretted that the fine substantial old edifice should be taken down. It much resembled Dr. Putnam's church on Roxbury Hill, and might have been as well preserved till the present day; but there being no cellar under it, furnaces could not be introduced, and it was not thought advisable to re-fit a building which must be warmed by stoves. It was also difficult for Mr. Knapp to preach in it. In 1848 the new church at present standing was built. The dedication took place December 1, 1848. The shrubbery around it was set out by Dr. Charles Wild, in the spring of 1849. In March, Dr. Pierce was seized with a sharp, sudden illness. Relief was obtained, but not a cure. He continued to suffer great pain, and as weeks passed on seemed gradually failing. During his long ministry he had lost only thirteen Sabbaths by ill-health, and several of those were in 1805, when he had a rheumatic fever.

He was a fine-looking, tall, large framed man, with a countenance " beaming with cheerfulness and benignity." His hair, from his early manhood, was almost white, and became beautiful in its snowy whiteness long before he was old. He remarked during his last sickness that for forty years he had not known what it was to have a physical infirmity worth naming. He had always had a habit of rising early, and either sawing or splitting wood, or working in his garden for two hours or more before breakfast. He was so vigorous a walker that when on an exchange anywhere within six or seven miles, he used to go out and back on foot, and without fatigue. He was temperate both in eating and drinking and economical without a shade of meanness or miserly tendency.

When it was talked of that Dr. Pierce was ill and might not recover, the community was shocked. The very idea of sickness was scarcely to be entertained in connection with such a personification of health and vigor. Nobody seemed to have thought that he could die, at least till extreme old age should gradually impair his energies.

He belonged to a long-lived family and though at an age when most men grow infirm, he was as elastic and vigorous as a boy, till the day of his first attack of illness.

All was done that love and skill could suggest to arrest the course of the disease, but in vain, and it soon became apparent that the beloved pastor and friend of the people was soon to be called away. Unused as he was to illness, there was no irritability or impatience, and with unfailing serenity and cheerfulness he waited for the end. In August of that year a new organ was placed in the church, and on Saturday the 18th, there was a trial of the instrument. This was of course an event of great interest to one so fond of music as the Doctor, and though he was too feeble to walk or ride, he was carried in his chair by some of his young friends, to the church. There he read some passages from the Scriptures and a hymn, joining heartily in the singing. At his own special request the tune sung was "Old Hundred," which Dr. Pierce used to say was " the best tune that ever was written or ever would be."

All rose and sung the hymn, standing, except the Doctor himself, who playfully asked that the old pastor be excused, as he no longer belonged to "the *rising* generation."

He was borne to his home by the same loving hands, never to be carried out again till he was carried for burial. Daily, however, he received the visits of a host of friends, who came laden with flowers, fruits, or other proofs of their affection ; and in the words of another, "wealth never purchased and power never won attentions of all kinds so devoted and loving as were gladly rendered without stint and in constant anticipation of his slightest wishes," not merely from his own society or townspeople but from all sects and many towns and the neighboring cities.

The great friendship between Dr. Pierce and Rev. Mr. Shailer, whom he often called his "oldest son," seemed to grow stronger as the former was drawing near to the close of life. For three months, Mr. Shailer visited him three times a week and carefully shaved him, and by reading or genial conversation beguiled the tedious hours of illness. Among his numerous visitors, were one hundred and twenty clergymen, representing seven different denominations.

His colleague, Rev. Mr. Knapp, was also one with whom he had most cordial sympathy, and whom he would have chosen to fill that place had the matter been left to him to decide. So that his people in deciding according to their own choice, had also acted in accordance with the wishes of their pastor.

Dr. Pierce failed very rapidly after his visit to the church, at the trial of the organ, but retained possession of his faculties and consciousness until the evening of Thursday, August 23. His last words were spoken that evening to Mr. Shailer, who with the family and two or three near friends were present. Mr. Shailer made an inquiry respecting the petition which he should offer for him in the evening prayer, to which he replied, " Entire submission to the Divine will." He never spoke again, but still reclining in the chair which he had occupied for weeks, without lying down, he quietly breathed his last at half-past eleven in the forenoon, August 24, 1849, aged seventy-six years.

The funeral solemnities took place at the church, on the afternoon of the 27th. There were no gloomy draperies, — they would have ill befitted the last offices for one who had been preëminently an apostle of cheerfulness, who had done his life's work well, and peacefully passed on.

The baptismal font was filled with white flowers, and a wreath was laid upon the coffin by one of the children of the Sunday-school.

The body was borne from the parsonage to the church by the same young men who had carried him thither a week before, attended by eight clergymen as pall-bearers. Rev. Mr. Shailer read the Scriptures, the venerable Dr. Lowell of Boston offered the prayer (in compliance with the special wish of Dr. Pierce), and Rev. Mr. Knapp, his colleague, delivered the discourse. The last message of the dying minister to his people was so beautiful, that we give it as repeated by Mr. Knapp on this solemn occasion.

"When you gather with my friends around my remains," he said, "read to them those cheering words of Jesus, 'I am the resurrection and the life; he that believeth on me, though he were dead, yet shall he live; and whosoever liveth and believeth on me shall never die.' and say to my people," he continued, "*my* faith and hope are there; that I do not feel that I shall ever die, but only pass on to a higher life. And beseech them," he added, "beseech them, if they love me, and would express their love, to do it by remembering me while they seek Christ as their Saviour, and strive to live as his disciples."

The services at the church were attended by a great concourse of people, many of whom were unable to enter it at all, but who followed the remains to the cemetery. Among them were the entire theological schools, students and professors, from Cambridge and Newton, the president and two ex-presidents of Harvard College. An old lady, upwards of eighty years of age, walked from Roxbury that afternoon, not having heard of his death, hoping to see him once more living, and arrived at the cemetery just in time to see the beloved face as it lay in the light of the summer sunset, before it was shut out from sight forever.

A simple white monument just within the cemetery wall marks his last resting place.

We have purposely omitted, hitherto, speaking of Dr. Pierce's theological views, preferring to give first his final message to his people. We now subjoin an extract from an article which appeared in the "Christian Inquirer," soon after his death, and which is considered by those better qualified to judge, a fair and just estimate of him as a preacher.

"He uniformly refused to be classed with any sect whatever, or to take any names except those of a 'Congregationalist' and a 'Christian.' He seldom preached doctrinal sermons. He had no taste for controversy; and hardly ever indulged in expressions of his belief clothed in any other phraseology than that of the Bible. For any party to claim him as a member on account of his opinions would be showing a sad want of respect to his memory, and an utter disregard of his feelings and wishes when alive.

"No one has any moral right to do for him that which he always refused to do for himself — class him anywhere as a theologian. He must be simply known as an 'eclectic Christian,' to use his own terms; and if this phrase is indefinite, it must be remembered that it has all the precision which he desired. On one point we may however be very explicit. He set his face like a flint against every form of sectarian exclusiveness and bigotry, and was only intolerant toward those who ventured to judge any body of believers in Christ, and to deny them the Master's name.

"Towards some views — more or less prevalent in New England of late years — he might have failed a little in preserving that 'Charity which is not easily provoked'; but on the whole, his catholicism was a marked trait in his character, which, often severely tried, was seldom found wanting. He was an earnest, plain preacher; dealing generally with practical subjects, without seeking originality of thought, or being remarkable for any graces of rhetoric.

"Perhaps, as we have already hinted, had his quotations from Scripture been more sparing, his discourses would have gained more in clearness. Alluding to this feature in his sermons, a friend remarked lately to us, 'that Dr. Pierce certainly preached the Bible.'

"But his style was that of former days; and few men have retained so much of their early acceptableness in the pulpit, owing to the impression he made upon his hearers of his own deep sincerity and unfeigned piety. You felt that he believed with his whole heart and soul everything he said, and was thoroughly in earnest. It was, however, by the daily beauty of his life as the faithful pastor, that Dr. Pierce won the confidence and affection of his people. . . . . With the same hearty simplicity he visited the rich and the poor, the refined and the unlearned, and though there were wide diversities in the social condition of the members of his society, there were none to charge him with partiality, none to doubt his friendliness and ready sympathies."

His memory has been kept fresh, and is still dear to all who knew him; and the recollections of the hallowed months of beautiful serenity and peace and faith, which made his sick room like the threshold of the heavenly kingdom, have been a ministry of holy influences to many souls.

The following lines were written for the family of Dr. Pierce.*

THE BURIAL.

LISTEN! the tolling bell
Rolls its deep cadence on the summer air;
And gathering mourners swell
The waiting numbers in the house of prayer.

Silence is on the throng, —
Save the deep organ-tones so sadly sweet;
Why lingereth so long
The pastor, ever wont his flock to meet?

---

* Inserted here by request of his daughter, Miss A. L. Pierce.

Hush! for he cometh now!
Cometh, — but not as in the days gone by;
Death's shadow marks his brow
And leaves its dimness in the half-shut eye.

He cometh, — not as when
His brisk, firm tread was heard along the aisle, —
But borne by sorrowing men,
And mourning hundreds hush their hearts the while.

The solemn service o'er
They bear him hence in silence and in tears;
Never! no never more
Those lips shall counsel as in other years.

Never! no never more!
Henceforth a void is left! A shining light,
A beacon from the shore
Is quenched, and sorrow shades us as the night.

Yet 'tis not quenched but gone!
Leaving a blank where late hath shone a star, —
But from the world unknown
The distant heaven, it shineth yet afar.

We mourn who loved him here,
And who that knew him e'er could fail to love?
Yet we would dry the tear
And strive to meet him in the world above.

The silvery locks are gone!
His voice can join our hymns of praise no more;
Heaven hath an angel won;
Father Divine! Forgive if we deplore!

In the words of his colleague, in his funeral discourse: "Simply thus to dwell upon the life of a good man is better than to have entered into a discussion of the mysteries of godliness."

MR. SAMUEL PHILBRICK.

The story of the First Church, as it was forty or more years ago, would hardly be complete without some allusion to incidents connected with the rise and growth of the anti-slavery reform and the manner in which some of the congregation were affected by it. Those who have come to mature years during or since the War of the Rebellion can scarcely have any conception of the difficulties through which the people of New England, and even our own vicinity, were educated up to the point of willingness to see slavery destroyed.

Mr. Samuel Philbrick, who was one of the pioneers in this reform at a time when a man must have had in him the courage and the perseverance of a martyr to dare identify himself with so unpopular a cause, was a worshipper at the First Church for years.

He was born and educated among the Friends or Quakers, but did not identify himself with them in later years, though his marriage was consummated according to the peculiar forms or usages of that sect. Mr. Philbrick never united with the Unitarian Church, as a member. He was a man of wealth and influence and occupied a central pew in the church. He was the friend of Garrison, May, Phillips, and others of the leading abolitionists of those days, and his house was one of the way-stations of "the underground railroad," which here and there gave brief shelter and rest for fugitives, on the way from Mason and Dixon's line to Canada.

Friend Isaac T. Hopper, whose delightful biography by Mrs. Child will be read as long as slavery is a remembered blot on our history, was often a visitor at Mr. Philbrick's house, and the Misses Grimké spent the winter of 1836–37 in his family.

These ladies, then young and wealthy, were the daughters of Judge Grimké of South Carolina. They had grown up in acquaintance with the abominations of the slave-power, and had voluntarily left their home of affluence to acquaint the people of the North with the danger which was even then threatening the nation.

They will be remembered by elderly people as the first ladies who spoke in public on this subject in this vicinity. Their first audience was composed of Brookline ladies assembled in Mr. Philbrick's parlors, which were thrown open for the purpose. It would have been impossible in the face of the prejudice of the times, to have obtained the Town Hall, or one of the churches for such a purpose. To have attempted it might have aroused a mob.

The announcement of the meeting was by cards of invitation sent to friends and acquaintances. At the appointed time the apartments were filled with ladies only, but in an ante-room, out of sight but within hearing, sat John G. Whittier, now the beloved Quaker poet, an intensely interested listener. Whether his presence in the audience would have embarrassed the speaker, or the large company of ladies would have abashed the shy and sensitive poet we are not informed, but he heard and went his way with new and fresh inspiration to write his lyrics of liberty.

During the winter which the Misses Grimké spent in Mr. Philbrick's house, a friend of the family solicited the sympathy and help of Mrs. Philbrick for a free colored woman in a neighboring city who was struggling to support herself and children. The result was that a little girl ten years of age was taken into the household to be made useful, and comfortably provided for.

On the following Sunday she was taken to church with the family and seated in their own pew, where, owing to her small size, her head did not reach to the top rail.

Mr. Philbrick had already incurred odium by identifying himself with the hated "abolitionists," and small as was the cause in this instance, it was the "fly in the pot of ointment," and conservative and aristocratic noses were elevated accordingly.

Great was the discussion and wide-spread the excitement before another Sunday, and when the day came it was necessary for the timid child to walk to church beside Mr. Philbrick's daughter that she might be protected from the insults of the boys. Even the children of the family were taunted by their school-fellows with being "*bobolitionists*," and annoyed in various ways.

The family were seated in their accustomed places, when a member of the society who could not see the child from his own pew, though he rose and stretched himself up to discover her, sent one of his children down the aisle on which he sat and up the other to look into Mr. Philbrick's pew, to ascertain whether she was actually there. To his intense disgust he learned that she was, and rising he summoned his whole family and left the church.

Viewed in the light of late events and modern times it seems too ridiculous to be true, and were it a solitary instance of negro-hatred it would not be historical. But it was the public sentiment of the times that was outraged, and the whole society, not to say all Brookline, was offended. It was a trying episode for Dr. Pierce, whose charitable spirit never allowed him to hate any human being because he was created of a different color or nationality from himself, and whose love of peace could ill endure a division and a quarrel among his people. Moreover he, like many another conscientious man of those days, could see no way in which the agitation of the slavery question could be of practical benefit to the slaves, and his motto was, "When you know not what to do, be sure not to do you know not what." Mr. Philbrick, the friend of the Grimkés and Garrison, and the slave, was beginning a dangerous agitation by bringing even a free negro child into the house of God with her friends and protectors. His course must be met with a remonstrance. Before another Sunday came he was waited upon by a committee of the society, and requested for the sake of peace, to send the child, if he must bring her to church, into the negro pew.

This, Mr. Philbrick politely but firmly declined to do. His stand on the negro question was taken, and he was not the man to commit the egregious inconsistency of not living up to it, nor to receive dictation as to the occupants of his pew. The little girl appeared at church again, and again the deeply exercised committee waited upon Mr. Philbrick, and more stringent arguments and exhortations were brought to bear. The result was that Mr. Philbrick no longer felt inclined to worship where what he considered a most unchristian spirit was being aroused, and he with his family withdrew and never entered the meeting-house again, neither did one gentleman of the family who took such great offense. The rest returned to their allegiance.

Mr. Philbrick continued to befriend the colored race whenever he could do so.

The celebrated William and Ellen Crafts were concealed for days in a back chamber of that house while the United States Marshal and his officers were hunting Boston for them. They were first taken to the Searle house in Cypress Street, where Hon. Ellis Gray Loring was then living, but it being feared that suspicion would point to that locality, they were conveyed secretly to Mr. Philbrick's, in the evening. After the hunt and excitement in Boston had somewhat subsided, the fugitives were removed from Mr. Philbrick's house by Theodore Parker, who with another gentleman and a lady, came in a cariage and started them on their way to Canada.

Mr. Philbrick outlived much of the odium attached to the name of "abolitionist," and saw their ranks swelled by thousands after the rendition of Anthony Burns. He died, however, in September, 1859, before the triumph of the principles for which he had sacrificed convenience and popularity.

In less than ten years from that time his son was supervising the industries and economies of the freedmen of South Carolina without molestation or hindrance.

The ministry of Rev. Mr. Knapp, which continued seven years, was unmarked by any striking events. He was much beloved as a pastor. He was succeeded by Rev. Dr. Hedge in October, 1856.

THE PARSONAGE. — POLLY HATCH.

We now pass to the story of the parsonage. To do so we must go back to an early period in the history of the town. The ground which has for almost a century been the site of the parsonage, was from the earliest dates till about the middle of the last century the property of the Gardners. It came into possession of the heirs of Judge Sewall, and was presented by Mrs. Walcott, as a site for the parsonage of the First Church forever. The house, in which Dr. Pierce lived and died, was built in 1781. It was first occupied by Rev. Joseph Jackson, who lived in it fifteen years. Dr. Pierce occupied it fifty-two years. It was refitted for Rev. Mr. Knapp, who lived in it during the whole of his ministry in this place. The new parsonage was built for Rev. Dr. Hedge, and the old one was sold and removed to Chestnut Place, where it still stands.

Closely identified with the family of Dr. Pierce, during the greater part of his long ministry, was an humble woman, whose obscure life better deserves a memorial than that of many a titled princess. To tell her story we must antedate the settlement of the Pierce family in Brookline.

In 1790 there came to Northampton, where the Tappan family resided, a country produce dealer, from Becket, who often supplied the people of that town with his wares. He was in great trouble, having been burned out, and lost everything except his family of a dozen children, and he besought Mrs. Tappan to take one child and give her a home and make her useful. The good lady consented, and the man brought down with him the next time he came, a little girl of six years whose name was Rebecca Hatch. There was a Rebecca already in the family, and this child was called Polly.

She soon discovered a wonderful aptitude for work, and a most grateful and affectionate devotion to the family, especially to Miss Lucy, who afterwards became Mrs. Pierce. The little girl learned to make bread when so small that she was obliged to stand upon a stool to knead it.

When Miss Tappan was married and came to Brookline, as the wife of Dr. Pierce, Polly came with them, and from that day, for forty years, no work was too hard and no sacrifice too great for this devoted servant and friend to make for them and theirs. Dr. Pierce's salary, as we have said, was but very small, and his family increased rapidly. Mrs. Pierce had enough to occupy her, with her domestic duties and the cares always belonging to a clergyman's wife, and Polly counted nothing toilsome or irksome that she could do for the friends she loved so well.

The little economies she practiced to help make the family income adequate were marvelous.

Her wages were small, as was common in those days, yet she laid up little by little her scanty earnings, spending almost nothing for dress, for which she seemed to care nothing, but wore whatever was given her by friends in the parish, and the relatives of the family. She was skilled in every branch of household work, and not only did faithfully the washing, ironing, cleaning, and cooking for the large family, but for years never slept without one child of the family under her care, and carried about a sickly infant of the family upon her hip, singing to it during her morning work. She was not required to do this, but chose to do it. At last there came to the family that saddest of misfortunes, a hopelessly imbecile and helpless child. Then shone out the beautiful spirit of devoted self-sacrifice which made Polly's life worthy to be written. She claimed poor unfortunate Benny as her charge, and took care of him for four years by night and day with untiring patience and love. The child was then sent from home to board for some years. At the age of eighteen he was taken home again as helpless as ever, and Polly resumed her care of him as before.

Yet she never abated her energy in other directions, but went on with all the household work, in a manner that made her name a synonym for efficiency, in the parish as well as in the family, and the idea that she was equal to almost any emergency was laughably illustrated in a curious incident.

When the church was struck by lightning, August 12, 1834, there was a town meeting being held in the old stone Town House. A venerable gentleman, who was one of the Selectmen, ran down to the parsonage, calling out "Polly! Polly! Polly!" As if Polly could put out a fire on the roof of the meeting-house. The fire was extinguished without serious damage.

The terrors of the fire which deprived her of her home in her childhood so impressed her mind that she never retired at night till she had seen the last light extinguished, not even trusting Dr. Pierce himself to take care of the fire and lights. Long before the dawn of day she was at her tasks; pleasure-seeking, in the common acceptation of the term, she entirely ignored. She was always cheerful, but she found her pleasure in serving others. In the goodness of her heart she used to go on Mondays, once a month, to the church and sweep it, before the Sunday fires were out, to assist Mr. Stone, the sexton, because he was poor, and had many young children, and her assistance would save his time for his business as a carpenter.

Many a longed-for toy, or book, or pleasure which the children of the family would have otherwise been obliged to forego, was purchased out of Polly's little store. All these years she had heard no word from her own relatives. They seemed to forget or give her up entirely, having moved out of the State, and she did not even know whither they went. Polly had several lovers in her youth, plain though she was, and quaint and antiquated in her dress at all times. But she met none of their advances with favor, her heart seeming to remain untouched. With all her hard work and plain appearance, and narrow round of duties, Polly was not an ignorant woman, though she had little school education. But she was cultivated in her taste for books, and had an innate refinement which shrank from coarseness of any kind. Her knowledge of books was acquired more by listening than by reading, as she delighted in having the children of the family come to the kitchen and read aloud while she pursued her various avocations. Often they followed her from room to room, reading Scott, or other authors to her. In this way she learned and could repeat from memory large portions of "Marmion," "The Lady of the

Lake," "Lord of the Isles," the whole of Parnell's "Hermit," and much of the poetry of other authors.

An evidence of her remarkable memory was discovered in her early youth, when she was living with the Tappan family at Northampton. Mr. Lucas, a Brookline gentleman, came to that town with Dr. Pierce. He was on his way to Deerfield, and he told the young folks of the Tappan family that if any one of them would commit to memory the twenty-sixth chapter of the book of Acts, so as to repeat it to him on his return, *verbatim*, he would give the successful one a silver dollar. All the children tried, but only Polly won the prize.

When some of Dr. Pierce's daughters were in their gay days of youth, there was a sleighing party in the winter, to which they were invited by young gentlemen from Cambridge. After the party had been gone some hours, a sudden and severe snow-storm came on. It proved to be so formidable that the young people started for home, but the snow blocked the roads so that the horses could scarcely make their way through it. Polly sat up waiting their return with fire and lights.

Before they came, the snow lay two feet deep between the front door and the street. Twice, she went out alone in the dark and driving storm, and shoveled a path from the door to the gate. But her benevolence did not stop there. She knew it would be impossible for the young gentlemen to reach Cambridge that night, and the horses must be taken care of. She therefore made her way with a lantern, to the barn, and actually shoveled away the snow which prevented the door from being opened, and when the young people arrived past midnight, chilled through, and the exhausted horses ready to drop, she had all things in readiness for the "entertainment of man and beast," took care of them all herself, in spite of every remonstrance, and was on the alert early in the morning as if nothing unusual had happened.

Nothing ever seriously disturbed or made her unhappy but opposition in her self-sacrifice for the family. If refused, or prevented from carrying out her purposes in this respect, her quickly starting tears bore evidence how genuine was the feeling that prompted them.

Her practice of often spending money for the young people of the family was sometimes very embarrassing to them, but no remonstrance was of any avail. In this particular she would have her own way. An inconvenience always severely felt at the parsonage was the want of a cistern to hold soft water. Dr. Pierce at one time went away upon a journey, and during his absence, Polly secured the coöperation of Capt. Benjamin Bradley, who was a carpenter, and before the Doctor's return, a cistern was built for the sum of fifty dollars, and paid for out of Polly's money. When the Doctor came home, and learned what had been done, he insisted upon paying Polly for the outlay at once. But she burst into tears, insisted that she had had it done for her own convenience, and a pleasant surprise to him, and that it would break her heart if he insisted upon it further. The matter was allowed to drop, but a long time afterwards the Doctor found an opportunity of making it up to her.

At the marriage of each of Dr. Pierce's children, a present was bestowed upon the bride by Polly, quite equal to the gifts of other friends, in those times. At the birth of each grandchild, till there were ten, she deposited in the bank five dollars for the new comer. This practice Dr. Pierce positively forbade, but it was vain to try to prevent the devoted creature from impoverishing herself for others.

At one time when a poor divinity student, who had

been often to see the Doctor, was leaving the house, the Doctor inquired why he wore no overcoat on so cold a day. He confessed that he had none. Polly overheard the conversation. Shortly afterwards, the young man received a present of a new overcoat. It was Polly's gift, but the recipient never knew whence it came, and even the family were not aware of this act of generosity for many years. It was finally disclosed by the person whom she deputed to make the purchase.

In 1830, when Polly had lived in the family of Dr. Pierce nearly thirty years, a person from a neighboring town, who had been on a trip to western New York, called to see Dr. Pierce, to inquire respecting her. He had met with a brother of hers, who finding that he was from the vicinity of Boston, made inquiries respecting "Rev. Mr. Pierce," who had taken Polly from Northampton. It was over twenty years since she had known whether she had a relative living. It was washing-day, and Polly stood at the tub, when the Doctor announced the startling news that she had two brothers and a sister living, and that they had taken the trouble to inquire respecting her. Polly was like one thunderstruck. She stood in silence for a moment, and then fell senseless upon the floor. It was some time before consciousness returned, and the manner in which she was affected was the more remarkable, from the fact that she was never known to faint before. Nothing would satisfy her but she must go and see her kindred, wholly forgetful of their long indifference to her. Her visits had been confined to annual trips to Boston all those many years, but nothing daunted, she set out on her journey, found her people, made them a four weeks' visit, and then returned to the parsonage.

A few years after, Polly asked leave of absence for a

whole year. This was granted, and she went to her friends, and devoted herself to their interests with her time and money.

At the expiration of that time she returned. Polly had scarcely ever had a letter in her lifetime, but now letters began to come, regularly and often, so that one day the Doctor returning from the post-office with a letter, said jokingly, as he delivered it, "What is the matter, Polly? Are you *engaged?*" "Yes sir," said Polly, meekly, and burst into tears.

Had the earth opened in front of the parsonage, the astonishment would scarcely have been greater. Polly, almost fifty-nine years of age, and as much identified with the parsonage as one of the rafters, about to launch her fortunes on the uncertain sea of matrimony!

It is doubtful if any engagement since then has created a greater sensation in the little circle concerned.

A lonely widower, a New York Dutchman, by the name of Schermerhorn, had found the way to Polly's sympathies, he was "so lonesome and she pitied him so;" yet warmly as her heart went out toward him, there was a link at the old parsonage that must not be broken.

There was poor Benny, and the infatuated lover could not have Polly without he would take Benny also, if the pastor's family would consent to let him go.

The terms for his board were agreed upon, satisfactorily to all parties. It was a service such as money could not buy, and only pure love could suggest, and as such it was appreciated by the family. The difficulty of removing him was less than might be supposed, as he had never grown beyond the size of a delicate child of twelve years. Polly's lover was about seventy years of age, and too feeble to make the long journey to take his bride; and it was arranged that her nephew should come on and take her and her helpless charge to their destination.

Polly had to undergo some bantering respecting the arrangement of going to her lover, instead of being carried thither as a bride by himself, but her serenity could not be disturbed, and she made her preparations, and bade farewell to Brookline and the parsonage forever.

She was married in her husband's own house, October 1, 1843. When she had been married a year, she wrote her old friends, that she was "more troubled by the bad grammar spoken by the people around her than by anything else." Trouble of that nature would be as light as one could reasonably expect in this life, it would seem.

From that time forward, Polly was visited once a year by one or more of Dr. Pierce's family, greatly to her delight. Her devotion to poor Benny continued unremitting, and her husband — who seemed so adapted to Polly's own heart, that one could well apply to them the adage, respecting the celestial origin of matches — was as kind to him as she could desire.

After six years, when Benny was thirty-two years of age, he was found one morning, dead in his bed, having given no signs of illness. The same Providence which had mysteriously darkened his intellect, and made his earthly life a blank, had doubtless wakened him to the full joys of a complete existence; for if He careth for the sparrows when they fall, surely He careth for such.

Mr. Schermerhorn was a Methodist, and held daily family worship. It was his practice to sing a long hymn after reading the Scriptures. Polly could not sing a note, but she sat beside her old husband, who held her hand in his, and gazed up in his face with a love and reverence that redeemed the situation from ludicrousness, and might have gone far toward convincing youthful skepticism, that the heart never grows old. Thus they lived for twenty years, and then the tie which had united this peculiar pair was broken by the death of the wife. Polly died of congestion of the lungs, in December, 1863, the same disease of which Mrs. Pierce, after years of serene and beautiful old age, had died not long before.

Her life had been one long, devoted service to others. Those who disbelieve in pure, unselfish love, and deny the existence of disinterested benevolence, may make what they can of the simple, unvarnished story of Polly's life.

One cannot but wonder how such a nature could be happy in heaven with no misery there to alleviate, no sorrow with which to sympathize, and no laborious services to perform.

Three years later the widower followed the partner for whom he sincerely mourned, and a memorial stone marks the last resting-place of Polly and her husband, and poor Benny.

The one text for an epitaph, fitting for her memory, suggested itself to the minds of her old friends at the parsonage, and was inscribed upon the stone: "Many daughters have done virtuously, but thou excellest them all."

CHAPTER XIV.

THE GARDNER FAMILY AND HOUSES. — THE BOYLSTON, OR HYSLOP PLACE (COLONEL LEE'S). — THE ACKERS PLACE. — OLD INDIAN BURIAL PLACE.

THE ancient Gardners of Brookline were large landowners, and once formed no inconsiderable part of the population. As they were chiefly gathered near the church and parsonage, though some branches of the family settled further off, perhaps this is the proper place to introduce them.

The early inhabitants of Brookline were recorded on the documents of the town of Roxbury as often or oftener than on those of Boston. The Gardners are traceable, in births, marriages, and deaths, on the Roxbury records. The name of Thomas occurs earliest and oftenest, like Robert among the Sharps, Ebenezer among the Davises, and Samuel, among the Clarks.

The first Thomas Gardner died in 1639, being "an householder." He of course was an Englishman, and from the records it would seem that he was the head of the large and wide-spread family which bears his name.

The second Thomas Gardner, son of the above, was also born in England. He married Lucy Smith of Roxbury in 1641, and settled in Brookline. He was a member of the Roxbury Church in 1650, and paid an annual tax of thirteen shillings for the support of a Roxbury school. This was probably kept in the ancient schoolhouse which formerly stood where the gas-works now are, as that part of Brookline was then in Roxbury. This man being the father of eight children, would doubtless take an interest in the support of the school. No school was then kept in Muddy River.

In 1672, when the people of Roxbury decided to build "a nue Metting-hous," and permit the people of " Mudi-river" to share in its privileges if they would bear one fifth of the expense, we find the list of Brookline taxpayers for this object headed by Thomas Gardner, who paid ten pounds, that being the largest amount paid by any man in the place. The amount raised was £104 13s. His brother Andrew paid five pounds.

Thomas Gardner died in 1689. He left a will providing for his sons Thomas and Joshua, and his four daughters who survived. His daughter Mary had married Thomas Boylston, one of the earliest of an old Brookline family. The school mentioned above was kept by Andrew Gardner, probably a nephew of Thomas, in 1698.

Andrew Gardner's son Andrew, was a preacher in Lancaster in 1696. He was accidentally shot by a soldier in that town in 1704. The account given in the "Boston News Letter," is as follows: —

"*Boston.* In our Number 28, as we then received it, we gave you the account of the Death of the Rev. Mr. Gardner, Minister of Lancaster; and having since had a perfect and exact account of the same from Eye and Ear witnesses; we thought it expedient to insert it here, to prevent various reports thereof. And is as follows: —

"That a man being killed the day before, between Groton and Lancaster, and the Indians being seen the night before nigh the town, Mr. Gardner, (three of the men belonging to his Garrison being gone out of Town, and two of the remaining three being tyred with Watching and Travelling in the Woods after the Indians that day), being a very careful as well as courageous man, concluded to watch that night himself; and accordingly went out into the little watch-house that was over the Flankers, and there stayed till late in the night, whence and when he was coming down (as it was thought) to warm him. The man that shot him, who was not long before sleeping by the fire, came out and whether between sleeping and waking, or surprised with an excess of fear, fired upon him as he was coming down out of the watch-house through a little trap-door into the Flanker, where no man having the exercise of his Reason could suspect the coming of an enemy, or suspect him to be so when in a clear Moonlight he was so nigh him.

"Mr. Gardner (though his wound was in his Breast being shot through the vitals), came to the door, bid them open it for he was wounded; after he came in he fainted away, but coming to himself again, asked who it was that shot him, and when they told him he prayed God to forgive him, and forgave him himself, for he believed he did not do it on purpose; and with a composed Christian frame of spirit, desired them that were bitterly lamenting over him not to weep but to pray for him, and comforted his sorrowful wife, telling her he was going to Glory, advising her to follow him; and in about an hour Dyed, leaving his sorrowful friends to lament the loss of so worthy and desirable a person." *

Thomas, another of the sons of the first Andrew, was a captain in the Canada expedition, under Sir William Phipps, in 1690, in which he lost his life, as did Robert Sharp, and other Brookline men.

The third Andrew Gardner born in this town was a graduate of Harvard College, in 1712, and was ordained minister of Worcester in 1719. He was subsequently settled in Lunenburg, but after his removal from that town in 1732 we lose trace of him.

Peter Gardner, brother of the second Thomas, was also a resident of this town, and had a large family of children. His son Samuel was killed by the Indians when nineteen years of age.

* *Boston News Letter*, No. 31, November 20, 1704.

There was also a Thomas, but the third Thomas in the regular line of succession, born in 1676, bore a more prominent part in the affairs of the town, and was chosen first deacon of the First Church. Of him we have more to say hereafter.

Joshua Gardner, his brother, married Mary, daughter of John Weld of Roxbury, in 1681. His house stood a little east of the present parsonage on ground now belonging to Mr. Kennard. This house of Mr. Joshua Gardner, according to Judge Sewall's journal, was burnt on the night of Sunday, January 11, 1691, and two of his children perished in the flames. What a glimpse of domestic vicissitude in those early days this incident thus barely and briefly mentioned, opens to the imagination. How did the fire originate? Where were the parents? Who came to help, on seeing the red light of the flames above the thick woods, for there was neither bell, nor engine, nor means of relief — and why were the little ones not saved, curiosity asks in vain. Nearly a year later, the Judge enters in his journal the following, under date of December 21: —

"Went with Mr. Addington and wife to the new house of Joshua Gardner, where were Mr. Walter and wife, Mr. Dennison and wife, Sir Ruggles and Mrs. Weld. At dinner Mr. Walter asked the blessing, and Mr. Dennison returned thanks on account of completing their new house."

This Mr. Walter was the Rev. Nehemiah Walter, then minister of the church on Roxbury Hill. Sir Ruggles Weld was doubtless Mrs. Gardner's uncle. In this house lived afterwards the Caleb Gardner who gave the land for the First Church.

It was a little singular that when Brookline was thinly inhabited, and fire by no means a common occurrence, three different dwelling-houses owned and occupied, by the Gardners should have been burned. Mr. Nathaniel Gardner, a son of the deacon previously mentioned, was a merchant in Boston, and lived in a house on the spot now occupied by the house of Mr. Chapin opposite the Reservoir. The Boston "News-Letter" of April 17, 1740, contains the following: —

"Last Monday, A. M. 14 April 1740, the house of Nathaniel Gardner of Brookline, next to the Meeting-house in that town took fire and was burned down, but most of the household goods saved. It was occasioned by a chimney's being on fire, the sparks falling on the roof catched in the shingles, which being very dry burnt so violently, as 'twas impossible to put a stop thereto."

The third Gardner house which was burnt was that of Isaac Gardner in Brighton Street, of which an account was given in the account of that street. He was a grandson of Deacon Thomas Gardner.

We now return to Deacon Thomas Gardner, also called Lieutenant (probably in the Indian wars). His name is one of the first on the petition for a separation of this town from Boston. He was evidently a man of property and much influence. He married Mary Bowles, daughter of Elder John Bowles, and had seven children. In 1718 he built the old house now owned by the Goddard heirs, and occupied by George W. Stearns. His three sons, Solomon, Caleb, and Benjamin successively owned and occupied it after him. Benjamin was succeeded in it by his son Deacon Elisha Gardner, who however sold the place to Mr. John Goddard, and removed to the old Walley house, — it was new then, however, — where he spent the rest of his days, and died in 1797. Captain Benjamin Gardner having left the house above mentioned, to his son, built a house for himself early in the last century, on Heath Street, almost to Newton line, next the house known as the old Richards Tavern. He died in 1762, leaving the house to his son Samuel, who, however, died about ten years afterwards at the age of forty-three. His son Caleb, then only sixteen years of age, was the next heir. The Revolutionary War was coming on, and the boy, too young to bear arms, but too old to submit to stay peacefully at home in those exciting days, went as attendant upon General Wesson, and followed his fortunes during the various campaigns in which he engaged. After the war was over he returned, married Mary Jackson of Newton, and settled upon the old place. He died in 1807, at the age of fifty-two. His widow lived to be ninety-two. Of his six children, the wife of Deacon Timothy Corey was one, and two of the other daughters are still living in this town. His son Samuel Jackson Gardner was a graduate of Harvard College, class of 1807, having, after such advantages as the Brookline schools could give, been fitted for college at Leicester Academy. He made the law his profession, and for twenty years did a prosperous business in Roxbury, which town he represented in the Legislature. He subsequently removed to Newark, N. J., where he became editor of the "Newark Daily Advertiser." He was an old Whig, a Unitarian of the Channing school, and possessed a mind peculiarly adapted to the pursuits of literature. Genial, witty, and versatile, he won hosts of friends. He died while on a visit to the White Mountains, in July, 1864, aged seventy-six, and was brought to Brookline, and laid in the Gardner tomb.

His son, Dr. Augustus Gardner, still living in New York, is the last male descendant of this line of the old Gardner family. He is known as the author of several books, on various subjects, among which is a treatise on "Copper," also a book of foreign travel, entitled "New Wine in Old Bottles."

The ancient house of Capt. Benjamin Gardner, still standing on Heath Street, is shaded by a grand old elm, which was set out and protected by the Gardners of the last century.

The ancient house in which Deacon Thomas Gardner lived in his last days, and where he died, was sold as above mentioned, by his grandson, Deacon Elisha Gardner, to Mr. John Goddard, the father of the late Benjamin Goddard, and has ever since been in that family.

The land which originally belonged to Caleb Gardner, after his father's death, and was attached to the house now occupied by George W. Stearns, included all the Goddard lands, and Bradley's Hill (before Mr. Walley's time), extending northward to the brook, and eastward to Cypress Street, as when Cypress Street was laid out it was ordered, that it should run "through the land of Thomas Cotton, and thence through the land belonging to Caleb Gardner.

As Boylston Street was not laid out till within the present century, the old Gardner house, standing just at the curve of the old Sherburne road, had only green fields and thick woods lying about it, there being no other house in sight, except Nathaniel Gardner's house, — on the site of the present residence of Mr. Chapin.

Deacon Gardner built his house for two centuries at least, judging from the substantial work he put into it. There is very little cellar room, for the good reason that nearly all that might have been cellar is chimney-work. The three stacks of chimneys contain bricks enough for a moderate-sized modern house. The walls of the house are laid in large coarse brick, plastered with clay, between the outside and inside, to the very roof. The immense timbers are of solid oak, as are also the floors. The rooms are sheathed with paneled woodwork, presenting a painted surface, which might well dismay a modern housekeeper. The doors are braced with long and strong iron hinges, reaching half across their width, and some of them were opened by great wooden latches which lifted by a string, one of which remains till the present time. Closets of all sorts in most unexpected places, were planned for the good housewife's convenience. Each of the front rooms had a recess, closed up with doors of paneled wood-work, concealing a bed turned up against the wall. A deep window seat was also provided with a cover to lift, disclosing a box or chest; the fire-place in this room is surrounded by blue and white Dutch tiles, covered with the most grotesque illustrations of Scripture history. Nearly all are perfectly intelligible, but in a few the "high art," baffles modern ingenuity to explain. The L on the north side was at first but one story high, and a second story window in the main house, which looked in that direction, was of diamond panes in leaden sash, evidently brought from England, as the house was built long before glass was made in this country, — this window is now closed up. Trap-doors in the floors, in the second story, indicate the method of "getting up stairs," before stairs were built. After the present occupants had lived twenty-one years in the house, a secret room in the second story was discovered. It was perfectly dark, and only accessible by a ladder, after removing a sliding board. No time was lost in exploring the unknown apartment, but nothing was found except an ancient sword, bearing a device, which might be explained by one who understands heraldry. It may have been the coat-of-arms of the old English Gardners. This room had been used by former occupants of the house as a place for secreting valuables, but had been forgotten, or never mentioned, so that its discovery by the present occupants was a complete surprise. Further investigation during the progress of some alterations, which were being made for convenience' sake, resulted in the exhuming of an old cannon ball, from between the chimney and the beams, where it had lain for perhaps a century. Samuel Parkman was a resident of this house for several years. Hon. Jonathan Mason made it his country seat for several summers. These residents hired it of the late Benjamin Goddard. Scores of people have been born under this humble roof, and very many have been carried out through its doorway to their last narrow house. Perhaps none of these thus indicated, have brought more honor to an humble home than George Theodore Stearns, the eldest son of the present tenant, who went at his country's summons to defend the imperiled government in the late Rebellion. Opposed in taste and principles to war and fighting, he did not volunteer, but when drafted, no persuasion could induce him to send a substitute, "because," he said, "he would peril no other man's life to save his own, if his country needed his services." He went like a hero, and like a hero fell, in the blood and fire of the Wilderness. He was carried from the scene of carnage to a Washington hospital, where he lingered a little while, and then passed on to his reward, as truly a martyr for conscience' sake, as a Reformer burned at the stake.

The gambrel-roofed house, opposite the Reservoir, now occupied by Mr. Chapin, was built in 1740, by Nathaniel Gardner, the same year that his first house was destroyed by fire. It was afterwards owned by Deacon

Benjamin White, who was contemporary with Thomas Gardner in the office of deacon of the First Church.

The next owner was Jeremiah Gridley, Esq., a graduate of Harvard University in 1725. He was a lawyer of note, so much so that President J. Q. Adams spoke of him as among the most distinguished in his profession. He several times represented the town in the State Legislature, and held various other offices of trust and importance in the town. He lived a single life, and died in the house of which we are writing, in 1767, at the age of sixty-five. Dr. Pierce quotes Rev. Dr. Elliott, author of "New England Biography," as saying, "that his legal knowledge was unquestionable;" but adds, "he died poor because he despised *wealth.*"

The next person who inhabited the house was Henry Hulton, Mandamus Counselor for the British Government. He was one of the five commissioners appointed by Parliament to receive the revenue derived from the odious stamp act, and the tax on tea, paints, etc. He arrived in Boston, "clothed with a little brief authority," in November, 1767. He purchased the house in question for his country-seat, and spent his summers here, and his winters in Boston.

Parties of British officers often rode out to his house — and their visits kept the people of Brookline in a constant state of irritation. As one after another of the hated acts were passed, and the spirit of rebellion burned deeper in the hearts of the people, the "Mandamus Counselor," who was quietly pocketing their money for King George, grew more and more distasteful, till finally the boys of Brookline assembled and smashed his windows. The father of the late Charles Heath was one of the party. One can imagine the gusto with which they did it, and the satisfaction they felt going home. Very likely they were wholesomely reproved by their parents for an act which so far as it went was the outgrowth of the same spirit which marshalled their fathers on Lexington Green a few months later.

Counselor Hulton subsequently took up his quarters in Boston till the Colonists made that place too hot for him, and then he returned to England, and his Brookline property was forfeited to the government, he being a refugee. Two or three other owners, of no special note, followed, each occupying the place but a short time, and then it was for several years owned by William Hyslop, a wealthy gentleman. His estate included land afterwards owned by the Murdocks on Warren Street, and now a part of the grounds of Ignatius Sargent, Esq. He gave to the town the triangular piece of ground in the fork of the roads, west of the church, for a site for the old brick school-house in 1793.

Next came John Carnes, who owned the land on the hill in the rear of the Unitarian Church, and of him the society purchased the building lot in 1805.

Mrs. Elizabeth Partridge, a wealthy widow, was the next occupant, and then came Thomas Sumner, Esq., who lived there many years, and ended his days under its roof. He was one of the Selectmen of Boston when Boston was a town. He used to relate an incident which occurred when he held that office, when at the March meeting one after another left, till only twenty men remained. The annual appropriations had been left till the last article, and this important business for the great town was disposed of by these twenty.

The results might have been startling under some circumstances, but we do not know that any harm arose from it.

Mr. Sumner's land extended as far as where the parsonage land begins, on **Walnut Street**. It was well supplied with fruit trees, and the kindly disposed old gentleman gained popularity with the boys of the stone school-house and protected his fruit, by appropriating a sweet apple tree, and two or three cherry trees exclusively to their use.

He took delight in seeing a tree full of boys shouting with pleasure, as they availed themselves of his generosity, and neither bored them with lectures on the dangers of climbing, nor cautioned them about breaking the limbs of the trees, but gave them the unchecked freedom of the trees. The boy would have been tabooed by his school-fellows who could have been mean enough to touch other than the tree thus generously assigned them.

Mr. Sumner occasionally appeared on the great rock next the sidewalk, nearly opposite the school-house, with pockets laden with apples which he tossed among the boys to see them scramble for them.

His white locks and affable manners will always be kindly remembered by the boys whom he thus propitiated, as well as by many others.

NEIGHBORHOOD OF THE RESERVOIR, THE BOYLSTON PLACE.

On the site of the present residence of Mrs. Bowditch, near the Reservoir, formerly stood a large house, owned and occupied by Richard Sullivan, Esq. He was succeeded by Judge Jackson. He was judge of the Supreme Court ten years. He also rendered important services on the Commission which reported the Revised Statutes of Massachusetts, in 1835.* Both these gentlemen were distinguished for their elegance of manner and genial traits, as well as for high culture, and the house was the resort of many distinguished persons. The place was next owned

* Allen's *American Biographical Dictionary*.

by the late John E. Thayer, who removed the old house and made preparations for building a new one, when the work of constructing the Brookline Reservoir was commenced, and it was thought it would damage the location, and consequently he chose a new site and built upon Warren Street. Mr. Benjamin Howard of Boston next purchased this fine place, built the present house, and lived here eleven years. During the time of his residence here, his son Chandler Howard, at that time a rising young merchant, widely known, and much beloved for the excellence of his character, lost his life by an accident with his horse while riding to Boston over the Mill-dam. Within a few years after, a sister of Mr. Howard met the same fate in almost the same way, while riding near the Cook place on Warren Street. Two such tragedies in one family in a short time, were enough to overshadow the brightest household, and the remnant of the family left Brookline not long afterwards. The place was then purchased by its present owners.

The ground now covered by the Reservoir was a large meadow lying lower than the level of the street. The embankment on the side next the street is wholly artificial. Instead of being a disadvantage to the vicinity as many persons feared, the great improvement caused by the Reservoir is apparent to all.

The part of Boylston Street, from the gate-house of the Reservoir to the junction of Heath Street and Brighton Street, it should be remembered is a part of the old road, and was merely widened when the turnpike was built, but was not turned from its course. On the north side of it, between these points, are three very old and interesting places.

The large, old-fashioned wooden house on Boylston Street, opposite the westerly end of the Reservoir, now owned by Henry Lee, Esq., was known for many years as the old Boylston house, — afterwards, for many years more, as the Hyslop place. It is one of the most interesting historical places in the town.

Thomas Boylston came to this country from England and settled in Watertown in 1635. His son Thomas, born in that town in 1644, became a surgeon. He took an active part in the Narragansett war. He married Mary Gardner of Muddy River, in 1665, and settled upon the place which we are describing, and from that time forward the Boylstons were identified with Brookline. There were twelve children of this marriage. His son Peter inherited the homestead. One of the daughters, Susanna, married John Adams, of Braintree, and was the mother of John Adams, second President of the United States. The second child of Dr. Thomas Boylston, was the eminent Dr. Zabdiel Boylston, born in 1680, who acquired wide celebrity and at first a most unenviable one, by the introduction of inoculation for the small-pox. His memoir has been written, and is full of interest.* The small-pox was making fearful ravages in Boston in 1721, when the Rev. Cotton Mather communicated to Dr. Boylston an account of the transactions of the Royal Society respecting inoculation as practiced in Turkey. Instead of allowing the disease to be taken in its natural way, the chances being that more than one sixth of the patients would die, the matter was forestalled by preparing the system for it by medical treatment and then scarifying the skin and applying the virus under a nutshell. Under inoculation it was seldom that a patient lost his life. The practice was not even begun in England when Cotton Mather suggested it to Dr. Boylston for experiment. He introduced the subject to the attention of other physicians in Boston

* See *American Med. Biography*, by J. Thacher.

and vicinity, and was met with violent opposition; the medical men, both in this country and in England, taking the ground that it was a crime which came under the classification of poisoning, while the clergy preached against it, and wrote pamphlets, arguing that the small-pox was a judgment from God for the sins of the people, and that to try to check its sway would only "*provoke Him the more.*"

A sermon was preached by a Rev. Mr. Massey, in 1722, against "The Dangerous and Sinful Practice of Inoculation," from the text, "So Satan went forth from the presence of the Lord, and smote Job with sore boils from the sole of his foot unto his crown," — from whence he argued that *the Devil was the first inoculator and Job his first patient.* Some fifty years afterward an epigram appeared in the "Monthly Miscellany," on this sage opinion of the Rev. Mr. Massey, as follows: —

> "We're told by one of the black robe,
> The Devil inoculated *Job;*
> Suppose 'tis true, what he does tell,
> Pray neighbors, did not *Job do well?*"

The inhabitants of Boston and vicinity became so excited, that men patrolled the streets with halters, in search of the Doctor, threatening to hang him to the nearest tree. The Doctor was secreted fourteen days in his own house, in a hiding-place known only to his wife. During this time the house was repeatedly searched for him, by day and by night, without success. One evening, a hand-grenade was dashed through the parlor window, where his wife and children were sitting. Fortunately the fuse was knocked off against a piece of furniture, and the family escaped death.

The Doctor could only visit his patients in the night, and in disguise. Yet, notwithstanding all this violence, he was brave enough to persevere with his experiments, being sanguine of success. He inoculated his own child and two servants, and though they all had the disease mildly and recovered, the authorities of Boston summoned him before them to answer for his practice. He underwent repeated examinations, and received insults and threats. During the year, however, he inoculated two hundred and eighty-six persons, of all ages, from infancy to old age, of whom only six died, while of five thousand seven hundred and fifty-nine, who took it in the natural way during the same period, eight hundred and forty-four died. The success of the practice was established, but the opposition did not cease. During this time the Doctor was in correspondence with the court physician in England, Sir Hans Sloane, and was invited to visit London. This invitation he accepted, and on his arrival he was treated with great attention, and was made a " Fellow of the Royal Society," one of the first Americans thus honored. He remained in England a year and a half and then returned.

As he grew somewhat infirm with years, he retired from his profession, which had kept him much in Boston, and devoted himself to his farm in Brookline, which he bought of his brother Peter, and on which he built the present house. He was greatly interested, and very successful in improving the breed of various domestic animals, especially horses, for which his farm became celebrated. He often broke the animals himself, being a fine horseman. His biographer speaks of him as having been seen in Boston after he was eighty-four years of age, riding a fine colt he was breaking. He lived to see inoculation universally practiced. This custom prevailed till it was superseded by vaccination, as practiced by Dr. Waterhouse, in Cambridge, and Dr. Aspinwall, in Brookline. He died at the age of eighty-seven, and was buried in Brookline Cemetery. His epitaph is said to be a just and appropriate one: —

"Sacred to the memory of Zabdiel Boylston, Esq., and F. R. S., who first introduced the practice of inoculation into America. Through a life of extensive benevolence, he was always faithful to his word, just in his dealings, affable in his manners, and after a long sickness in which he was exemplary for his patience and resignation to his Maker, he quitted this mortal life in a just expectation of a happy immortality, March 1st, 1766."

It is said that Dr. Boylston, in his will, bequeathed his house and farm to the town, as a home for the poor, on certain conditions, to which one of his relatives was expected to accede, but this not being complied with, the town missed the donation.

From Dudley Boylston, a brother of the Doctor, who married Susanna Gardner, descended the first wife of the late Deacon Joshua C. Clark. Her daughters are the last of this old family, in Brookline. From Thomas, another brother, descended Thomas, who died in London, a wealthy merchant, who made bequests to the city of Boston. His sister Mary married a Hallowell. One of her sons became Admiral Sir Benjamin Hallowell, of the British Navy. Another of her sons, preferring the family name of his mother to that of his father, changed his name to Ward Nicholas Boylston. He became a merchant of London, acquired great wealth, and was distinguished for his liberality. He returned to his native place, and lived for several years in Roxbury, and afterwards in Princeton. He gave large bequests to many charitable enterprises, and munificent donations to Harvard College and the Boylston Medical Society and Library.

Thomas Boylston, the son of another brother, settled in School Street, Boston, and was identified with Brattle Street Church. He endowed a Professorship at Harvard College. He directed his executors to purchase the homestead of his ancestors in Brookline, and convey the same to the First Church in this town, on condition that the church officers would allow his nephew, Joshua Boylston, to live upon the place, for which he should pay a rent of ten pounds annually to the church. The estate was to be entailed in the male line from this heir, in the same way from generation to generation, and failing the heir, who should have the right to live upon it, it should go to the church. But the property was in the hands of Mr. William Hyslop, who had bought it of the Doctor's heirs, and the Brookline Church never received the intended bequest, neither did Joshua Boylston ever have a male heir, and with him the family name became extinct in Brookline.

THE HYSLOPS.

Mr. William Hyslop, the purchaser of the Boylston house, was a native of Scotland. He came to this country in his youth, and began business as a peddler of dry goods, which he carried from house to house in a pack upon his back. He was very successful in this humble beginning, and having invested money in goods at a fortunate time and way, he was able to enter the dry goods trade still more extensively, and became very wealthy.

He had a son of the same name, the one mentioned as having lived for some years in the house now occupied by Mr. Chapin, a son David, and one daughter, Elizabeth, who became the wife of Governor Increase Sumner.

There was a Scotch Presbyterian clergyman with whom Mr. Hyslop was acquainted in the old country, who emigrated to Massachusetts with twenty or more of his parishioners, and settled in Worcester. His name was Abercrombie. After a residence for some time in Worcester Mr. Abercrombie removed with his people to a more congenial situation on the Pelham Hills. When this good man could number eleven " olive plants round about his table," he was suddenly left a widower. The youngest had been named Mehitable, for Mrs. Hyslop, and when the little girl was six years of age Mr. Hyslop adopted her as his own, and she remained in his family till her marriage. Mr. Hyslop's business called him occasionally to Europe, and on his return at one time he brought with him a slab, or pier table, which was supported by a pair of large spread eagles, the claws of which each clasped a round ball. It was placed between the parlor windows. This was a highly ornamental piece of furniture for those days, and as such was much admired and prized. When the Revolutionary War broke out, Mr. Hyslop was in Europe, and the contingencies of the war were such that he could not return till it was over, without imperiling his life. While the British troops occupied Boston, a great alarm was one day created in the upper part of Brookline, by a man who rode up the old road furiously, on horseback, telling all whom he met that the British troops were at the church green. This was at the green in front of the church on Roxbury Hill; but the people of the upper part of this town naturally enough supposed that the Brookline church green was meant, and great was the terror that ensued. The first impulse was to flee for safety; the second to carry off something valuable; but like distracted people at a fire, who throw mirrors out of the windows and carry mattrasses carefully down-stairs, they seized upon anything but what the British would have taken had they come.

The table with the spread eagles was hurriedly torn from the wall and laboriously carried up into the woods, which then covered the whole hill back of the house, and there buried by the servants. The little adopted daughter was not to be outdone by the rest of the family, and she secured a new pair of red bellows which hung beside the fire-place, and never let them go during the flight and the temporary absence.

Colonial troops were afterward quartered in the house; and the family took refuge in Medfield, from the fortunes of war. When a return was safe, and the buried eagles were dug up, for restoration to their proper place, one was broken. It was mended and the table replaced, being fastened to the wall with nails instead of screws, thus making the thing legally a part of the house, and not a movable article. Not many years ago the eagles were claimed by Governor Sumner's descendants as a part of their inheritance, but it was shown that they were a part of the house, and the demand was not allowed. They remained there at the last accounts, and are an appropriate adornment for the ancient and curious house. Mr. Hyslop returned after the war was over, and died in 1796, aged eighty-five years.

His son David inherited the homestead. This singular man is well remembered by many persons now living. He was lame, of uncouth figure, and such excessive homeliness of countenance as is seldom seen, amounting almost to hideousness. He also had an impediment in his speech, or rather never learned to speak plainly, always articulating his words like a little child, and the order of his mind being below the average he never acquired much education. But he inherited great wealth, and this consideration, in the eyes of many, counterbalanced all his defects.

> "Oh, what a world of vile, ill-favored faults
> Look handsome in three hundred pounds a year."

He found a wife, notwithstanding his personal peculiarities, was left a widower, and when quite advanced in years, married a lovely young girl of great personal beauty, who was sacrificed to her father's ambition for wealth. Mr. Hyslop was not a bad man, however, but his singularities were a source of annoyance or amusement to all with whom he had any dealings. He had a strange aversion to music of all kinds, and especially to the instruments used at church, and the anthems so much practiced in those times and which he always called "*tantrums*." He would not attend church on Thanksgiving days, on account of the "*tantrums*," which formed a prominent part of the service. Soon after the old gentleman brought his young bride to Brookline, a bassoon was added to the orchestra at church by Captain Robert Davis, who played well.

Mrs. Hyslop lingered one Sunday after service to hear the choir practice a little, while her husband went out for his horse. As soon as he was ready, however, he made his appearance at the church door, and beckoning to his wife he called out loudly in his broken speech, "Jane! tome! tome along! don't 'tay there to hear the *bagpipe*."

It was his custom to make a long prayer every morning before breakfast, at which every member of the household was requested to be present. He always prayed with his eyes open, and the consequence was that material things and spiritual were apt to get decidedly mixed. On one occasion, while thus praying he happened to see, through the open door into the kitchen, a monkey which he kept, making free with the sausages which had been set frying before the morning worship began. Pausing in the prayer, he interpolated a direction to "Hetty," that the sausages should be protected, and went on with his prayer without the slightest perception of anything ludicrous in the situation. His remark must have had a peculiar effect on those who had not observed the performance in the kitchen.

In the third story of the house at the southwesterly corner was a small room which was dark and only accessible through another room, and not easily noticed. (Perhaps this was where Dr. Boylston was secreted from his enemies.) This room Mr. Hyslop called his "iron 'tudy," — and it was the only "study" of which he ever made use. In this he hoarded up all the old iron he could collect on the premises, and quantities of other things useful and useless. The key he always carried with him. Articles of daily domestic use often disappeared. Inquiries and search were of no avail. After weeks or months, perhaps, the proposal often before made, that he should look in his "iron study," for the missing article, resulted in the restoration of it, as composedly returned as if no inconvenience had arisen from its absence.

Anything on the place, from a silver spoon to a bread trough, a rake or a halter, was liable to spend a season in the "iron study." His peculiar ideas were also evinced in his management of his fruit. The place abounded in choice fruit, especially peaches, plums, and cherries. These he could not use, would not sell, and did not give away. Bushels upon bushels of the finest fruit lay and perished under the trees every year.

There were two daughters and one son by this marriage, and both the former died in childhood. The son, who was a fine lad, lived till within a few days of his twenty-first birthday.

While John Adams was President of the United States,

he came to Brookline, and was the guest of Hon. Jonathan Mason, who lived on what is now Colonel Lyman's place. While there he spoke of the last time he had passed along that road as riding on horseback, carrying his mother on a pillion behind him. He never lost his interest in this home of his ancestors, and in 1821, when he was very aged, and so infirm that he was unable to walk without assistance, he expressed a wish to visit once more the old place where his mother was born, and where his grandparents had lived and died.

Accordingly, Mr. Hyslop made a dinner party, and invited the venerable ex-President, Governor Brooks, General Sumner, and other distinguished guests. It was a grand affair, and passed off with great *éclat*, but there was something pathetic in the sight of the almost helpless old man, supported by his grandson, going feebly about the place, and taking a last look of scenes once so familiar to his boyhood.

Mr. Hyslop died in 1822, at the age of sixty-seven, and thus ended the Hyslop name.

His widow married again; her second husband being Mr. John Hayden. There were no children; she survived her husband, and at her death, the Hyslop wealth, which comprised much real estate in Roxbury and Chelsea, as well as the place in Brookline, went to the heirs of Elizabeth Hyslop, and by them the homestead was sold to the present owner.

THE SEAVER, OR HAMMOND PLACE, AND THE ACKERS PLACE.

West of the old Boylston house, on the crest of the hill, was built in 1742, a house which stood until since the purchase of the place by the late Francis Fisher, Esq. All the land, as we have before mentioned, from Cypress

Street to Brighton Street, and from the old road to the brook, was held among the Gardners. John Seaver married a Gardner, and lived on the place we are describing. His son Nathaniel built the house above mentioned, and it was afterwards occupied by his son of the same name. This Nathaniel Seaver was twice married, and there were eight children; from one of the sons descended the present Seavers of Boston (Highlands). The late Mayor, Benjamin Seaver, was one of them. Nathaniel, the only son of the second marriage, was on board a vessel as supercargo, when it was wrecked, and he with the captain and part of the crew, were cast away on a desert island, where after great sufferings and hardships he died. A book was afterwards written by Captain Ockington, his brother-in-law, who was rescued, containing an account of their strange experiences, and of the death of young Seaver. His mother died young, leaving two daughters, who were afterwards married, the one to one of the Gardners, the other to Mr. John Goddard, the father of the late Benjamin Goddard. As none of the Seavers settled upon the old place, it was sold to John Deane, and afterwards to John Lucas. This man had become wealthy in the business of a baker, and retired to enjoy the fruits of his industry upon this beautiful place. He lived many years in Brookline, was an attendant upon Dr. Pierce's ministry, and showed his great regard for him by frequently taking him on journeys or short trips, bearing his expenses, and always bespeaking the best of hospitalities for him on the ground that he was his " *wife's minister.*"

Mr. Lucas died in 1812, and the place was next owned for many years by Samuel Hammond. The mansion house stood a little in front, and east of the old farmhouse which still remains, and the terrace on which it stood is still to be seen.

On the site of the house built by the late Francis
Fisher, stood a large old-fashioned house, known as the
Ackers house. John Ackers was a resident of Muddy
River in 1656, and for more than two hundred years his
descendants, to the sixth generation, have lived on or
near that spot. The first house built by this first John
Ackers, was on the west side of Brighton Street, then
called " the lane from the country road to Cambridge"
(Brighton it must be remembered was then a part of
Cambridge). This land was an interesting piece of
territory, and still is, from old associations. In 1648,
it was " Voted that Jacob Eliot should have the swamp
that joyneth to his allotment at Muddy River next to
Cotton Flax (sometimes spelt Flack's), he receiving
lybertye to cut Hedgyng wood in it for the Common
fence that runneth through the said swamp." The " Common was a part of the five hundred acres set apart by
the town of Boston at Muddy River for perpetual commonage ;" but which in time was all of it alienated, or
taken up and improved. This Jacob Eliot was the
brother of John Eliot, the famous Apostle to the Indians.
He was a deacon of the Roxbury Church, of which his
brother was minister. About the year 1640, Jacob Eliot
was appointed to lay out a highway from Boston to
Cambridge, which was laid out and trees spotted along
the old Indian trail as far as " the falls of Charles River."
All the territory on the north and northwest side of
the river, being for several years called Cambridge.
This road led along what is now Walnut Street, Heath
Street, Pound Lane, and Reservoir Lane, to Nonantum
Hill. At this place was an Indian village, or settlement
of " praying Indians," and an Indian burying-place was
located on what John Ackers bought for his farm, on
the west side of Brighton Street, including Ackers'

Avenue, and all the ground now occupied by the Irish population. There was probably an Indian village here also, as many Indian relics have been ploughed out, on this ground, as well as at Nonantum Hill. Many years after all the Indians were gone from this locality, some old Indians travelled a long distance from the west to visit these old graves of their fathers. Jacob Eliot's " Swamp," it is quite evident from old deeds, included all the meadow land from Ackers' Avenue to the new Reservoir. This Jacob Eliot died in 1651, leaving among other children a Capt. Jacob Eliot (also a deacon) and a daughter Mary, who married Theophilus Frarey of Boston. It seems that this Captain Eliot and his brother-in-law Frarey retained this property, until the death of the Captain in 1693 rendered it necessary to sell it in settlement of his estate. A curious old deed, still in possession of the Ackers family, written in 1698, bears the names of Theophilus Frarey, and the widow and children of Deacon Jacob Eliot, who joined in deeding a part or all of this land (twenty acres) to John Ackers. The cellar of the original Ackers' house was traceable within the memory of persons now living.

One of the children of Deacon Eliot, whose name with her husband's appears in this old deed, was the wife of Elizur Holyoke. This couple were the parents of Edwark Holyoke, afterwards President of Harvard College.

Three years previous to this purchase John Ackers had bought of Samuel Ruggles a tract of land on the east side of "the lane," or Brighton Street, now belonging to the heirs of the late Jacob Pierce.

These old deeds are in excellent preservation, the one containing the signature of the Eliots, bearing heavy black seals. John Ackers married *Desiretruth Thorne* of Boston, and their children " Desiretruth and Elizabeth," perhaps twins, were baptized and recorded in Roxbury in July, 1666. There were afterwards several other children, including two sons, John and William. The father afterwards moved to Dunstable, and the son John occupied the homestead. This John was a thrifty farmer, frequently buying tracts of land around him as well as woodland and marsh lands, as the ancient deeds prove. All the Ackerses have been farmers through seven generations. In the mean time, on the corner of Brighton and Boylston streets, where Mr. Fisher's house now stands, was the house of Joseph White. Nathaniel Holland married one of his daughters, and to him the place was deeded in 1695. In 1705, the same year that the town was set off and incorporated, John and William Ackers purchased the house and land.

The names of these two men and that of their father appeared on the petition for the separation of Muddy River from Boston the previous year. In 1735 William Ackers, son of the last named John, then a youth of seventeen, brought from the woods, upon his shoulder, and set out, the fine elm tree which now casts its luxuriant shadow upon the lawn. In 1744, John Ackers built a fine large house on this spot, which was quite imposing for a farm-house in those days. In Revolutionary times it was occupied as barracks for colonial troops, but the family did not leave it, as many families left their houses, but divided with the soldiers and bore the inconvenience. The old road was then much narrower in front of the house than at present. The well, where a sweep was poised for lifting the water in "the old oaken bucket," was at the foot of the grassy slope, and all the water was carried by hand with much toil, to the house and barn up the hill. The road has since been widened, and the old well is now under the sidewalk. Mr. William Ackers, second, died in 1794, at a good old age. His son William, the third of the name, was the next owner of the house. He married Mehitable Hyslop Abercrombie, the adopted daughter of Mr. William Hyslop.

Mr. Hyslop gave her a great wedding, which was a grand event in the town for those times, and was not only a theme for tea-table chat, but was remembered, talked of, and written about, long after. The sons of this marriage were outlived by their father, who died in 1841, the last male member of this ancient family.

The place was sold by the heirs to Mr. John Howe, and was purchased from him in 1850 by the late Francis Fisher. The old house was taken down, and though it had stood for more than a century it was in excellent preservation. The present fine house was built the same year.

The great elm has been preserved with assiduous care. In 1839, during a gale of wind, a large lower branch was torn from the tree and fell upon the end of the house, breaking it through. A large cavity was left in the trunk, which had increased by the action of the weather and natural decay, till the very existence of the tree was threatened. Mr. Fisher immediately set about the work of rescuing it. The cavity was carefully excavated to the solid wood; all the decay being removed, the opening was then carefully filled with bricks laid in cement, and the whole covered with a plate of lead to protect it from the weather. The dead and unsightly branches were removed, the bark scraped to destroy moss and insects, and a flower bed opened near it to admit of a constant supply of nutriment to the roots. The result was a complete renovation of the patriarchal tree. It commenced growing again with vigor, and new wood formed which from time to time pushed out the bricks till the opening was greatly reduced in size, while the girth of the tree was much increased. In 1829 the large tree nearer the street was broken in two by a weight of ice. This also was suffering from neglect, but a similar course was the means of its preservation, and new bark has nearly obliterated the marks of the injury.

It is a curious coincidence that Thomas Stedman was one of the abuttors upon the Ackers farm in 1698; and that Mr. Fisher, who is a descendant from that family, on the mother's side, should, without design, come to live in this neighborhood of his ancestor, so far removed, and beautify the grounds so familiar in their primitive wildness to his predecessors of more than a century ago.

CHAPTER XV.

THE HOUSE OF SAMUEL WHITE, ESQ., AFTERWARDS THE HEATH PLACE. — AUNT WHITE. — THE WINCHESTERS.

THE first White who settled in Brookline was John White, who came from Watertown very early in the days of the Colonial settlement, and from him all the old families of Brookline by that name have descended. He settled in "the village." Major Edward White, of whom an account has been given, was his son, as was also Joseph White who lived on the corner of Brighton and Boylston streets, before the place was purchased by the Ackers brothers. Joseph and Benjamin White both signed the petition for the separation of Muddy River from Boston, and both were prominent in founding the First Church.

Samuel White, son of Joseph, built a house on the site of the one now occupied by Mr. Cabot, between Heath and Boylston streets. This was a century before Boylston Street was opened, and the land belonging to the house extended northward across what is now Boylston Street and abutted upon "the lane," or Brighton Street, and the Ackers' lands. On the opposite side of Heath Street it extended to the Reservoir ground, which was then a part of the "Commons," or five hundred acres set apart by the town of Boston "for perpetual commonage at Muddy River." Samuel White married Ann Drew, an energetic woman of those early days, who made a practice of arranging her toilet on Sunday mornings over a tub or pail of water for lack of a looking-glass, and then walked to "Roxbury meeting-house," to attend a long day's service. After the Brookline church was established Mr. and Mrs. White were identified with it during their lifetime. In 1759, about a year before Mr. White's death, he gave by deed to the Selectmen of Brookline twenty acres of woodland at Needham, " to supply the minister or ministers that may be settled in the town from time to time." This deed was witnessed before the eminent lawyer Jeremiah Gridley, Esq., then residing in the present Chapin house, and was probably written by him. Ann, a daughter of Samuel White, became the wife of Henry Sewall, grandson of Chief Justice Sewall of this town. She had three sons, Henry, Hull, and Samuel. The two former each died at the age of twenty-four. Samuel, who outlived his parents, inherited his father's property, or the homestead. At the breaking out of the Revolutionary War, this young man, being a Loyalist or Tory, abandoned his native land and took refuge in England. The banishment act was passed in 1778, and our Brookline Tory, being proscribed as a refugee, never returned. After the close of the war the confiscated property was sold by order of Government. It was purchased by Mr. John Heath and thus passed into the hands of those from whom it afterward took the name of "the old Heath house." Samuel Sewall died unmarried at Bristol, England, in 1811.

Susanna, the other daughter of Samuel White, was the wife of Ebenezer Crafts of Roxbury, who built the house known as "the old Crafts house," on the Roxbury road, now Tremont Street. Its date, 1709, upon the chimney, is familiar to all. Mr. John Heath married Mr. Ebenezer Crafts' daughter, and thus, by this purchase, Mrs. Heath came to live in the house of her grandfather. One branch of the Goddard family (Samuel Goddard) also descended from this daughter of Samuel White. There was also an intermarriage several years before between the White and Crafts families. Mrs. Elizabeth (Crafts) White was one of the most interesting of the many occupants of this old White or Heath house. She was born in 1746. In her childhood, books were rare, and the opportunities for the education of girls very limited. The Bible and the Almanac were almost her only literature. But her mind was of the order that must grow, and will not be repressed. She read and re-read the Bible till her knowledge of it was wonderful. As other books came scantily into her possession, she read and studied them, and from her small stock culled a larger store of information and gained more strength of understanding and real thought than is often gained by those who skim swiftly the boundless surface of the light literature of modern times. She had a superior memory and wrote remarkable letters, and occasional verses. Her husband was a young man of education and unusual promise. Early in their married life, however, he was stricken down by a fever which deprived him of his reason and he died by his own hand. This sorrow overshadowed the whole life of the widow thus bereft. She never married again, but lived to a great age beloved and respected by all. As she advanced in years she came to be called "Aunt White" by a host of friends, and is still so called in affectionate remembrance.

Several slaves were kept in the Crafts and Heath families. A bill of sale of one of these is still extant among old papers. It reads as follows: —

"To all People to whom these presents shall come, I Richard Champion of Boston, in the County of Suffolk, of ye Massachusetts Bay in New England School-Master, sendeth *Greeting*, Know ye that I the said Richard Champion for and in consideration of the sum of one hundred pounds in good and passable bills of New England aforesaid, the receipt whereof I do hereby confess and acknowledge . . . . have Bargained and Sold, Released and granted and confirmed and by these Presents do bargain and sell unto Ebenezer Crafts of Roxbury, Cordwainer, a Negro Girl named Dina, about eleven years old, together with all her wearing apparel, To have and to hold the said Negro Girl unto the aforesaid Ebenezer Crafts, and to his heirs and assigns forever."

This is dated in 1739.

This Dinah proved well worth the hundred pounds which her master invested in her at eleven years of age, and during sixty years she faithfully served those who claimed her allegiance.

At the death of Dinah, in 1803, Mrs. White wrote the following lines, which show not only her feeling, but the view of slavery, which she held even then, before the anti-slavery agitation had even begun in New England: —

"Tho' now no pensive father mourns her death,
Nor tender mother her departed breath,
No brother kind, no child nor sister dear
Sheds o'er her silent grave one friendly tear,—

"Yet once the tears her parents' cheeks bedewed
When human monsters, worse than tigers rude
With hearts unfeeling as the direst fiend
Snatched her from every joy and every friend.

"How were their bleeding hearts with anguish torn,
When she was o'er the raging billows borne,
No more to see her native land again,
But distant far, to feel hard Slavery's chain.
Tho' black her skin as sky where clouds deform,
And temper boist'rous as the wintry storm,
Yet sometimes mild as summer eve was she
And oft her ebon visage smiled on me.

> "In days of yore when in my infant state,
> Her weary arms did oft sustain my weight,
> And oft with trifles did she win my love,
> Ere lapse of time had taught my feet to move.
>
> "And shall no tear fall on the lifeless clay,
> Of one who has in servitude grown gray?
> Forbid it heaven! My breast shall heave a sigh,
> While trickling tears descend from either eye.
>
> "Rest, rest in peace, thou relic of a slave!
> Soft be thy slumbers in the silent grave,
> And may'st thou rise washed in the Saviour's blood,
> Spotless and white at the great day of God."

There are other verses extant which this lady wrote when nearly ninety years of age. Her taste for books and writing continued to the end of her life. The greatest recreation for these quiet wives and daughters of the Brookline farmers in those old days was to look on at the gayeties of "Commencement Day," at Cambridge, or witness the display made by those who could attend and participate in it. Mrs. White and others of the Crafts family who came to live in Brookline were in the habit of going to the old Crafts house on the Roxbury road, — before the bridge to Cambridge was built, — on Commencement Days to see the gay riding, which all passed through Roxbury and Brookline on these occasions.

Mrs. White died in 1838, aged ninety-two years.

John White, another son of Joseph, and brother of Samuel, born in Brookline, in 1677, became a minister and settled in Gloucester. Letters written by Rev. John White, more than a hundred years ago, but when he was at an advanced age, addressed to his brother Samuel, are still preserved, and manifest the devout and affectionate spirit which characterized him. He died in 1760, aged eighty-three.

The papers left by the venerable Mrs. White have been a means of the preservation of various bits of family or local history, and some amusing incidents which would otherwise have been lost. A complete genealogy of the Crafts, White, and Heath families is thus preserved, and many interesting letters. In one of the latter there is an account of an accident which occurred in Cypress Street, in the last century, which just missed of being a tragedy, and resulted in a comedy.

It will perhaps be remembered by many persons, that that part of Cypress Street where the railroad crosses, and the brook passes under the street, was formerly three or four feet lower than at present. The great oak tree at the entrance to Tappan Street, stood, within the last thirty years, on ground that was walled up at least three feet; and it was then easy to drive a horse down through the brook at the west side of the road. In the time of the incident we are about to relate, the brook always ran over the road, when swollen by the rain. The letter from which we gather the story, is dated March 9th, 1795, and was written by Mrs. White to a member of the family, who was away from home.

It seems that on the Saturday night previous, March 7th, there had been a great southerly storm which had melted the snow and caused a great freshet, which made Cypress Street impassable. Rev. Mr. Tappan of Cambridge was to preach in the First Church for Rev. Mr. Jackson, who was then out of health. Not knowing the unsafe condition of the street, or "the New Lane," as it was then called, he attempted to ford the torrent with his horse and chaise, his son being with him. But the horse went off the bridge, and chaise and riders were plunged into the flood. The son came very near being drowned, but having finally struggled out of his predicament he set off to Captain Croft's, to call assistance.

The letter goes on to say: —

"Your brother has just come in from Town Meeting. He says that Mr. Jackson told him that after Mr. Tappan had sent his son to call assistance, he stayed in the water while he disengaged the horse from the carriage, and then mounted barebacked, followed his son, borrowed a saddle, and rode round by White and Sumner's store " (at the foot of Walnut Street).

"This accident happened at first bell ringing. He did not get to Mr. Jackson's till after the second began. He was so surprised and fatigued, he could not give much account of himself, only that he had been in the water. Mr. Jackson dressed the poor unfortunate man in a suit of his clothes, but as his small clothes did not cover his knees, he was obliged to wear his wet ones. . . . .

"David Hyslop said he was very sorry he did not send to him for a pair, but as 'the legs of the lame are not equal,' if one knee had been covered the other must have been bare. But he dried and fixed himself as well as he could, and went clumping into meeting in borrowed shoes just as Mr. Jackson had done his first prayer.

"Mr. Jackson's cloak was so short for him he could not look very buckish. Although there were some circumstances a little diverting, it was really a serious affair. Mr. Jackson prayed in the morning and at night; both times he returned thanks that they were preserved when in imminent danger, and prayed that their health might not be injured. Mr. Tappan put his notes and his band in his book and put them on the cushion behind him when he set out from Cambridge, but the current was so rapid that they were all carried off. Notwithstanding, he preached two excellent sermons from notes which he happened to have in his pocket. The chaise, which he borrowed of the President,* was very much damaged. It seemed as if fire and water were against them, Sunday. His son stayed at home in the forenoon, to dry himself, left his shoes in the sitting room, and went out to the kitchen fire.

* Rev. Dr. Willard was President of Harvard College at that time.

Meanwhile, a brand fell down on one of them and burnt the heel quarter almost up. But Mr. Jackson was kind enough to look up one that answered, so that he followed his father to church in the afternoon."

There is an additional appropriateness in the name of *Tappan Street* of which we had not been aware till the above incident suggested it.

In Mr. John Heath's family were two old slaves, Cuff and Kate, and one Primus, of whom various anecdotes are related. Mr. Heath, who was fond of quizzing Primus, asked him one day which was the heavier, a pound of lead or a pound of feathers.

"A pound of lead, Massa," said Primus, promptly. "Course, a pound of lead is de heaviest."

A laugh ensued at Primus's expense.

"Don't you b'lieve it, Massa? You go stick your head in de fireplace and let Primus go up a top de house and drap a pound ob fedders and a pound ob lead down de chimbley on your head; den see which de heaviest."

On the occasion of the great alarm in this part of the town in Revolutionary times, occasioned by a party of British "regulars," riding out into Roxbury, and the announcement being made that they were at "church green," there was a general stampede from the Heath house, as well as from all the other houses in the neighborhood. Everybody, white and black, sought a hiding place in the woods, except poor old Kate, Cuff's wife, who was too old and infirm to run away. She squeezed behind the tall, old-fashioned clock, which stood in a corner, and stayed there for hours, and there the family found her when they returned. The only article carried off by the family for safety was *a bag of salt*, which was seized by one of the female members of the household in the moment of flight.

This part of the town was very social in customs in the old times, and the quaint, old-fashioned style of visiting prevailed, long after it was discontinued in the more thickly settled portions of the town. Persons now living can remember when it was the fashion to send a child early in the morning with her mother's " compliments," to some neighbor, and say that " if it was convenient, mother would come and spend the afternoon." By two o'clock, the visit was begun, and often the small spinning wheel was carried, instead of the sewing, but how the necessary amount of talking could be done with two or three spinning-wheels in motion, we, of the days of sewing machines, are at a loss to understand. By "milking time," the visit was over, and the guests gone home to their chores and their early bed-time.

It is easy to perceive, when familiar with our early history, as a people, how the New England habit of talking about everybody and their affairs grew up as a natural consequence of the mode of life and the state of the country. With no holidays, or public amusements, and few recreations of any sort, with a few great common interests, as the church, the crops, and the state of the country, — with many common inconveniences and privations growing out of the newness of the country, and the difficulty of communication with England, it is no wonder that when they met, the interest or the misfortune of one neighbor, which was the interest or misfortune of all, was the common subject of discussion.

It is easy, too, to perceive how the very habit which grew out of common human sympathy, and the needs of the heart, was liable to perversion by envy and uncharitableness, into the gossip and scandal which are even now the bane and curse of thinly settled towns, and small villages.

Out of this same common sympathy and need, has

grown also the prompt, quick, willing, helpful spirit which is never appealed to in vain for a case of real need, whether it is a private family stranded by adverse circumstances, a battle which has struck a blow to every household in the land, or a burnt city which stretches out imploring hands for help. If New England gossips over her tea-table, not the less does she empty her full hands into the lap of the needy, and help the struggling up into security and peace.

The journals or private diaries, kept for years by persons resident in this town, though cumbered with many family cares, are, a faithful transcript of the daily life which made the women of those times strong but not unfeminine, and left them no leisure to seek a share in the government, or administration of public affairs.

Mr. John Heath in his old age relinquished his farm to his son. A curious old deed of subsistence is still preserved in which are specified all the items for his maintenance. This method was not uncommon in former times, and seems to have been a wise provision both for parents and children. Mr. John Heath died in 1804, aged seventy-two.

Mr. Ebenezer Heath, the only son of Mr. John Heath, succeeded his father as proprietor of the homestead or farm. He married Miss Hannah Williams of Roxbury, and built the house now occupied by his daughters. The old house was rented for many years to a succession of tenants.

One of the daughters of Mr. John Heath became the wife of Dr. John Goddard of this town, who settled in Portsmouth, N. H.

After the death of this lady he married a second time, then a third, and finally for his fourth and last wife he returned to Brookline and took one from the same house whence he had taken his first, this time marrying Anne, the only child of Mrs. Elizabeth White. This lady survived her husband about three years, but not her venerable mother.

The wife of Mr. Ebenezer Heath was a woman of more than ordinary ability, and great strength and beauty of character. She brought up a family of nine children, and with all the household cares which a farmer's wife necessarily had in those days (and she was an accomplished housekeeper) she found time for the improvement of her mind, and the extracts which are extant in her own handwriting from religious and other books which she read, indicate her good taste, her humble, conscientious, and grateful spirit, and her tender sympathies.

She also kept a diary of noteworthy local events with many interesting comments, and recorded much of her own personal experience and reflection thereon.

The latter was for her own improvement and not for the eyes of others, but her growth in the traits which make up a beautiful and consistent Christian life, is unconsciously manifested upon almost every page. Under date of July 9th, 1826, she speaks of a party of friends meeting "to celebrate Lafayette passing by." The same week, she speaks of a visit from her daughter, with her husband and young child, in which great pleasure had been anticipated, but which was turned to grief by the illness and death of the little one. She writes, "Dr. Pierce returned from the funeral of President Adams, who had lived in this world ninety years, to pray with our little grandson who had lived but forty-two days."

Long years after Mrs. Heath's death, a voluntary tribute was paid to her memory and her worth, by one who had in early life, being an orphan, been placed in the family of Mr. Heath, a mere child, to earn his board on the farm. He has since been prospered till he is able to ride in his own carriage. The little kindly acts by which this excellent woman made the almost friendless little boy her devoted friend, were also strong in their influence upon him in his manhood, making him careful for the rights and the feelings of those in his own employ similarly situated. And so " the good, men do, lives after them."

A great affliction came upon this lovely woman in the death of her daughter Mary, a young lady of twenty.

During several of the last years of Mrs. Heath's life she was deprived of the use of her limbs and was otherwise much afflicted, but her cheerful and beautiful spirit was triumphant over all her sorrows. She died in 1832, aged sixty-one years. It was a little singular that two other ladies, members of the First Church, and noted in the community for their personal worth, were removed by death the same year; these were the wife of Mr. Richard Sullivan, and the first wife of Mr. Benjamin Goddard. Dr. Pierce remarked that " the loss of three such women was enough to impoverish any church."

Mr. Charles Heath, the eldest son of Mr. Eben Heath, took down the old mansion in 1838. It was one of the substantial square houses of the olden time, built for centuries, with low ceilings and narrow windows with seats in the deep recesses, now long out of date. A fence containing much timber, elaborately constructed, surrounded the yard, and the borders were hedged with box. Mr. Heath built the house which is still standing and now occupied by Francis Cabot, the same year, and occupied it many years himself.

Mr. Ebenezer Heath was for some time Town Treasurer. He died in 1845 at the age of eighty.

The late Mr. Charles Heath is so well remembered that scarcely more than a passing notice is necessary, yet his memory deserves the tribute of recorded worth. Like his excellent mother he possessed traits of character which won the respect and esteem of all who knew him, and though his quiet and retiring disposition prevented his bearing great public responsibilities, he was none the less an honored and valued citizen. His death called forth expressions of sincere regret from those who were not bound to him by the ties of kindred, as well as from those who claimed him as their own. He left the sum of two thousand dollars in trust to be used for the poor of the First Parish, or for such persons as his executors deemed worthy, they not being beggars or common paupers.

Among ancient papers of the Heath family there is an account of the famous " dark day." It is uncertain whose handwriting it may be, but it was evidently written immediately after the event.

"*May* 19*th*, 1780. Being Friday there were several small showers in the morning. About three o'clock the Clouds began to have a yellowish appearance, this brassy Colour kept increasing. A little before Ten, it began to look dark, and by twelve o'clock we were obliged to light up candles. It was as dark as at an hour after sundown. At one the darkness began to abate, and by half-past three the clouds blew over and the afternoon was as pleasant as usual.

"The night following was as uncommonly dark as the day. Before nine o'clock there was a total privation of light; though the moon was but just past the full it did not give one ray of light till it was more than three hours high. People that were not above thirty rods from home could not get home without the greatest difficulty.

"There were various opinions about the darkness. Some were exceedingly surprised and tho't the Conclusion of all things was come. Others that a Comet passed between us and the sun. Others again that it was a large body of Smoke that came from the woods that was on fire for many miles together at the westward. Others that it was a large Collection of Clouds and Vapors drove together by Contrary Winds."

On the site of the house built a few years since by George Bacon, formerly stood a large and handsome house, owned and occupied by Hon. Stephen Higginson, a member of the legislature in the last century under "the old Confederation." His descendants have lived in the town almost constantly since that time. Hon. Stephen Higginson died in 1828, at the age of eighty-five. The house was occupied for several years by Mr. Appleton, then by Dr. Warren, and was finally sold to Mr. Bacon, who removed the old structure and built the present house.

Nearly opposite this house stood a house built before the last century, by Joseph Gardner, one of that numerous family of whom an account has previously been given. Deacon Joseph White was the next occupant, and he died in 1777. His son Samuel (the one of whom an account has been previously given), succeeded him as owner, and then for a long period the house was owned and occupied by Jonathan Jackson. General Simon Elliot next bought the place, and built the present house in 1824. Simon Elliot Greene succeeded him, and more recently the late J. Sullivan Warren, who was held in high esteem in Brookline, as also in Boston, for many acts of liberality, and his general benevolence of character. This gentleman left a sum of money to be expended in beautifying the streets of this town with shade trees.

On the narrow lane which here crosses from Heath to Boylston Street, is the town "Pound," and it is generally known as "Pound Lane." This continues across Boylston Street and to Beacon Street, at the upper part of the new reservoir. Possibly parts of it are traceable further.

It is a part of the old highway from Dedham to "Cambridge Village," and originally led to a village of Elliot's "praying Indians," who lived at the falls of Charles River, between Newton and Watertown. It has recently been widened and graded, and is now called "Reservoir Lane." It was one of the wildest and most picturesque lanes to be found in the country, and it would be difficult to convince one who had never explored it that such a place could be found within six miles of the State House. It was narrow, winding, rocky, and steep; up hill and down dale, bordered with wild briers, and gay with wild flowers, or attractive with berries, according to the season. Two or three houses, difficult of access, built within fifteen or twenty years, stand along this lane, that was so secluded. Even now it is a retired and rustic place, but the great Reservoir is built and all the world goes to see it, and the little wild lane begins to be a thoroughfare.

To return to Pound Lane — there was little use for a Town Pound, comparatively, till about the year 1836, when Mr. Samuel Philbrick was instrumental in causing the town to pass a by-law, forbidding animals to be pastured along the streets. Previous to that time, cows, horses, and often swine, roamed at large, and grazed along the highways. Every avenue and driveway was necessarily closed with a gate to prevent the depredations of these marauders, and if a gate was accidentally left open, it was fortunate for the owner of the premises if his grounds were not invaded, and his fruit trees or garden damaged before the mischief was discovered.

Many persons fearing lest they should be called upon for damages for trespass, kept their children out of school, lounging by the roadsides to watch their cattle, and little barefooted boys and girls, with their cows, were a common feature of the landscape.

It would naturally be supposed that so great a public improvement as that proposed by Mr. Philbrick, would have been hailed with delight by our townspeople, but this was not the case. The most formidable opposition came from the very people best able to provide pasturage for their live stock, on their own grounds. Men who owned scores of acres of land, raised an outcry about being defrauded of their rights, and those who owned a solitary cow and no land, lamented the hard-heartedness of the rich who denied the poor the privilege of the wayside grass. But the law was enforced, and many an angry man made an irksome journey to the Pound, and reluctantly paid the necessary fee to get poor Brindle or Dobbin released from "durance vile." Remarks decidedly uncomplimentary to Mr. Philbrick were freely indulged, but law triumphed, and gates ceased to be a necessity.

West of Pound Lane, on the north side of Heath Street, was the extensive farm of Deacon Benjamin White, son of Joseph White and brother of Samuel. He was one of the original founders of the town and the church, and is sometimes called "Ensign" Benjamin White.

On this farm was the ancient house, which was taken down in 1809, between the floors of which was found the paper, of which a copy has been given, containing the names of all who were seated in the meeting-house in 1719. There were four Benjamin Whites in succession from this ancestry, but Moses White occupied the house last mentioned, after his father, and his son of the same name after him. It was purchased from him in 1792, by Hon. Jonathan Mason, who had previously lived in the old Goddard or Gardner house, opposite the Reservoir. He was a senator in Congress. He died in 1831.

An allusion to the politics of those times, occurs in an old letter dated in 1798, written by a lady of that vicinity.

The writer, mentioning two of her neighbors who called, says:—

"They spent the evening talking upon Politics. These troublesome times seem to take up every person's attention. I am almost sick of hearing the name of Federalists and Jacobins. We live in the midst of both. The upper and lower part of the Town are what people call Jacobins. They say those that live in the middle of the town are influenced by Mr. Mason and Mr. Cabot." [Hon. George Cabot at that time lived on the place now owned by the heirs of the late Samuel Goddard.]

"I am sorry for 'Squire Gardner who said he wanted to please everybody, for he did not please anybody. At Town Meeting he stood in the broad aisle and durst not go one side or the other till somebody told him to go one side or the other, and at last he went on Dr. Aspinwall's side. He has said since that he was sorry he went to Town Meeting."

The Federalists, it will be remembered, were the party who desired to reëlect Washington, but as he positively declined a third term of office, they had unanimously nominated and elected John Adams, whose political opinions were those of Washington. The Jacobins or Republicans believing the other party less devoted than themselves to the cause of popular liberty, had declared their preference for Thomas Jefferson, and the result had been the election of Adams to the Presidency, and Jefferson as Vice-president.

Hostilities between France and the United States were then impending, and party feeling, instead of subsiding, as is usually the case after an election is over, was rampant, and men and principles were handled without gloves, by everybody, from statesmen and their compeers, down to school-boys.

The people in the "middle of the town," whom the lady intimates to have been influenced by Mr. Mason and Mr. Cabot, were no doubt Federalists, as Mr. Mason had served in the Senate, under Washington, and was his personal friend and admirer, and Mr. Adams, as we have before stated, was a visitor at Mr. Mason's house.

An incident is connected with Mr. Mason's old house which is somewhat amusing. A colored woman, noted as a notorious thief, and a white girl in company, called at the house begging one day, and took the opportunity to steal some silver spoons. Mr. Mason had just before hired a new coachman. The man had been out, and on returning to the house was made acquainted with the loss. He instantly volunteered to go after the culprits and recover the lost silver, for he said that he had noticed them as he came along the road, digging dandelions in a field beside the way. It so happened that the persons whom the man saw, were indeed, by an odd coincidence, a colored woman and a white girl, but they were from Mr. Heath's family, Sukey, a trusty servant of theirs, and a young girl who was staying there.

The man made all possible speed down the road, and there in the field were the supposed vagrants. He jumped over the wall, and seizing them by the arms, ordered them to deliver up the silver they had stolen. As the terrified women stoutly denied any knowledge of what he meant, he compelled them to pour out their dandelions, and to empty their pockets, every few minutes giving them a grip and a shake. No silver was to be found, however, and he proceeded to search their clothing, the frightened creatures all the while protesting and asserting their innocence. Finding nothing, and being shown the house where they lived, the self-made detective finally let them go. Their anger and fright at being taken for thieves, and the whole ludicrous affair, made passing entertainment enough for the young people of the neighborhood.

In 1822, Benjamin Guild, Esq., purchased the house which Hon. Jonathan Mason had occupied. In 1841, it was sold to Hon. Theodore Lyman, formerly mayor of Boston, who took down the old house and built the present fine mansion. The beautiful trees which shade the avenue, were set out by Mr. Mason. Under the care of the various owners, all of whom have been gentlemen of taste, these beautiful trees and the fine lawn have been cultivated and brought to their present luxuriance. West of the house, the summit of the gradually sloping hill commands a magnificent prospect; in clear weather, Wachusett, Watatick, and other mountains being distinctly visible.

A little beyond this house, on the opposite side of Heath Street, formerly stood the school-house for this part of the town. It was a one story wooden building, low in the walls, and with few conveniences. In this for many years, a school was kept by a female teacher in summer, and by a male teacher in winter. In this building the Worcesters were for several years employed as teachers. It was small, and became densely crowded with pupils long before a new one was built, though it was only a primary school. The new school-house, for both grammar and primary schools, which was thought adequate for many years, has already been enlarged to meet present needs.

On the north side of the street the next house of olden

times was owned by Peter Gardner, another of the Gardner family, formerly so numerous in this part of the town. There were five houses occupied and owned by Gardners as early as 1688, of whom Peter was one.

After him it was owned by Benjamin White, who died in 1777, at the age of 70. He was one of the Selectmen for many years. His son Benjamin occupied the house for several years, but in 1790 he took down the old house, which had been standing more than a hundred years, and built the present large square house upon the same site.*

He died in 1814, and the large estate which had descended through three generations became now the possession of the fourth Benjamin White. He died in 1839, and the estate passed into other hands.

West of this house about half a mile further on, upon the other side of the street, was a very old house, which was once the property of Joseph Adams. Still further west was another owned by Nathaniel Stedman when Brookline first became a town. Both these houses were bought by one of the Benjamin Whites, and pulled down on account of their great age.

The next house on the same side of the street was also once the property of Nathaniel Stedman, and was sold by him to Ebenezer Sargent. It was purchased of him by Deacon Winchester (of whom more hereafter), and finally became the property of the same Benjamin White who seems to have owned a goodly portion of this part of Brookline. It was built before 1740.

The next house upon the opposite side, that built by Capt. Benjamin Gardner, was described in the article on the Gardner family.

* This has recently become the property of Mr. Cabot, who has built an elegant house upon the hill west of it.

The next house of any note, going westward, is the one owned for some years by Mark Sheafe. This old house has quite a history.

Among the earliest settlers of the town were John and Josiah Winchester. They were of Welsh origin. Elhanan and Henry Winchester appear in the second generation. Of Captain John Winchester we gave a sketch in an article on Harvard Street. Elhanan Winchester, above alluded to, lived in the house there mentioned, and was a member of the First Church, of which his ancestors had been the founders. This man and his son of the same name, for many years bore a conspicuous part in the religious annals of this town and vicinity.

Mr. Winchester was married three times; the first wife left no children, the second left six, and the third nine.

In the year 1744, when Mr. Winchester was a young man, there was quite an excitement in the First Church, of which Rev. Mr. Allen was pastor, and several persons left it, and established an order which they called "New Lights." They held worship in private houses, sometimes in the lower part of the town in the house of Nathaniel Shepherd, on what is now the Public Library ground. (This was before the Dana family owned it.) In the upper part of the town they met at the house of Mr. Winchester.

On Washington Street they sometimes met at the house of Mrs. Elizabeth Corey. They had a preacher, Mr. Jonathan Hyde, for about thirty years. Many of the laymen became exhorters, and among these was Mr. Winchester. In 1751 his first child, Elhanan, was born. He was a most remarkable child from his earliest years. When only five years of age he could read any English book with ease and fluency. He was a delicate, thoughtful, gentle child, caring little for play, but devouring books with the keenest avidity. The few books then adapted to children were entirely inadequate for the cravings of his mind, and he read and studied the Bible till his knowledge of it was wonderful.

Mr. Winchester was not able to afford other than common school instruction for his remarkable little boy, and he soon mastered all that he could obtain from this source. He then obtained a Latin grammar, and with one evening's study qualified himself to join a class who had been studying several weeks. When a little older he acquired with wonderful facility, French, Greek, and Hebrew.

An instance of his remarkable memory is stated by his biographer.* He had attended church one Sabbath with his father, where the building was in an unfinished state. (This was probably the old meeting-house at Newton known as "Father Grafton's.") The father sat below stairs, and the little boy in the gallery. The keen eyes of the strict parent, however, detected the child gazing about the building apparently engrossed with its details.

On returning home he called him to account for it, charging him with paying no attention to the sermon. The boy in self-defense immediately named the text and the place where it was to be found. The father however was not satisfied, and the boy proceeded to name the "heads" of the sermon, and repeated much that the preacher had said. The stern countenance of the father relaxed into something of complacency as the evidence of his son's attention and good memory was established, and the boy taking courage, continued, —

"And now, father, if you will not be offended, I will tell you the number of people, and the number of beams, posts, braces, rafters, and panes of glass there were in the meeting-house. I counted them all, and remembered the text too."

* Rev. Edwin M. Stone.

The father with difficulty repressed a smile, but assuming a look of gravity he warned the child to "give hereafter undivided attention to religious exercises when in a place of worship."

This remarkable child was overwhelmed at the loss of his mother, who was a most affectionate and excellent woman, when he was only eight years of age. In his later years he always spoke of her with an intensity of affection and respect.

It became inconvenient after a time for the New Lights to meet from house to house, and Mr. Winchester, who had been made deacon, was assisted by his religious brethren to build a large house which should contain a hall or apartment convenient for their use. This was the house long known as "Richards' Hotel," afterwards as the Sheafe place, and now occupied by many Irish tenants.

In this house the New Lights worshipped undisturbed. After a time, however, young Winchester, who had made a formal profession of religion when about eighteen years of age, became a Baptist. His influence with his father was so great that he too left the New Lights and joined the Baptists soon after. The work of disintegration went on, and the sect was broken up, some joining the Congregationalists, and some other sects.

In 1769 young Winchester was married to Alice Rogers of Rowley, Mass. Soon after this he entered upon the public work of the ministry, staying for a short time at Canterbury, Conn., and afterwards removing to Rehoboth, Mass. At this place was a Baptist church of open communion practice. Mr. Winchester's youth, his eloquence, his wonderful memory and zeal, attracted crowds; a revival followed, and he gathered a new church of seventy members.

In less than a year he so far changed his views as to

believe in close communion, and was excluded from his church for breach of covenant. This produced a great commotion, and a council was called which decided that Mr. Winchester had left an error to embrace the truth. He soon became one of the most successful and popular preachers in his sect, returned to Brookline, and preached among his old friends, till he preached nearly all the New Lights into the close communion Baptist faith. It was at this time that his father joined this sect.

The next year, 1774, he decided to visit the South. On this visit he received a call from a church at Welch Neck, S. C., to become its pastor. He accepted the call, and after a short stay returned for his wife whom he had left in Massachusetts. When they arrived at Fairfax, Va., Mrs. Winchester was taken sick, and being unable to accompany him he went on and resumed his duties with his church, leaving his wife in the care of a friend. The following spring he returned to carry her to his southern home. But when he arrived it was too late. She was laid away in her last rest, and he saw her no more. He did not return at once to his people, but came to Boston to visit his old friends, and spend the summer. During this summer he preached for Dr. Stedman. Before autumn he had visited Rehoboth and married Miss Sarah Peck, one of his former parishioners. He returned in the autumn to his church, where he was welcomed with great joy, — a revival occurred, and forty persons were baptized, among whom was Mrs. Winchester. He was then in the full tide of success and popularity, and in the enjoyment of great domestic happiness. In less than a year from his marriage he was again bereaved, and himself prostrated with a fever which nearly cost him his life.

The next year he was married again to a young lady of his own parish, and in less than a year she too was no more. Mr. Winchester often spoke of her as " one of the sweetest tempered women he ever saw."

He bore his solitude two years, and then married a widow of Philadelphia. In less than two years she had followed her predecessors. Mr. Winchester's friends, after this unhappy experience, advised him never again to enter into a matrimonial alliance, but he thought it best for a clergyman to be married, and after a year or two he married for the fifth time — taking a widow lady of Philadelphia, who led him an unhappy life during the rest of his days.

In 1780 he was called to Philadelphia, where he drew throngs, till the house was insufficient to contain them, and even St. Paul's, then the largest church in the city, was obtained, and immediately filled to overflowing.

Sometime before this Mr. Winchester had met with " Siegvolk's Everlasting Gospel," which held forth and illustrated the doctrine of Restoration, or what is now commonly called Universalism. He was half a convert to these views when he was preaching with such wonderful effect in Philadelphia. When it became a settled conviction in his mind that these views were true, he preached them without reservation. This of course produced a furore, and the crowds who listened were divided into warm friends and bitter persecutors. It would be amusing were it not lamentable, to note the change of sentiment which will seize and overpower one's best friends, in the bitterness engendered by diversities of religious belief. Some, seeming to consider themselves custodians of the truth, resent it as a personal affront if a friend honestly avows different sentiments, and many who claim in these modern times to be the most liberal in their views, are the most rancorous in their feelings when one of their number goes over to another sect. It amounts to just this, "Believe what you please and call yourself of *our sect*, and you shall be popular, but take another name and work with another sect, and though your sentiments be lofty, and your life pure, you shall eat the bread of persecution, and drink the waters of bitterness." It is also doubly rancorous, this spirit of sectarian hate, when the object of it has been a man of eminence in his own sect. We see frequent illustrations of it in our own day. In Mr. Winchester's time it was tenfold worse.

Rev. John Murray had been preaching the doctrine of Universal Salvation ten years, and quite an extensive correspondence had been going on between him and Mr. Winchester before they met. Dr. De Benneville, the first preacher of those views in this country, of French parentage, was also Mr. Winchester's friend. Dr. De Benneville had been imprisoned in Calais and afterwards in Normandy for preaching his views, and with a fellow preacher, Durant, was sentenced for execution. His companion suffered the penalty, but he was reprieved, and finally set at liberty, and after preaching in Germany and Holland, settled in this country, where he lived to a great age. Mr. Winchester's acquaintance with these two eminent men of his own faith, led him to desire to preach in Europe. He went to London in 1787, where he met with coldness and opposition at first, but his hearers continued to increase, and one place after another of larger size was required till he preached with wonderful success in the Parliament-Court Chapel. Mr. Winchester remained in England nearly seven years, and then went to France for brief visit. He returned to Boston in 1794, and immediately to Brookline. He was received with affection and respect by our townspeople, to their credit be it said, though probably scarcely a person in the town held the views which he did. But his personal popularity and the real respect upon which it was based, overcame religious opposition. The next day being Sunday, he attended the First Church. In the evening, though his arrival was so recent and there was so little time to make it known, he preached to a large audience at the " Punch Bowl Village." General Heath of Roxbury, and many others from that place were among his auditors. He preached during that autumn in many private houses in Brookline, Newton, and Cambridge, as well as in many churches of various denominations, and " wherever he went, large and delighted audiences hung upon the sound of his instructive voice." Among his converts at this time was his aged father, who seemed to follow the lead of his gifted son, from the excess of love and pride which he bore towards him.

The celebrated Dr. Benjamin Rush of Philadelphia was one of the most intimate friends of Rev. Mr. Winchester. Much of the correspondence which passed between them is preserved, and is of interest both on theological and political matters, for both held similar views on religious themes, and were ardent lovers of American ideas and institutions. Mr. Winchester was in England during the stormy times in Europe, in the latter part of the last century, and his observation there, led him to prize more highly than ever the newly-established Republican form of government of the United States which was then threatened with difficulty with France. He deeply lamented the part which England took in that war, and rejoiced in the neutrality preserved by this country, and its steady gain in prosperity.

As soon as his visit to Brookline and vicinity was over, he visited Western Massachusetts and Connecticut, preaching in many towns. He also wrote a "Defense of Revelation" in answer to Thomas Paine's "Age of Reason," an excellent work, as an answer to infidel opinions, and a strong weapon not for his own sect alone, but for all believers in revealed truth. This was reprinted in London within two years afterwards.

Early in the following year, 1795, Mr. Winchester started on a tour to Philadelphia, stopping on the way at Providence, where he preached in the Baptist Church to a crowded assembly. Having proceeded to New York he was detained there two or three weeks by the illness of his wife, and in a letter mentions an interview with Hon. John Jay. He says:—

"Of public news I need not inform you. You will see by the papers the clamors against the treaty and against Mr. Jay. I was this morning with Mr. Jay, and happening to mention these vexatious clamors, he replied, 'It was what I expected, but my trust is in God. I know that He rules and orders everything; and I shall endeavor to go on in the way of my duty and rest all events in his hands.' This speech he made with such manly dignity, that his very manner charmed me as well as the excellence of the speech itself."

Mr. Winchester preached to crowds in the Circus in New York during his stay there, and a subscription was started to build him a house of worship, but he proceeded to Philadelphia as soon as his wife's health would permit, and spent that autumn and winter preaching to his former people. Here he published a volume of hymns. In February he was attacked with a severe hemorrhage of the lungs, and his friend, Dr. Rush, was his medical adviser. He so far recovered as to go to New York the following June. This year he published a "Political Catechism," at the suggestion of Hon. Timothy Pickering. This work passed through many editions, and Governor Jay interested himself much in its circulation. It was adapted for use in high schools and colleges, and was designed to give instruction in true principles of government and liberty.

The following autumn, on his way north, Mr. Winchester stopped in Hartford, at the residence of a friend. He was still pale from his severe illness, but able to walk out and to speak somewhat in public. On the day of his arrival he walked out after dinner, and observing a funeral procession, he joined it and followed to the cemetery. The assemblage was large, and the scene solemn. Just as the coffin was lowered into the grave, he arrested the attention of the multitude by breaking forth in his musical, sonorous voice, with the sublime words of Jesus to the mourning sisters at Bethany, "I am the resurrection and the life." The effect was electric, and he went on in a strain of eloquence which held his audience spell-bound. The moment he ceased to speak there was the universal inquiry, "Who is he?" "Where did he come from?"

As soon as it was noised abroad that the stranger at the grave was Mr. Winchester, there was a general desire to hear him preach. He delivered one or two lectures, but no building in the city would contain his audiences, but the Theatre was soon opened for that purpose on Sundays, and on Wednesday evenings he preached in one of the churches. He was strongly impressed that his earthly course was nearly ended, and he spoke as one about to leave this world. Early in April he preached his last sermon, having chosen his text with the profound conviction that he should never preach again, from St. Paul's farewell address to the elders of the Ephesian Church (Acts. xx. 28-35.)

From that day he declined rapidly, but with his mind clear to the very last, even joining in a hymn which was sung at his request, a few moments before he died, on the morning of April 18, 1797.

On the following Friday he was buried from the Presbyterian Church, the funeral sermon being preached by Rev. Dr. Strong, who though of another faith was his intimate friend, and paid a fitting tribute to the lovely character and lofty piety of the deceased.

He was buried in Hartford, and his resting place is marked by a stone containing the following inscription: —

THE GENERAL CONVENTION OF THE UNIVERSAL CHURCHES IN MEMORY OF THEIR DEAR DEPARTED BROTHER
ELHANAN WINCHESTER,
ERECTED THIS MONUMENTAL STONE. HE DIED APRIL 18TH, 1797, AGED 46 YEARS.

"Twas thine to preach with animated zeal
The glories of the restitution morn,
When sin, death, hell, the power of Christ shall feel,
And Light, Life, Immortality be born."

Mr. Winchester left no children, those which he had having died in infancy. His aged father, still living at the old place in Heath Street, and holding the views of his eminent son, while the latter was living, but apparently without any settled convictions of his own, was now again afloat without chart or compass. He had been first a Congregationalist, then a New Light, then a Baptist, then a Universalist; a few years after his son's death, he turned *Shaker*, and left Brookline and joined that sect in Harvard, where he died "full in the faith," in September, 1810, aged 91 years.

Just before his death he sent word to some of his old friends in Newton, " In every other denomination I have had my doubts; but now I am sure that I am right."

When we see good men live noble and useful lives, and die triumphant deaths, holding views which other men just as good and living just as purely consider arrant heresy, it may well make us very modest in the assertion of any creed beyond that of " doing justly, loving mercy, and walking humbly with God."

The great house which Deacon Winchester had occupied, and in which he had brought up his fifteen children, was afterwards owned by Ebenezer White, and then by Joseph White, who sold it to Ebenezer Richards. He kept it as a public house for several years. When the turnpike to Worcester was opened, a toll-gate was placed across it in the rear of the tavern. It was a convenient resort for teamsters, and parties from Boston often went out there to have games at nine-pins. In its best days it was much frequented by gay parties, and Brookline balls were held there. It was discontinued as a tavern about 1830.

It was afterwards purchased by Henry Pettes of Boston, who made great improvements upon it, resided there for a year or two, and then sold it to Mark W. Sheafe of Portsmouth; it has since then been commonly called the Sheafe place.

The next house on the same side of Heath Street stands on the site of one which was built by Ebenezer Kendrick, another of the New Lights, being conveniently near their place of worship. The present house was built by Mr. Jonathan Hammond. There was quite a large tract of land in this vicinity, partly in Brookline, and partly in Newton, belonging to the Hammonds, from whom the pond and the cross street near by were named.

The Hammond house was for several years occupied by Madame Jane Coaifford, a French lady. She died in this house and was buried in Brookline Cemetery.

CHAPTER XVI.

HEATH STREET, CONCLUDED. — WARREN STREET. — ANECDOTE OF JOSHUA BOYLSTON, DEACON CLARK, MISS PRUDY HEATH, COLONEL PERKINS. — GODDARD AVENUE. — THE GODDARDS IN THE REVOLUTION. — A PATRIOTIC FAMILY. — COTTAGE STREET. — THE LEE PLACE.

HAVING arrived at the very limits of the town in this direction, we find a small settlement of Germans. Almost on the town line stood a little cottage or hovel, years ago, where lived an old negro, Nathaniel Hill, who was hired by the farmers around to do odd jobs. The place was bought by Deacon Ebenezer Crafts, who sold it to Rev. Jonathan Hyde, who came from Canterbury, Conn., where the Hydes abound, — to preach to the "New Lights" of Brookline. He built a house upon it in 1751, and lived here thirty-six years, the most of that time officiating as a clergyman, though there was not a regularly organized church, and was not probably wealth enough among them to build a meeting-house; the history of the sect we have given, so far as information could be obtained, in the chapters on the Winchesters. Of Mr. Hyde we can learn little personal history, but Dr. Pierce states that though nearly all his followers were, or became Baptists, he held to the doctrine of infant baptism to the end of his days. He died in 1787, aged 78. His son Thaddeus next owned the place, and died there in 1808, and his son Arba succeeded him.

The place and the men deteriorated together, and after the death of the last Hyde in 1841, the house was torn down by order of the selectmen. Since that time John Zecher settled upon the place, and quite a village of Germans has gradually grown up.

We now return to the middle of the town, and enter Warren Street, west of the Unitarian Church. This picturesque and beautiful entrance to the street needs to be seen coming *northerly*, instead of *going* in the opposite direction, in order to be fully appreciated. It would seem that in laying out this street, the fathers availed themselves of a natural depression in the rocky ledge for the street to pass through, as the rocks are high on both sides, but bear no traces of ever having been blasted. There is no bit of rock scenery in the town so picturesque as this, with the wild mosses and ferns growing from the crevices, and crowned with the woods on the one side, and the steep face of the little precipice on the other, covered with luxuriant vines, cultivated with all the resources of taste and skill.

The first house in the street on the west, standing formerly on the site of the house of the late Deacon Clark, was built by a John Shepard so long ago, that the date is not recoverable. The house was purchased by Dudley Boylston in 1722, who made it his residence. A few persons still live in the town who can remember it. One venerable lady, who was often in it, in her early childhood, describes it as a black, gambrel-roofed house, standing end to the street, fronting toward the place now owned by John L. Gardner. The sills were sunken level with the ground, and to enter it, one needed to step down instead of up. The whole interior was in keeping with the external appearance.

Dudley Boylston was a son of the Peter Boylston

often before mentioned, — and a brother of Dr. Zabdiel Boylston. He was born about 1688, and married Elizabeth Gardner of this town. He was the town constable for some time, and an old military commission issued in the time of Francis Bernard, Captain-general and Governor-in-chief, indicates his rank as "first adjutant of the first regiment, whereof Jeremy Gridley is Colonel."

There was a lifelong sorrow in the family of Dudley Boylston, in the insanity of his daughter Mary, who was thus afflicted from eighteen years of age to eighty, when she died.

After the death of the father, the homestead became the property of his son Joshua. He was a bachelor of reserved and stern manners, but a sagacious and practical man. The story of his courtship and marriage is a curious one. When he was nearly fifty-five years of age, in 1783, he being one of the selectmen or school committee, was at the annual dinner of that board of officers, which was then always served at the "Punch Bowl." It was then kept by Eleazer Baker, whose sister Abigail, a cheerful, trim little body, about forty years of age, was attending upon the guests at table.

Esquire Sharp, the town clerk and justice of the peace, — also a bachelor, was present. The two were well bantered by the rest of the merry company for their celibacy, and some one pressed Mr. Boylston for a reason why he had never married. He replied that he could find no one who would have him.

To the astonishment of all present, Miss Abigail instantly remarked, —

"I would have you, Mr. Boylston."

"Would you?" he asked incredulously.

"Yes, I would."

"Squire Sharp!" said Mr. Boylston, "do you hear that. Publish us next Sunday morning."

There was a laugh, and the matter was dropped as a mere joke.

On Sunday morning no publishment appeared, and Mr. Boylston, taking an early opportunity to see Squire Sharp, desired to know the reason.

"Why," said the Squire, "are you in earnest? I thought it was only a joke."

"Publish me next Sunday, or I'll prosecute you," was the gruff reply of the sturdy old bachelor. The next Sunday morning the town was astonished at the announcement which hung up in the vestibule of the little old meeting-house. Three weeks of probation passed, and all the gossips had enough to amuse them.

Mr. Boylston appointed the time for the wedding, to which his affianced agreed, at seven o'clock the following Monday morning, at Parson Jackson's.

Mrs. Jackson had her bed "in the best fore-room," and she had barely made herself and her room ready, when the couple made their appearance at the gate, each on foot, coming alone from their opposite homes. There was a few moments' conversation, and then Abigail came in, while her Joshua hastened down the street. He had forgotten to get a certificate! With due speed he found Squire Sharp, obtained the necessary document, and reappeared at the parsonage. A few moments more and Joshua Boylston ceased to be a bachelor. They lived together, as the story-books say, "in happiness ever after," — for twenty-six years.

There was one child by this marriage, a daughter Rebecca. Mr. Boylston died in 1804, at the age of 79. His widow lived till 1814.

Deacon Joshua C. Clark purchased the old Boylston house, and took it down in 1809, the Boylston family living at that time in the house on the corner of Washington and Cypress streets. He had a new house built for him by Nathaniel Murdock, on the old site, and when completed in all but the last details, it took fire and burned to the ground. The loss fell upon the carpenter, who had not delivered his completed work to the owner's hands. The townspeople rallied and raised a handsome sum towards remunerating him for his loss, and in a few months the present house was built, and Mr. Clark married Rebecca Boylston, and took possession of the house, in May, 1810.

The yard of the old house contained great rocks, and all the space from the west side of the house to the great ledge in Mrs. Bowditch's garden in the rear of the greenhouse, and so westward over what is now called Lakeside, was thickly wooded. The ground around the house was leveled by filling the spaces between the rocks even with their surface, retaining only the one projecting end of the ledge, which now helps to make this old place so picturesque, overrun with climbing vines.

We can hardly leave the Clark house and its inhabitants, without brief mention of one of its former inmates, an elderly maiden lady, known as "Miss Prudy Heath." She was from the Roxbury branch of the Heath family. There were no striking events in her life, or especially strong points in her character, to form the subject of a biographical sketch, yet she was just her own peculiar self, and as such was identified with Brookline, and particularly with the First Parish. In this connection, her figure should stand in the picture of the times in which she lived, as an incidental part of the whole, as the milestone, the rail fence, or the wayside burdock is introduced by the artist in a corner of his canvas.

Miss Prudence Heath was born in 1751; lived many

years in the family of the last Robert Sharp, received a small property from her nephew, Mr. Samuel Gore of Roxbury, and then settled herself for life among the Clarks, living first in the house of Deacon Samuel Clark, at the corner of Walnut and Chestnut streets, till his death, and then removing to his son's house in Warren Street, where she spent the remainder of her days.

Miss Prudy was not only quaint and unique, seen in the light of modern times, but in the days in which she lived, she was always, whatever might be the prevailing fashions, at least twenty years behind the times. She was a curiosity to children and strangers, whatever she might be to accustomed eyes, — with her immense black leghorn bonnet, and her great green silk umbrella, which she usually carried. There are persons to whom the sight of the plant known as succory, or blue vervain, which is still to be seen in waste spots, and along roadsides, often recalls the memory of Miss Prudy. This plant she gathered and dried, using its leaves as *tea*. Perhaps she would have resorted to its roots, had she known that it would become the famous chicory of modern commerce, which forms no inconsiderable part of the coffee now drank by the multitude.

So far as Miss Prudy's own living and habits were concerned, her Christian name might have been a synonym for her character, but to others she was truly generous, though a little vindictiveness flamed up occasionally, towards certain persons who had been unjust to her in her earlier days. One of her greatest pleasures was to entertain her friends at tea, a ceremony which always took place at four in the afternoon. Then the " young Hyson," which was carefully hoarded for these festivities, sent up its steaming fragrance, the choicest cake, and the " preserved squince," in which she delighted, were brought forth from their hidden retreats, and Miss Prudy was as happy as the presiding genius of the most aristocratic festal board in the town. Once a year, at least, Dr. Pierce honored her humble apartment with his presence on such an occasion, sometimes taking one of his family with him, and very often Miss Prudy remembered her minister with a generous gift from her small income. Two silver cups are still in possession of the First Church, which were presented by her in 1818.

This old lady was neither witty nor even facetious. She took life very much in earnest, yet her quaint speeches and queer ordering of words unawares, were sometimes as amusing to her friends as wit might have been. When the Providence railroad was opened through Roxbury, at the crossing of Tremont Street, it passed through the farm of her nephew, Mr. John Heath, and necessitated the removal of the house which he then occupied. Miss Prudy did not admire railways, — they were modern innovations upon which only the seal of evil was set, and her mind was a good deal exercised thereby. She visited in Roxbury at the old Gore place, by the crossing, and there examined the track, and came home convinced of its dangerous and mischievous tendency. The word "cars," she could not remember; "stages," were her idea of travelling conveyances. "Would you," she asked of her friends again and again, "*would* you ride in one o' them ravin' stages?" for to her imagination doubtless a Revere disaster might be a daily occurrence.

Poor old simple-hearted Miss Prudy, born in the middle of the eighteenth century, lived long enough to see something of the grand march of the nineteenth, in which she at least had no part. She died in 1839, aged eighty-eight, a character as impossible to be reproduced in these times, in this vicinity, as the ichthyosaurus, or the megatherium of geology.

A little southeast of this house, on the same side of the street, stood for many years, in the earlier history of the town, a house owned and occupied by Josiah Winchester, Jr. His son Caleb, and afterwards John Seaver, were his successors. The house was purchased and taken down during the last century, by the original proprietor of the house now owned by the heirs of the late Samuel Goddard.

The wooded hill opposite was formerly the property of Deacon Samuel Clark. About the year 1822, Captain Benjamin Bradley built a house below, and in front of the woods. He rented it for some little time to various tenants, and at last sold it to Mr. Jacob Eustis, an elderly gentleman who removed here from Saugus.

Mr. Eustis had two sons, both of whom survived him, the one well known as Judge Eustis, who took up his residence at the South, returning often to Brookline to spend his summers. The other, William Eustis, was educated for the profession of a physician, but being of a sensitive temperament, and also predisposed to insanity, his mind became somewhat affected by troubles in his early manhood, and he never followed his profession. Instead, however, he devoted attention to horticulture, built a fine greenhouse, and ornamented the place with choice vines and plants. He also was a teacher and afterwards superintendent of the First Parish Sabbath-school for several years. His beautiful attention to his aged and widowed mother, his kindness and delicacy of feeling made him warm friends in all who knew him well, though by the unsympathizing world at large he was smiled at for his little peculiarities, and perhaps generally undervalued. His health was gradually undermined, and he sank away and died without any visible disease. His mother did not long survive him, and the place soon passed into other hands. The house has lately given place to a modern and much larger one.

The house now owned by John L. Gardner was built by Captain Ingersoll early in the present century. Charles Tappan was the next owner of this place, and occupied it like his predecessor, ten years. His successor was Deacon Thomas Kendall of Boston, who also held a ten years' ownership. He was a prominent member of the Charles Street Baptist Church (then Dr. Sharp's) for many years. After some years' residence in Brookline he connected himself with the Baptist Church in this place, in which he continued an influential and honored member till his death, at an advanced age.

Deacon Kendall was the Representative of Brookline in the State Legislature for several years. He died in November, 1850.

The house which has for many years past been the residence of the late Samuel Goddard or his heirs, was built in 1792, by Nehemiah Davis.

At this time there were no other houses on the entire street, except the old Boylston house and the houses of the Winchesters, one of which, as mentioned before, he bought and took down. The farm connected with this place was very extensive. Mr. Davis occupied the house till his death in 1785. The next owner of any note, was Hon. George Cabot, a member of Congress, and afterwards Secretary of the Navy, in Washington's time, and a Federalist, in the old days when political animosity ran high between the conservatives and the democracy then just coming into power. The rancor between "Federalists" and "Jacobins" was as strong as anything which as yet marks the conflict between the supporters of Republican and Democratic candidates, and each party called the other as unlovely names and was as unscrupulous as to truth and falsehood in politics as their descendants seem to be.

Mr. Cabot was a retired sea-captain who had seen much of the world, and he bore hearty testimony to the desirableness of our town as a place of residence in his day, and to its many attractions. Mr. Cabot died in Boston in 1823, aged seventy-one. He left three sons, and a daughter who became the wife of President Kirkland of Harvard College.

Stephen Higginson, Jr., was the next owner of the place for a few years, but sold it to Captain Adam Babcock. The land which now comprises all of Mr. Gardner's place was sold off this estate to Captain Ingersoll, who married Captain Babcock's daughter. Both these gentlemen were also retired sea-captains. Mr. Goddard was Captain Babcock's successor in this house.

Mr. Goddard was one of the wealthy men of Brookline. In early life he had been engaged in mercantile pursuits in Manchester, England. He returned to this town about 1838, where he resided till his death, in March, 1871. He was nearly eighty-four years of age.

On the opposite side of the street, several acres of ground were once included in the Cabot estate. This was the corner lot bordering on Warren and Cottage streets. An old building, partly house and partly barn, stood on this lot, and was occupied by one of the first Irishmen who settled here. All that was between this and the estate before mentioned as Dr. Eustis's place, was early in the last century the property of Mr. Elhanan Winchester, grandfather of the preacher of that name. The old Winchester house stood almost on the site of the present Murdock house. His son Elhanan (who died a Shaker) was the next owner, and he sold to John Seaver and removed to the upper part of Heath Street as before mentioned. Mr. Seaver's estate went through many changes, and this lot of land became the property of the Hyslops. In 1799, Mr. David Hyslop sold the land to Nathaniel Murdock, a young carpenter, who had come into the town and was building the house of Hon. Stephen Higginson. The land sold included what is now the house lot of Mr. Charles D. Head. The house was built for Mr. Stephen Perkins, son of Samuel G. Perkins of Brookline.

Mr. Murdock raised the frame of his own house (which still stands) on the last day of the last century, December 31, 1799. On the first day of the year 1800 he boarded it in, and in the spring it was completed, and he occupied it from that time till his death, in 1837.

A house which stood next it and was removed a few years ago by Mr. Sargent, was built by George Murdock, son of the former.

The Cabot estate included all the land which has for many years past been the property of the Warren family. In the early settlement of the town, however, this place was the property of Josiah Winchester, father of Elhanan, who lived upon the Murdock place. The ancient Winchester house was destroyed before the close of the last century. The descendants of the Winchesters still live in Brookline.

On this place also stood an old gambrel-roofed red house, said to have been moved out from Boston. From the size and quality of the timbers and chimney, and the manner of building, it would seem to be very ancient. Mr. Warren, on purchasing the place, lived for a short time in this house till he could erect another, and then sold the old one to Captain Benjamin Bradley, who removed it to his hill. It was the first house placed on the hill. In this house lived for many years Mr. Celfe, an excellent man, well remembered as the skillful gardener for Richard Sullivan, Esq., and Judge Jackson, and afterwards for the late John E. Thayer, in whose service he died, at an advanced age. Long before his death, however, he had changed his residence. The old house was removed from Bradley's Hill at the time the other buildings were transferred to Sewall Street, and is still doing service at " Hart's Content." Whether it has finished its travels or still has further journeys before it, remains to be seen.

The house in the corner between Warren and Cottage streets, was built for Samuel G. Perkins, brother of Colonel Thomas H. Perkins.

The land upon the same side of Warren Street for many years past so highly cultivated and so beautiful in many attractions, including the estates of James S. Amory and Mrs. Winthrop, were never built upon until purchased by the present owners, and the whole area was known for many years as "the old huckleberry pasture." There are people now living in town who have gathered bushels of berries upon these places.

COLONEL T. H. PERKINS.

Colonel Thomas H. Perkins, though not a native of Brookline, was for so many years a resident and large tax-payer, that a brief sketch of his life seems in place in this history.

He was born in Boston, December 15, 1764. His mother's father, for whom he was named, was a dealer in hats and furs. The family lived in King Street, now State Street, and in full view of the events of the "Boston Massacre" in March, 1770. Colonel Perkins throughout his life remembered with great distinctness the impression made upon his childish mind by the sight of the dead bodies, and the blood which lay frozen upon the ground the next day. His father died when he was but six years old, and his mother, a woman of great energy, continued the business, and brought up her eight children with great credit to herself and to them. Her eldest son, James, on coming of age, went to the Island of San Domingo, in a ship of which his mother was part owner, and there was soon established in mercantile business.

Thomas Handasyd, the second son, was educated for college, but being much more strongly inclined to an active business life than to a quiet literary one, he joined his brother in San Domingo. Having remained there for a time, the climate being unfavorable to his health he returned to Boston, where he attended to the business of the house in the United States, while his younger brother, Samuel G. Perkins, took his place in San Domingo.

In 1788 he was married to the only daughter of Simon Elliot, Esq. (who afterwards came to reside in Heath Street). Mr. Perkins commenced married life in a most economical manner, as a matter of necessity, but soon turned his attention to the tea trade in Canton, to which place he made one voyage himself. During his absence our government was organized under the new constitution of 1789, and though heavy duties had been established, a stability had been given to trade which led to great mercantile prosperity.

In 1792 the great insurrection of the slaves in San Domingo broke up the prosperous business of his two brothers, and obliged them to return to Boston, having narrowly escaped with their lives, and suffered great losses. They began anew in Boston, their trade being with China and the northwest coast, and eventually established a house in Canton. Colonel Perkins received his military title as commander of the battalion which forms the Governor's escort, he having previously held a lower rank in that body.

Mr. James Perkins settled at what is known as "Pine Bank" on the shore of Jamaica Pond. The house was the one which now stands opposite the Town House, owned by Robert S. Davis, and lately occupied by Dr. Sanford. It was sold, and removed from Pine Bank about thirty years ago.

Samuel G. Perkins settled at the corner of Cottage and Warren streets.

Colonel Perkins about the beginning of the present century was chosen President of the Boston branch of the United States Bank, which was then quite a distinction, when there were so few banks. His own business was too pressing to admit of his holding this situation long, and he resigned after a year or two, and Hon. George Cabot was chosen in his stead. In 1805, Colonel Perkins was chosen a member of the State Senate, which place he held for nearly twenty years.

He was very active in establishing the Massachusetts General Hospital, and the Insane Hospital, his contribution and his elder brother's being each eight thousand dollars for these purposes, an amount for those times equal to a very much greater one at present.

In 1838 Colonel Perkins withdrew from business with a large fortune, and devoted his time to various public matters which interested him. He was especially noted as the generous patron of the Blind Asylum, to which he gave a fine large house in Pearl Street, Boston; of the Mercantile Library Association, and of the Boston Athenæum. He was naturally a lover of the beautiful both in nature and art, and spared no pains in the importing and cultivating of choice plants and trees on his beautiful place in Warren Street, which was quite a resort for visitors from many places. He sometimes went far out of his way to enjoy an extensive prospect or examine a fine tree.

An incident is related of the interest which he felt in the preservation of our Brookline elms. There was a row of magnificent elms through "the village," on the south side of the street from the lower part of Walnut Street, to the town line, — though this part of the village was then in Roxbury. Colonel Perkins riding by one day noticed a certain man who then lived in that neighborhood about to cut down two of them. He stopped and inquired into the necessity for such an act, and was informed that they shaded some cherry trees (two miserable little specimens not long set out). Colonel Perkins begged the man to spare the trees, telling him he would furnish him with cherries as long as he lived, but the obstinate old sinner, who seemed to delight in doing what annoyed others, especially rich men, persevered, and not only cut down the two, but after a time, all the rest which bordered his land, thus depriving not only his own generation, but those which have succeeded him, of the grateful shade which would have redeemed that unattractive region of half its repulsiveness even now, had they been spared.

Colonel Perkins being in Washington in 1796, was there introduced to General Washington, who invited him to his home in Mt. Vernon, where he spent two days. Some interesting incidents of this visit are related in his Memoirs.*

Colonel Perkins outlived both his brothers. His brother Samuel had died blind, and one of his own eyes was covered by a cataract for twenty years. The other

---

* *Memoirs of Colonel Thomas H. Perkins*, by Thomas G. Carey. This highly interesting volume is in the Brookline Public Library.

eye became affected, and he was in danger of total blindness. A successful operation by Dr. Williams of Boston removed it, however, and he who had done so much for others who were blind, was saved from that sad calamity himself. He was able to keep his books with his own hand till the last few months of his life.

Colonel Perkins was a remarkably noble looking man, with the dignified manners which characterize the gentlemen of the old school, now too seldom seen.

In 1852, Daniel Webster presented him with a set of his published works, accompanied by a most complimentary note in his own handwriting.

Colonel Perkins was not confined to his bed by illness a day, but died quite suddenly of prostration caused by a surgical operation, on the 11th of January, 1854, in the ninetieth year of his age.

As early as 1740 there was a house standing upon that part of Colonel Perkins' place where his farm-house has since stood. It was owned at that time by Christopher Dyer, and afterwards by his son William.

Afterwards Joseph Woodward purchased it, and it finally passed into the hands of John Lucas, who at one time owned a large amount of real estate in this town. The rest of the land belonging to the Perkins' and also the Cabot place, was formerly the property of Hon. Jonathan Mason, Jonathan Jackson, Mr. Heath, and others, but was not occupied by dwelling houses until purchased by the above-mentioned gentlemen. At the time Colonel Perkins built his house the site commanded an uninterrupted view of Boston, and Colonel Perkins so planned his house as to command the fine prospect from his parlor windows. The whole line of the Mill-dam, and the beautiful expanse of Charles River and the Back Bay were included in this extensive panorama. Trees and buildings long since interposed a barrier which shuts out this lovely view, and miles of streets with solid blocks of brick and stone houses, stand where the tide then rose and fell, and obscure Boston Common from all the high points which once overlooked it.

The old Cabot house, which stood upon the site of Mr. William Gray's present residence, was built for Mr. Samuel Cabot in the year 1806, by Mr. Murdock. During this year occurred the total eclipse of the sun, still remembered by aged persons for the great darkness which prevailed, so that fowls went to roost and cattle returned to their various places of shelter. The workmen upon this house abandoned their tools, and in common with everbody else went out to witness the impressive spectacle, — all but one youth; who declined to thus far trouble himself. This hero was the future Capt. Benjamin Bradley. Those who remembered the man, will recognize the incident as characteristic. The old family nurse indignantly expressed her opinion that "that fellow would live to be hanged."

The next house was built in 1824 by Colonel Perkins, for his daughter, Mrs. Cabot, by whom it is still occupied.

COTTAGE STREET.

In continuing our sketches of Warren Street, we passed Cottage Street without mention. We now return to that street, as upon it was one of the earliest settlements in the town.

Nearly upon the site of the late Captain Cook's cottage was the residence of Thomas Buckminster, who came hither from England in 1640. This ancient family dates back as far as 1216 in the English records. Thomas Buckminster, grandfather of the one who settled in this town, was the author of an almanac printed in London in 1599, and a copy of this curious old book has been preserved in the family down to the present time.

Thomas Buckminster of Muddy River was made a "freeman," as in the old meaning of the term becoming a communicant of the church was called, and received from the General Court a grant of a tract of land valued at ten pounds.

His descendant, Mrs. Eliza Buckminster Lee, for many years a resident of Brookline, in writing of her ancestor, says : —

" If we may infer anything from the selection of Thomas Buckminster's farm in Brookline, he must have had an eye for picturesque beauty. His dwelling stood at the foot of wooded heights, covered with a dense shrubbery, and fringed all up the rocky sides with delicate pensile branches and hanging vines. A rapid brook descending from these rocky heights, ran past his door, spreading out and winding in the meadows in front. Jamaica Lake, a quarter of a mile distant, embosomed in beautiful undulations of hill and valley, slept tranquilly in full sight of the house."

This place and neighborhood even yet retains much of the rural beauty which distinguished it in those remote days, and culture has added new attractions to the surroundings.

The elder Buckminster died in 1656. His eldest son, Lawrence, returned to England.

The wills of both these gentlemen are recorded in the Suffolk Probate office. Joseph Buckminster succeeded his father upon the farm in Brookline. His son Joseph married Martha Sharp, the daughter of the brave Lieutenant who fell in Sudbury fight, and removed from Brookline to Framingham. A further sketch of this branch of the Buckminster family is to be found in the chapter on the Sharp family. From this Brookline couple descended the Buckminsters of Rutland, Mass., and afterwards the eminent Dr. Buckminster of Portsmouth, whose distinguished son was pastor of the Brattle Street Church, and whose daughter, Mrs. Eliza Buckminster Lee, was the wife of Thomas Lee of this town, who brought his bride to this home of her remote ancestors to live on a part of the original Buckminster farm.

There seems to be much obscurity about the history of this old place for many years, but in 1740 it was owned by Henry Winchester. For more than eighty years it was owned by his descendants, his son Joseph and his grandson Nathaniel being his successors. The last of the Winchesters who resided here died in 1808. The old Winchester house, as it was called, was taken down in 1826.

Captain Cook purchased the place and made it a tasteful and beautiful residence. He also built two houses near his own for his two sons, — one in the valley, and the other on the opposite side of the street. One of them lived in the cottage a short time only, and the other died without ever occupying the residence intended for him. The Captain and his wife both lived to a great age, and died in the house in the valley. The original place which he beautified, now the property of Mr. Jerome W. Tyler, is known as "Linden Terrace."

The Lee place lies in Brookline, though the entrance to it is from Perkins Street in Roxbury. Mr. Lee was a great lover of natural beauty, and preserved the forest trees which adorned his place, and admired the natural rocks with their wild mosses and vines about them, too much to permit them to be removed by blasting. What a man of less taste would have regarded as blemishes, he looked upon with the true eye of one who lived close to the heart of Nature, and won from her many a secret.

On this beautiful place his gifted wife wrote several of the volumes which have become a part of the literature of the land, and in the unpretending cottage she died but a few years since.

This place has since Mr. Lee's death become the property of Ignatius Sargent, Esq.

GODDARD AVENUE.

This beautiful avenue, diverging at right angles from Cottage Street on the south side, takes its name from one of the old Brookline families. The original road was only a farm lane or cart-road leading to the farm and dwelling of the Goddard family. The principal entrance to this place from Brookline, however, was through land now on the Winthrop place on Warren Street. There was an old road through the woods also, toward Jamaica Plain, in the earliest days of the settlement, and a new road has been quite recently laid out over almost the same track. The part called Avon Street is of recent date. The old Goddard house still standing dates back a hundred years, but the original house, like the original family, was far more ancient than that. The family genealogy, which has been carefully traced out and published, dates back to William Goddard, a citizen and grocer of London, who came to Boston in 1665. His wife and three young sons came the following year. They settled in Watertown, and there Mr. Goddard was hired as a teacher. An old record of that place reads as follows: —

" *March* 27, 1680. These are to certify that Mr. William Goddard of Watertown whome the said towne by covenanting agreed to teach such children as should be sent to him to learn the rules of the Latin tongue, hath those accomplishments, which render him capable to discharge the trust (in that respect) committed to him.

(Signed) JOHN SHERMAN, *Pastor.*"

The second son of this William Goddard, Joseph, born in London in 1655, was the first of the name who settled in Brookline. He married in Watertown, Deborah Treadway, and came to Brookline in 1680, and settled upon the farm where his posterity still live.

His son John, and afterwards his grandson of the same name, succeeded him on the place. The latter, born in 1730, was a distinguished citizen of this town. During the Revolutionary War Mr. Goddard was a commissary-general for the American army in this vicinity.

During the seige of Boston Mr. Goddard was intrusted with the command of three hundred teams, which worked in darkness and by stealth in constructing the fortifications on Dorchester Heights, now South Boston. The absolute silence of the men, the promptness and efficiency with which they labored, and the success which crowned their efforts, were no doubt largely owing to the firmness, courage, and tact of the sturdy patriot in charge. Captain Joseph Goddard, who at that time was a boy of fourteen, was a driver of one of the teams under his father's direction, and often described the event to his children and friends now living.

Not a whip was allowed among the men on that moonlight March night when the fortifications on the Heights were the scene of such busy excitement, lest some incautious crack might betray them, but the oxen were urged on with goads. The saplings for the fascines were cut in the woods between Dorchester and Milton, and combined with fresh hay, made a light, though bulky material, easily piled up. No wonder that General Howe, looking over from Boston the next morning, thought that "the

Americans had done more in one night than his whole army could do in weeks." He did not know what had been going on in the woods within six miles of his army. Four or five pieces of cannon which had been concealed under the hay in Mr. Goddard's barn for weeks, were on this night stealthily removed to their destination, being taken round through Heath Street in Roxbury, and placed in position on Dorchester Heights.

In a shed or shop-building opposite the house, were several hundred pounds of gunpowder stored in the loft. A garrison of several soldiers occupied this building, living in the lower story, while they and the patriotic heroes of the house knew that one unfortunate spark might at any moment blow them all into eternity. All this time a sentinel was kept on the Goddard place to guard the premises.

The British officers (who were often out to Mr. Hulton's where Mr. Chapin now lives) and who were frequently entertained at the expense of a female Tory, who lived on the place now belonging to the family of the late Samuel Goddard, occasionally rode through the woods and about among the farm-houses, but they failed to discover anything which compromised the wary patriots. A British deserter, however, found his way through the woods to this retired place one day, and coming in sight of the house, which was then quite new, and was handsomely painted, unlike most of the houses of the vicinity, was afraid to go to it. Seeing some men at work on the place, he ventured to approach, and inquired if that was " the Governor's house." He was taken to the house, his wants were kindly provided for, and after a good night's rest he was able to proceed in his laudable purpose of putting all the space possible between himself and King George's troops. Had one traitorous Tory or half-hearted, corruptible friend, discovered those cannon being drawn quietly by night up that farm-lane to the hiding place, it would have cost the brave old farmer his life.

There was reason to believe, however, after a time, that suspicion had been roused respecting the concealed army stores, and they were removed to Concord, Mr. Goddard himself driving one of the teams the whole distance.

On one occasion when passing on horseback over Charlestown Neck, he overtook a loaded team. The driver was in some difficulty respecting his oxen, and Mr. Goddard dismounted to help him. He stepped between the oxen, but in a moment his horse was startled, and he sprang forward to seize him. At the same instant a ball fired from a British frigate in the river struck the ox-yoke and shivered it into fragments.

Mr. Goddard was an eye-witness of the battle of Lexington, and on that memorable day a Brookline man who had no gun, but was eager for the fray, borrowed of Mr. Goddard a fowling-piece, which he carried into the fight. During the action, however, the gun somehow was lost. Several years afterward when Mr. Goddard was one day on his way to Sherborn, he stopped at the "way-side inn." There, on a rack over the wide chimney piece, he saw what he supposed to be the identical gun which had been lost. He asked permission of the landlord to examine it, and at once on handling it, identified it beyond dispute. The landlord being convinced, gave up the gun to its rightful owner, who brought it home, and kept it till his grandson (our late Representative) was old enough to use it, when he gave it to him as a Revolutionary relic. It is still in existence among the Goddards, though it has gone from Brookline.

When the American army removed from Boston to New York, General Washington was urgent that Mr.

Goddard should accompany them, but his large family was a sufficiently strong reason why he should decline such service.

When the Federal Government was established, Mr. Goddard was chosen as the Representative of this town in the State Legislature, from 1785 to 1792.

Mr. Goddard was twice married. His first wife lived but two years; the second, Hannah Seaver, a most excellent, energetic, and highly esteemed woman, brought up a family of sixteen children. When some inquisitive or sympathizing friend in later years asked how she managed with such a host of little ones, she laughingly replied that she " put leather aprons on them all and turned them out to play."

Mrs. Goddard is still remembered, and her virtues are often recounted. Mr. Goddard removed in the latter part of his life to the house now occupied by George W. Stearns, opposite the old Reservoir, and in this house he died, in 1816, at the age of eighty-six years. Mrs. Goddard also died at the same age, in 1821.

John Goddard, born 1756, the eldest son of this couple, was a child of delicate and sensitive organization, but great powers of mind. When less than nine years of age he had committed to memory and recited to Rev. Joseph Jackson of the First Church, the whole book of Proverbs, and the 119th Psalm. He attended the Brookline schools, and entered Harvard College just before the Revolutionary War. He was interrupted in his course by a long and severe fit of illness, and by the events of the war, but notwithstanding maintained a high rank in his class. He graduated in 1777 as a physician, a student with the highly esteemed Dr. A. R. Cutter of Portsmouth, but owing to his delicate health preferred to commence business as an apothecary. He obtained a situation as surgeon on one of our armed vessels, intending thus to go to Spain to procure his stock, which the war prevented him from purchasing in England. On the way, however, the vessel was captured by the British, and he with the rest of the officers were carried as prisoners to one of the West India Islands. Here he was brought to the verge of death by a terrible fever, which so emaciated his body that when convalescent he crawled through a port-hole of the prison-ship and escaped by swimming to a vessel which put him on his way to the United States. Just before he reached home, however, this vessel was captured, and he was again a prisoner. Another exhausting fit of sickness followed in the same prison-ship from which he had escaped. He so far recovered as to make his escape once more, and this time reached home in safety, but the shock to his constitution was so severe that he never fully recovered from it.

After the war was over he married Susanna Heath, daughter of Mr. John Heath of Brookline, and settled in Portsmouth, where he engaged in the drug business. His talents every way fitted him for eminent public life, and he was, contrary to his wishes, elected Governor of New Hampshire, which office he however positively declined to accept. He was also chosen Senator to Congress, but being as decided in this as in the former case, the country was deprived of the services of an excellent man. He also enjoined upon his sons a similar abstinence from public life; for what reason we are not informed. One can hardly help wishing such delicacy might oftener prevail, but not in cases where it would deprive the country of the services of true and competent men.

Mr. Goddard was married four times. His second marriage, to Miss Jane Boyd, was soon terminated by her death. The third wife was a daughter of Dr. Langdon of Portsmouth, formerly President of Harvard College. The fourth was Anne White of Brookline.

Mr. Goddard died in Portsmouth, but some of his children have returned to reside in this home of their ancestors. One of the sons of Dr. John Goddard is the Rev. Warren Goddard of Bridgewater, a graduate of Harvard College, in the class of 1818. He was for some time Preceptor of Princeton Academy. Rev. Mr. Goddard is one of the oldest and ablest ministers of the New Church, or the denomination oftener known as Swedenborgian. His son, Rev. John Goddard, of Cincinnati, is also a distingished exponent of the same faith.* Richard Langdon Goddard, another son of Dr. John Goddard, is a merchant of New York. These gentlemen were sons of the third Mrs. Goddard, President Langdon's daughter.

Mr. Joseph Goddard, who settled upon the farm of his father in Brookline, was, during his long and prosperous life, a prominent citizen of Brookline. He was a justice of the peace for many years, and was captain of the militia of the town. He married Mary, a daughter of Samuel Aspinwall, of this town. Of the twelve children of Mr. Joseph Goddard, several are widely known. The eldest daughter married Captain George W. Stearns, and their numerous descendants are among our highly respected townspeople. One of his sons is our late Representative, and another is Samuel Aspinwall Goddard, of Birmingham, England, whose name deserves to be held in perpetual and honored remembrance, for the invaluable services rendered our country by his patriotic pen during the late rebellion. Though from his early manhood he has been a resident of England, and was even naturalized there by act of Parliament, he has ever retained a pro-

---

* Rev. Warren Goddard of High Street Church, Brookline, is a younger son of Mr. Goddard of Bridgewater. (1874.)

found respect and love of his native land, its government, and its institutions, worthy of the son of his distinguished and patriotic ancestry.

From the beginning of the Rebellion, when England in unfraternal haste was eager to recognize the Southern Confederacy, with its basis on slavery, and rebel emissaries both Southern and English were filling the columns of the British papers with false statements respecting both North and South, Mr. Goddard's pen was untiring in its refutations of these falsities. His clear and extensive knowledge of his native country, and of England, his familiarity with history, his utter detestation of any tyranny of man over his fellow man, and his fearlessness in daring to write the truth, the whole truth, and nothing but the truth, over his own signature in the face of opposition and hate, all fitted him to wield the pen, for the cause of right, with a force that made it mightier than the sword. If his grandfather, toiling by night within range of British bullets, did faithful service in establishing our national freedom, not the less did his own powerful pen do glorious service in guarding that freedom against British plotting with home traitors to overthrow it. To no one man's efforts are we more indebted for the failure of the British to recognize the Southern Confederacy among the nations, than to those of Mr. Goddard. John Bright himself recognized and acknowledged the strength which he received in his own honorable course from Mr. Goddard's able statements and unanswerable arguments.

Mr. Goddard received his only school-education in the old brick school-house near the Unitarian Church, but he may be called a self-made man. To a man with his powers of mind, all of life is education, and strength is gathered from a thousand resources scarcely known to the mere student of the classics. The boy who has awakened in him a love of books, and knows how to use them, holds the key to all knowledge, and life and nature will be his teachers.

The articles which he wrote for the various British papers have been reprinted in a large volume, and will form a valuable reference book for the future historian. This work has been presented to our Public Library by A. W. Goddard, Esq., and is worthy of a place in every library.

Captain Joseph Goddard was a man of energetic health, until the last few months of his life. He died in 1846, aged eighty-six.

Another prominent citizen of this town, born in the old house, was Mr. Benjamin Goddard, who lived opposite the Reservoir. He was a man of intelligence and much influence, though he never would accept or hold any public office. He acquired much wealth and lived to a great age, being over ninety-five years of age at his death. His brothers, Nathaniel and William Goddard, were successful merchants. A son of the latter is one of the owners of " Bradley's Hill." * There are branches of this family in Worcester County and other places, all of whom originated in Brookline, from the first Goddard family. Mr. Samuel Aspinwall Goddard, having occasion to investigate a case in England, which led to researches into the remote history of his family, a few years since, was successful in tracing back this old family in an unbroken line to the time of William the Conqueror. On this side of the water, the name bids fair to exist as long, at least, as that of any other family of New England. No other house and land in Brookline, except the Aspinwall possessions, have been so long in one family.

* Now called " Clifton Hill."

The first Joseph Goddard found this place in possession of William Marean, son of Dorman Marean, who was the first white settler upon it. From Joseph Goddard's time down to the present, there have been six generations born upon the place. The present old house was built in 1761, but has been kept in thorough repair and subjected to occasional improvements, so that it would not be supposed to be more than half that age. From the retirement of this secluded Brookline farm-house, have gone forth men whose strength of character has made them a power in society, both at home and abroad.

CHAPTER XVII.

CLYDE STREET. — NEWTON STREET. — " PUTTERHAM." — THE
CRAFT PLACE (NOW THE DENNY PLACE). — THE OLD SAW-
MILL. — SOUTH STREET. — ANCIENT HOUSE ATTACKED BY
INDIANS. — JAMES GRIGGS. — THE KENDRICKS.

CLYDE Street dates back to the year 1715, when it was voted, November 21: —

"That there should be an open way laid out from the south-west part of Brookline (to wit), from the road that leadeth from Jamaica to Erosamond Drew's saw-mill, across to Sherburne Road, so called, which accordingly was effected by the selectmen, viz., Captain Samuel Aspinwall, Thomas Stedman, and John Winchester, Jr., who have agreed with all the proprietors, and the damage by running said way through their property, has been paid as appears in the account book of said Town of Brookline. The aforesaid highway, beginning at the road leading from Roxbury to Mr. Drew's saw-mill, as aforesaid, near Isaac Child's house, on the east of said house as it is staked out, and running northwardly through Isaac Child's land, to the land of Samuel Newell, and then turning a little toward the east, running through the land of Joseph Dudley, Esq., then turning northwardly and running through or upon part of Joshua Child's land, being part of the 'Bowers Farm' so called, then entering upon the land of Thomas Woodward to the land of Joseph White, then turning a little toward the east, running to the land of the heirs of Jonathan Torrey, late of Brookline (alias Muddy River, deceased), then running northwardly to the road or lane, known by the name of 'Woodward's Lane,' to the road commonly known by the name of 'Sherburne Road.'"

It seems to come next in order, though not in date. "The road that leadeth from Jamaica to Erosamond Drew's saw-mill," was what is now Newton Street; the lane known by the name of "Woodward's lane," was that part of Warren Street leading from the present westerly entrance of Clyde Street to Heath Street.

There was no house on Clyde Street until after this date. The corner lot now owned by Mr. Cowan* was formerly a part of the estate of John Ackers, being used by him for a pasture. There was land on both sides of the street, belonging to Joseph White. The lot on the west side of Clyde Street, just north of the avenue leading to the estate of W. H. Gardner, was in the early part of this century owned by John Lucas, and was called "the Lucas pasture" long after it became the property of Timothy H. Child, an eccentric old man, known as "Daddy Child," though he was never married. He sold the pasture to Mr. Cabot some twenty-five years ago.

On the land lying between Mr. Gardner's place and the "Stock farm," so called, where there is now a young grove growing up, stood one of the earliest houses built in the street, probably the very first. This was built by Andrew Allard, afterward occupied by William Woodward, and last by "an old countryman," probably a Scotchman, named Vaughn. This man died at a very advanced age in 1775, and the old house was not long after demolished. The house now occupied by George Goldsmith was built by John Woodward, brother of William, at some time previous to 1740, as it was then standing. The Woodwards were a numerous family in this part of the town a hundred years ago. After the Woodwards, Deacon Joseph White owned it, and then John Corey, a distant connection of the Coreys of Washington Street.

* Now by the heirs of the late Mr. Cowan.

He died in 1803, and a cabinet maker, Erastus Champney, was the next owner. John Dunn, a gardener to Mr. Higginson, next owned it, and sold it to the present proprietor.

The old house on the extensive place formerly known as "the Stock farm," now Clyde Park, was built previous to 1740, by Samuel Newell. He left it to his son John, who was succeeded by Gulliver Winchester.

Another house a few rods to the east, on the same place, was begun by Robert Holt, the next resident of the old house, but was completed by Dr. Spooner, of Boston, who lived here in summers for many years, but died in Boston in 1836. After him it was occupied for a while by Curtis Travis, a butcher, who moved away and died. There have been many residents upon this place, but none who have specially identified themselves with the interests of the town. On this place, however, was born Hon. George S. Boutwell, late secretary of the treasury. William B. Spooner of Boston was also born on this place. The stone posts and iron gates at the entrances to the avenues were originally at the Park Street and Charles Street corners of Boston Common. When the iron fence was built around it, these were sold and brought to the Spooner place.

The land at this end of Clyde Street, on both sides, was, at the time of the laying out of the street in 1715, the property of Isaac Child. At this point we enter Newton Street, but to describe the places on this ancient street, in their order, we will begin at the point where Newton Street enters Brookline, from Roxbury. This was one of the early highways of the town, and had as many, if not more houses upon it a hundred and more years ago, than it has at present. There are two or three old and somewhat poor looking houses near the town line.

Nearly on the site of one of them, which looks like an old country school-house, formerly stood a house built early in the last century by Timothy Harris. It will be remembered by many Brookline people as the residence of Alvin Loker. It was destroyed by fire more than twenty years ago. Next it is a small, old-fashioned house close to the street, on the site of one also owned a hundred years ago by Timothy Harris. The present house was built in 1805, by his widow, and was afterwards occupied by the eccentric old bachelor, before mentioned as "Daddy Child," or Timothy Harris Child. Various anecdotes are related respecting his oddities, as leaving off his farmers' frock on a certain day in the spring, by the calendar, without regard to the weather, and putting it on in the autumn, equally regardless of the season. Between these dates he was never known to wear it. He had a certain routine, which he followed, in taking down a pair of bars, and from which he never varied. It would seem quite desirable that a mind so inclined to run in grooves should get started in the right ones, but perhaps the best thing he ever did, was one the most unlooked for. He was for many years addicted to the excessive use of liquors, and returning from the store one day with his customary black jug of rum, he met one of his neighbors, who said to him: —

"Mr. Child, I'll tell you what is the best possible use you can make of that black jug of yours."

"What is that?" he asked.

"Why, you just carry it up to the top of the hill there, and bury it," was the reply.

"Well, I'll do it," said the old man, and he carried the black jug to the top of the hill, dug a deep hole and buried it, and never dug it up again. From that time forward he drank no more liquor, and was as steady as the most faithful adherent to a temperance pledge. One might wish many modern jugs and bottles could share a similar fate.

NEWTON STREET, "PUTTERHAM."

Passing westward on Newton Street, we reach "the old Walley place," so called, afterwards known as "the Tilden place." This old, square, hip-roofed house has had many owners. It was built early in the last century, but is still apparently in tolerably good condition. Joshua Child was its first owner and occupant. His descendants, of another name, still live in our town. The Hon. Samuel H. Walley was for many years a resident here, and the place took its name from him.

The high hill, now known as Mount Walley, was during the Revolution one of the outposts of Washington's line of circumvallation around Boston, and from here a watch was kept (as from all the principal hills) upon the enemy's movements. A local tradition has always been preserved that Washington at one time visited this outpost, and entered the house of Joshua Child.

Soon after passing this place, we come to the point where the new extension of Goddard Avenue opens upon Newton Street, thus making a — we had almost said, *direct* communication with Cottage Street, through the once secluded acres of the Goddard farm. We consider again and write *circuitous*, instead of direct. Perhaps there were the best of reasons for the remarkable curves which this street describes, only it seems a little singular that when so much pains and money are spent to *straighten*, at the expense of fine shade trees, in some parts of the town, there should be such an apparent enthusiasm for curves in other places where it is difficult to discover anything gained by them. But we leave the problem for the initiated.

The next house upon the street, dating back any length of time, is the one now owned and occupied by W. A. Humphrey. This house was built by Isaac Child, who had died and left it to his son Isaac, previous to 1770. There are no traditions of historical interest that we can learn respecting it. It was occupied, after the time of the Childs, by Elisha Whitney, then by Major Asa Whitney, his son, and afterwards for many years by Samuel Hills. The house has been raised and greatly improved by its present owner, and is one of the most attractive places on the street.

A long avenue on the opposite side of the street, led in, to a remote house owned and occupied in the last century by Robert and John Harris. The third and last John Harris died at a great age in 1831. It must have been somewhat like pioneer life to have lived in this out of the way region, even within the last fifty years.

On the northwest side of the street, at some distance further on, stands the little, one-story temple of learning, long known as "Putterham school-house." The origin of this name, "Putterham," which long clung to this picturesque part of our town, has been for years a problem, unsolved, to the minds of the dwellers in the lower and populous part of the town. There seems to be an innate love of applying absurd, ridiculous, or grotesque titles to certain localities, and hardly a country town but has its "Purgatory," or "Squash End," or "Grab Village," or "Skunk's Misery," or some other ill-savored appellation for some particular spot. But the euphonious title of "Putterham," seems to have been exclusively reserved for the southwest part of our beautiful town.

In seeking to sift the matter to its origin, we have been informed by more than one of the old inhabitants that there was, or is a little spot of meadow land beside Newton Street, about half-way from the school-house to Newton line, on which a hundred years ago, a man, who was a sort of shiftless do-little, might be seen "puttering," from day to day the season through, by any passer-by. But no results ever were to be discovered, and that lot of land received the nickname of Putterham, which gradually extended over a much wider region, till it became common for the dwellers in the populous parts of the town to designate all this sparsely settled section of the town as Putterham, and the school-house and the saw-mill also shared the title. A better taste is now casting this old name aside.

The little old building above alluded to stands on the site of one which was no ornament to the neighborhood, and was destroyed by fire some fifty years ago. The present building, though small, has of late years been kept in repair, and meets the wants of the thinly settled neighborhood. The beautiful woods and rocks by which it is environed, afford the children delightful recreations not to be found in the neighborhood of elegant public buildings and concrete pavements. "Foot-ball" and "tag," ought to be at a discount where the wild vines cling and the velvety mosses and gray lichens grow, and the oaks drop down their shining acorns, and the bold and saucy squirrels chatter almost within arm's reach.

Many a beautiful lesson may be learned in this wild region not set down in "Colburn's," or mapped out by Guyot, but perhaps quite as useful in cultivating eye, and head, and heart, and quite as strength-giving against the weary days that are sure to come to us all sometime.

> "Still waits kind Nature to impart
> Her choicest gifts to those who gain
> An entrance to her loving heart
> Through the sharp discipline of pain."

A few rods west of the Newton Street school-house, on the opposite side of the street, there stood formerly an old house which was built and occupied by William Davis, who died there in 1777. The house had many owners afterwards, and was, when too old for further use, demolished in 1809. Traces of the old cellar are still to be seen. On the west side still further on is a somewhat old house still owned and occupied by members of the Woodward family. The next really old house is on the opposite side of the street just above the junction of South Street. On the site of it in the early days of the settlement stood a small house, owned — as was the farm with which it was connected — by Abraham Chamberlain. His heirs sold the farm, excepting the house and ten acres of land, to Caleb Crafts.* The remaining land and the house were bought by Thaddeus Jackson. On the same spot, after taking down the original house, Joshua Woodward, an uncle of Mrs. Jackson, built the house. It was occupied by him for some time and he died there during the Revolutionary War; Thaddeus Jackson, too, resided there till his death in 1832, at a great age. This old house stands endwise to the street, and has a long sloping roof in the rear.

The next house is interesting for its great age and the old families connected with its history. This is the old Crafts house on the Denny place. It has been thoroughly repaired and painted, and now looks not unlike the old houses seen on country roads, that were formerly kept as taverns. Its great age would not be suspected by a casual observer. This house was built by Vincent Druce in

---

* This name is quite as frequently spelt Craft.

the latter part of the seventeenth century or beginning of the eighteenth, and is therefore nearly two hundred years old. Obadiah Druce, son of John, and probably a nephew of Vincent, inherited the house and spent his days there. John Druce, the third of the name, was a graduate of Harvard College in 1738 and settled as a physician in Wrentham.

An interesting item is preserved respecting the first John Druce. It seems that he was a soldier in Captain Prentice's company, a troop of horse, in King Philip's War, and in July, 1675, was mortally wounded in the battle near Swanzey. He was brought home and died in his own house; he was but thirty-four years of age. His son John, who was but a child then, was probably the father of the doctor who settled in Wrentham.

Deacon Ebenezer Crafts of Roxbury, next purchased the house. This family in all its branches in Roxbury and Brookline traces its pedigree in this country to Griffin Crafts, who came from England among the earliest settlers in this vicinity. His son Ebenezer was the builder of the old house opposite Hillside on "the Roxbury road" or Tremont Street, which bears its date, 1709, on the chimney. In this house the Deacon Ebenezer Crafts above mentioned, lived in his youth. He married Susannah, daughter of Samuel White, Esq., of Brookline. The descendants of this couple have been and still are prominent among the inhabitants of Brookline.

Elizabeth Crafts, a daughter of theirs, born in 1747, was the lady long known as "Aunt White," a sketch of whose life has been given. There is an old letter written by her in her youth to a young friend, inviting her to come and visit her at the old farm-house on Newton Street. It is written in rhyme, and describes the domestic life of those days with quaint simplicity.

Her brother Caleb, a few years older than herself, held

a lieutenant's commission during the War of the Revolution. Many of the old military orders which he received are extant. Among them is the following: —

NEEDHAM, *Jan.* 31, 1778.

Sir, as the TransPorts are Soon Expected for the purpose of Carring Burgoynes' army to Europ — I am directed to detach from my regt 86 men repair to Castle Island to do doty there untill the troops are embarked and gone out of the harbor. You are directed to detach from your Company one Corporal and five men for the above Purpose and see that they are armed and accutred according to Law with a good Blanket and two days Provision and hold themselves ready to march on the shortice nots to the above Postes, Let no Time be lost.

"your humble serv't

" WM. MCINTOSH, *Col.*

" P. S. The fine is ten pounds if they refuse to march or Procure some able Bodaid man in his roome in twenty-four hours after he is detached as aforesaid."

The old pay-roll of a company of twenty-five Brookline men who served under Lieutenant Crafts at Dorchester Heights contains the names of Williams, Weld, Gore, Wiswell, Mann, and other well-known names in this vicinity.

All the men wrote their own names but one, who was obliged to make his " mark."

A list of men who enlisted as " six months' men " in the service for special duty in the Northern or Canada department, contains their agreement to provide themselves with " a good effective fire-arm, and if possible a bayonet thereto, a Cartridge box and blanket or in lieu of a Bayonet a Hatchet or Tomahawk."

During a great part of the Revolutionary War, Lieutenant Craft commanded under Captain Thomas White, in the Brookline Company, but among the curions old documents of those times is a note from a Captain Mayo, under date of Roxbury, July 4th, 1778, as follows: —

"*Sur*, Mr. Coller is cum to Do Duty in room of his Sun for a few days for won of the men of my Company, I Expect that you will have another man to-morrow.

"To Lieut. Craft in Dortichter,
"Thomas Mayo, *Capt.*"

Under date of 1782, July 9, we find a notice from the Selectmen to Lieutenant Crafts as follows: —

"*Sir*, The within is the fifth class in said town, which we the subscribers have classed in order to procure a man for the Continental army for three years or during the war agreeable to a resolve of the General Court of March last of which we have appointed you the head.

B White
John Goddard } *Selectmen.*"
W Campbell

"N. B. You are obliged to Notifie all the Inhabitants of your Class to meet within four days in order to procure a man or you will be oblidged to answer for all deficiencies."

On the inside are the following names: —

Caleb Crafts	57 £.
Wm Hyslop	122 "
Abr Jackson	8 "
Thad. Jackson	45. 15
Sol. Child	49. 10
Nath'l Griggs	1. 5
John Harris	29. 15
Isaac Child	50.
Mary Boylston	24.
Gulliver Winchester	39.
Isaac Gardner	74. 10

Several names of non-residents follow variously rated.

Under date of Brookline, August 23d, 1782, we find the following action taken upon the above order: —

"This certifies that I Samuel Whipple of Hardwick in county of Worcester and State of Massachusetts Bay do Engage and oblige myself to procure two Good and Lawful able bodied men to Inlist and Serve as Soldiers for the Town of Brookline in the county of Suffolk and state aforesaid for the Term of three years for the Consideration of sixty pound for Each man, viz, for Class No 3 & No 5 Whereof Benjamin White and Caleb Craft are heads. Said men are to be inlisted and mustered at or before the thirteenth day of September next and in falier thereof I Do Promise and oblige myself to pay all Damage that Shall arise on Sd Classes thereby as witness my hand,

"SAMUEL WHIPPLE."

Several orders issued before and during the Revolution bear the autograph of Captain, afterwards General William Heath.

We turn from the military experience of the old Craft family for a brief glance at the domestic life of those ancient days, for nothing seems to bring the past so completely within the scope of our apprehension as a glimpse of the little daily vicissitudes which came to them as to us, small things in themselves, and yet which make up a large part of life.

Deacon Crafts' family, like other well-to-do people of this colony in those times, employed slaves. He had bought a negro girl named Flora, for the sum of one hundred and five pounds. We copy the following letter, now nearly a hundred and forty years old, in all its quaint simplicity. It was written by Flora's former master to Deacon Craft.

"Sr, I am sorey you did not Lett me see you yesterday. I perseve you still meet with troble with the Negro which I am Exceeding sorey to hear as I told you at your houes I intended you no harme but good. I did bye you as I wold be done by & I still intend to do by you as I wold be done by if I ware in your

Caess, but however you must think as to the Sale of the Negro it is — by means of selling her to you for it is all over town that your discurege and wold give ten pounds to have me take her agane. I apperehend I had better given you twenty pounds than ever you had been consarned with her I would not a thanked anybody to have given me an hundred pounds for her that morning befor you carred her away but however seeing it is as it is, we must do as well as we can I wold have you consult with the Justes and Consider my case allso and do by me allso you would be done by. if I had your money as the Justeses bond I should be under the same consarn that I am now pray Lett me see you if you please and if we can accommodate the matter to both our Sattesfactun I shall be verey free in the matter that is if I hear no Reflecsions for I do declare I was sensere in the whole mater.

"from yours to Serve,

"EBENEZER DORR.

"*January the* 6 1735-6."

An uncomfortable servant for whom one had paid over a hundred pounds was not so easy to get rid of as a disorderly Bridget from the intelligence office whose place might be filled in three hours by one still more recently imported, and matters getting worse, the case was left out to referees consisting of " Messrs. Edward Ruggles of Roxbury, Thomas Cotton of Brooklyne, and Mr. Joseph Warren of Roxbury," who were to ascertain the particulars of the case and decide upon the best settlement of it between Mr. Dorr and Mr. Craft. It was decided by them in the course of a fortnight, that Mr. Dorr should take " the said Flora," back, and Mr. Craft should give him fifteen pounds in bills of credit, and Mr. Dorr pledged himself in case he should sell the girl to any other party for over ninety pounds that " the overplus of the sale shall be returned to said Ebenezer Craft, and the said fifteen pounds to Remain to me." And so the troubled domestic waters probably ran smooth again.

Edward Ruggles first appears in Brookline on this wise, in the town records: —

"Agreed with John Winchester, Jr., for his man Ed Ruggles, to keep school at the new school house two months, he beginning Wednesday January 23, 1711-12, allowing for his services £4 per order of Selectmen."

From time to time allusions to him occur in old papers. No doubt "Ruggles Street," indicates the vicinity of the place where this old Brookline school-master or his children settled, or at least owned lands. There were Ruggleses in Roxbury, however, in 1632-37. The old Dinah mentioned in connection with the White family was a slave in this Craft family all the earlier part of her life.

Deacon Craft was eighty-six years of age at the time of his death, in 1791. His son Samuel received from his grandfather, Samuel White, Esq., the gift of a farm on what is now South Street in this town, and has ever since been known as the Craft place. He was about to marry Ann, daughter of Deacon David Weld, and intended to occupy this place, but he died in 1775, aged thirty-nine, and the farm came into his father's possession.

In 1791, it was purchased by the lieutenant, Caleb, his brother, who continued to live in the Druce house on Newton Street, till his marriage in 1812, to Jerusha, daughter of Benjamin White, who had married Sarah, daughter of Captain Samuel Aspinwall. From this marriage descended the present Craft family in South Street. His second marriage was to Sarah, daughter of Robert Sharp. From this marriage descended the Craft family on Washington Street. Caleb Craft lived, like his father, to be above eighty years of age. He died in 1826, in the house which he built in South Street.

His son Caleb, also a grandson of the same name, lived upon the farm in South Street; the Newton Street house was sold by his son Samuel, who removed to the lower part of the town. All of his children have settled in other places, and there are no young people growing up in the town to keep up this respected old family name.

"EROSAMOND DREW'S SAW-MILL."

On the western side of Newton Street there is an extensive tract of land which is comparatively an unknown region. Once heavily timbered, the original forest was cut away, and no heavy timber has since been allowed to grow there, yet it is an unreclaimed wild covered with birches, alders, red maples, and many trees of larger growth. Bears lingered there long after they were exterminated elsewhere, and foxes, musk-rats, minks, owls, and other wild game have until recently, and do perhaps still tempt adventurous sportsmen to tramp through these rocky and swampy fastnesses.

The land lying hereabouts, on both sides of the street, both in Brookline and in Newton to the extent of several hundred acres, was in the year 1650 conveyed by Nicholas Hodgden of Boston and Brookline, to Thomas Hammond and Vincent Druce, the same who built the old house before described.

Erosamon Drew, whose name is spelled in six different ways in old documents, came from Ireland in his youth. He married Bethiah, Vincent Druce's daughter. The elder Druce, who seems to have been a wealthy man for those times, left his son-in-law considerable property.

A most curious and elaborate old deed dated in 1683 conveys a tract of sixty-four acres of woodland for fifty-five pounds to Erosamon Drew from "Vincent Drusse and Elizabeth his wife," in which an imperfectly scrawled V for his name, and E for hers, are their only attempts at penmanship.

An examination of the new map of the town will show a slight curving bit of road-way near Newton line, diverging from the street on the left, and joining it again at Newton line.

The passer-by upon the street would scarcely notice the grassy entrance to this curve, and perhaps fail to observe, unless attention were called to it, an old roof, to be seen almost on a level with the street, below the brow of the hill. Yet this curved bit of road was the original street or old road dipping down into the valley, for what good reason nobody now living knows, unless it was because down here was "Erosamond Drew's saw-mill," and there must be a way to get to it.

A brook which is the natural outlet of Hammond's Pond, flows through the swampy lot opposite and under the road. It is nearly concealed by rank bushes and young trees, beyond which is a large open meadow, which still annually yields many tons of hay. This extensive tract is the property of numerous owners, and is designated in ancient deeds as "the Grate meddows," also "Saw-mill meadows," and far and near colloquially as "Ponica." These meadows were flowed to obtain water-power enough to run the saw-mill, on leaving which after passing under the old road-way, the water emptied into another tract of land called "Bald Pate Meadows," there forming a mill-pond for another saw-mill which stood a short distance below, many years ago, in the edge of Newton. Its site was plainly to be seen a few years ago (and may be still), though it long since yielded to the superior advantages of its Brookline rival.

Below the level of the road down the declivity of the hill, and standing endwise to the now deserted and grassy old road-way, is a low house (the roof of which was above mentioned), falling into ruins, though still inhabited.* It is not less than two hundred years old, and perhaps more. This was Erosamon Drew's house, and over the brook close to it stood his saw-mill, and here all the sawing of boards for miles around was accomplished. The owner of the saw-mill was evidently a thrifty and good citizen, as he held various offices of trust in the town, being one of the selectmen, assessor, a member of the grand jury, and one of the committee on building the First Church.

There were three sons of Erosamon and Bethiah Drew who died young, or at least unmarried.

Ann, the only child of this parentage who lived to marry, was born in 1683. In 1710, she became the wife of Samuel White, Esq., and was the Madam Ann White of whom an account has been given.

Ann White, a daughter of this marriage, became the wife of Henry Sewall, son of the chief justice of that name.

One of her sons married into the Sparhawk family of Cambridge; there are also descendants of one of the daughters still living bearing the names of Walcott, and Ridgway; from one of the sons comes a branch of the Goddard family, so that there are still lineal descendants of Erosamon Drew in existence, in several names, or families, as it will be recollected that in the history of the Craft family, it was stated that Deacon Ebenezer Craft married Susannah, daughter of Samuel and Ann White (Drew).

An old deed of Isaac Hammond in 1693 conveys land bordering on the saw-mill lot, to Erosamon Drew. By another deed in April, 1731, Drew conveyed ten acres of his land to his son-in-law, Samuel White, " by reason and

---

* Since the above was written we learn that the building has been demolished.

in consideration of the Love, good-will and affection which he hath and doth bear toward him," which was certainly a very substantial proof of his satisfaction with his daughter's marriage.

This deed was witnessed by James Allen, the first minister of this town, and " hugh seot," but Erosamon Drew's signature, alas, was only " his mark," a round scrawl, for he could not write his name.

The deed was acknowledged before " Samuel Sewall, J Pacis," and rounds off in sonorous Latin, " Annoq Regnis Regis Georgius Magna Brittanica quarto," etc.

In August of the same year by another deed he gave his house and all his movable property to his son-in-law, wife and two children, for his being " helpful to him in his old age." In fact, from 1711 to this last date he seems to have been at short intervals bequeathing all his worldly goods to this beloved son-in-law. The grave-stones of all the Drews are still to be seen in Newton cemetery. The last of the Drews was gone before the middle of the last century, and large portions had been sold off the Druce and Hammond property, and that part of Samuel White's land which he inherited from his wife's father.

In the Revolutionary times this great tract, which still lies wild, was in the hands of Tories, who it is said secured some of King George's cannon and hid them in the thick woods, intending when the right time came to use them for the royal cause. But that time never came, and the Tories were forced to escape to the British Provinces, where they stayed till their property was confiscated. It was sold, and divided among many owners, and so remains. The old saw-mill came into the hands of Captain Curtis of Jamaica Plain, and afterwards of Edward Hall, who formerly was a blacksmith on Washington Street.

For many years Erosamon Drew's old house was called

"the huckleberry tavern," because the tenant then occupying it was skillful in making a kind of wine from the abundant huckleberries of the surrounding pastures, and on election days and other festive occasions, the scattered residents of the adjacent parts of Brookline and Newton often resorted thither for the mild stimulants of society and huckleberry wine. The old saw-mill was taken down about twenty-five years ago; Time with the slow fingers of decay is taking down the old house. It is a curious old place, the roof behind sloping almost to the ground. A part of the old flume and some of the stone underpinning of the saw-mill are still to be seen.

The extensive meadows through which the brook flows, and which were once rich with cranberry vines, are now all bush-grown. The old road down which teams drew heavy logs and took away the finished boards, is so narrow, rough, and winding, as to be almost unsafe. At the side of the road near the end of the house is a little patch fenced with brush, which was this very summer* blooming and gay with purple amaranths and other well-kept flowers, which lent a bit of brightness to the lonesome and otherwise neglected spot. The picturesque old place is a fit one for the location of the scenes of a poem or a novel.

SOUTH STREET.

South Street, formerly known as the old upper road to Dedham, extends from Newton Street to the extreme southerly corner of the town, where it enters West Roxbury. Several years ago a short cut was opened from Newton Street to South Street, beginning nearly opposite the old school-house on Newton Street, and ending on South Street at the Craft place, materially reducing the distance and avoiding a hill, in the journey from Brookline

* 1872.

to Dedham. This short street, which as yet has scarcely a house upon it, is known as Grove Street. The old way through the upper end of South Street is very little used, and probably few of the modern inhabitants of Brookline have explored it. It is such a road as one finds in mountain regions or backwoods, narrow, rough, and crooked, and heavily bordered with wild bushes, vines, and trees, nearly concealing the low, mossy old stone-wall laid up by the forefathers. It is a wild, picturesque, country road, such as few frequenters of the City Hall would believe to be in existence within six miles of that renowned locality. There is no need of exploring Berkshire or the White Hills for retirement or country scenes, while South Street is unvisited by county commissioners and their inevitable followers, the surveyors, and the corps who reduce the face of nature with the axe, the pickaxe, the shovel, and the tip-cart.

It will be curious to observe, when once a railroad crosses this section of the town, with what rapid strides the changes which have quietly bided their time for two hundred and forty years, will walk through South Street.

On the corner of Newton and South Street, stood a century ago an old blacksmith's shop, the property of Abraham Jackson, who was farmer and blacksmith. Being right on the way to the saw-mill, there was probably quite a business in his time, a hundred years and more ago, and till since railroads have been built, much teaming from Newton and travel to and from Dedham passed this corner. In 1712 Abraham Jackson was one of the surveyors of the highways. The old house which stood on South Street, on the same spot now occupied by Mr. Goodnough, had double or folding doors in front, and persons who can recollect it well remember how battered those heavy oaken doors were by tomahawks of the Indians, in a desperate attack made upon it. Thaddeus Jackson, Jr., who was his grandson and lived in the old house, often related the tales of those stirring old times which he heard from his grandfather, in whose day Indians and bears were not unfrequently found prowling about these parts of Brookline.

A few rods south of the present Crafts house stood a house once owned by Samuel White, Esq., who gave it to his grandson Samuel Crafts (as mentioned in a previous chapter), which was once occupied by "Hugh Scott," whose name appears frequently on old documents, but of whom we can ascertain but little. The old Crafts house near the corner of South and Grove streets, was mentioned on a previous page as having been built within the present century, by Caleb Crafts. On the opposite corner, around the modern house built by his grandson, grow many beautiful things which find their way to the charming exhibitions in Horticultural Hall. This is the last house in the town. On the opposite side, a little further south, on land which is now included in the Crafts and Weld places, stood, two hundred years ago, a house which was the dwelling of James Griggs, one of the early inhabitants of the town, the same who was appointed to "seat the meeting-house," was "tithing-man," and altogether, probably, a good church-goer of the old orthodox type till he became a "New Light" in Rev. Mr. Allen's day, and went off with the seceders to listen to Rev. Mr. Hyde's preaching in the old Winchester house. From thence we hear little of him. He was a relative of the families of the same name in other parts of the town.

Thomas Kendrick built a house a few rods south of the one last named, which would now be considered a curiosity, its site being but a few rods from the boundary line of the city of Boston. It was one story high only, of but two rooms. It was lighted by little windows of diamond-shaped glass in leaden sash, which swung on hinges, like doors. There was no paint within or without and the best room was papered with old newspapers, not being even plastered. The only ascent to "the loft" was through a trap-door by a well worn ladder, and in a similar way access was had to the cellar. Thomas Kendrick married a Griggs, from the family above mentioned, and James Griggs' son George, at one time lived here. After the death of Kendrick his widow married Jacob Hervey or Harvey.

The Kendrick family, not now represented in Brookline, will be remembered by many, chiefly by an old lady who died about twenty or more years ago, after a long and helpless illness, during which she was supported by the town, yet during all this time had successfully concealed several hundreds of dollars, which of course reverted to the town by way of compensation, after her death. This person was the wife of Thomas Kendrick, Jr. Jacob Harvey, his step-father, was a soldier in the service of the town in Revolutionary times. An old document, dated 1781, is still preserved, in which eight of the old citizens of the town " promise to pay Jacob Harvey on conditions of his serving as a soldier in the Contenantal army for the term of three years unless sooner regulerly discharged . . . the sum of fifty hard dollers and three thousand seven hundred and 50 of the oald Contenantal Dollers and to deliver at his hous in said town Four Cords of good Fire wood." This was to be repeated each year or fraction of a year thereafter that he remained in the service. An old receipt for a part of this money signed by his wife " Marey Hervey X her mark," is also extant. Mr. Hervey died in 1812 aged 63 years.

Thomas Kendrick, Mrs. Harvey's son, distinctly remembered seeing men at the time of the Lexington and Concord battle running across lots in this neighborhood guided by the sound of the firing, and jumping fences in their eagerness to reach the scene of the fray, taking their course back of Walnut Hills and through Newton.

The old house became so dilapidated that Mrs. Harvey for the last ten years of her life spent her winters with a married daughter in Boston, but she was always impatient for Spring to come that she might return to her country residence, or "hut" as she called it. After the old lady died, in 1826, the house was taken down. The land on which it stood is a part of the Weld place. It is a rocky and beautifully wild country place thereabouts, on one side of the street almost covered with forest trees. There are no other buildings in the town on South Street, and this closes the description of the town in this direction.

CHAPTER XVIII.

HIGH STREET CHURCH. — CHURCH OF OUR SAVIOUR. — GOSPEL CHURCH. — LOCAL INDUSTRIES.

THE churches of Brookline, which have been established within the last quarter of a century, can hardly be reckoned among the fitting subjects of a series of sketches belonging almost exclusively to the past, yet to omit a part of them simply because they are modern, might seem an invidious distinction. There are other reasons also, why a sketch of the High Street Church, more generally known as the Swedenborgian, may be presumed to be of some interest, for there is probably no religious society in the community of which so little is known by outsiders, nor of which such mistaken ideas are prevalent.

A few members of the Boston Society of the New Jerusalem, in Bowdoin Street, became residents of Brookline twenty or more years ago. There was then no public conveyance on Sundays, and these few worshippers, of a like faith, met for occasional religious services, and a little Sunday-school, in private parlors. Sometimes an omnibus was chartered, and these persons thus resorted to their own church on such occasions as seemed desirable.

In 1852, worship was first held in the Town Hall, the numbers increased, and in April, 1857, a society was formed. The first minister was Rev. T. B. Hayward. His connection with the church continued until 1861. He was succeeded the same year by Rev. Mr. Ager. In

1862, the temple in High Street was built. Mr. Ager continued with this church until 1864, when he was called to the pastorate of the society in Brooklyn, N. Y., where he still officiates. He was succeeded in Brookline by the Rev. S. M. Warren. Mr. Warren being called away to Europe for an indefinite period, his place was temporarily filled by Rev. Abiel Silver, who divided his time between this church and a little body of worshippers at Boston Highlands. A society was soon formed there which outgrew in numbers and means, the little church in Brookline, and soon took occasion to appropriate the services of the pastor altogether to their own needs. Since that time the Brookline society has been without a regular minister, except as various clergymen have been hired for longer or shorter periods.* The question is often asked, "What do the Swedenborgians believe?" We append the following "Doctrines of the New Church," from the Liturgy or Book of Worship, page 69.

1. "That there is one God; that in Him is a Divine Trinity, called the Father, the Son, and the Holy Spirit; that these three are distinct, and at the same time united in Him, as the soul, the body, and the operation are in man; and that the one God is the Lord Jesus Christ.

2. "That saving faith is to believe in Him as the Redeemer, Regenerator, and Saviour from sin.

3. "That the sacred Scripture is Divine Truth; that it is revealed to us as a means by which we may distinguish between good and evil, by which we may be delivered from the influence of evil spirits, and by which we may become associated with angels and conjoined with the Lord.

4. "That we must abstain from doing evil, because it is of the devil and from the devil; and that we must do good because it is of God and from God.

* Rev. Warren Goddard, Jr., of Bridgewater, was installed as pastor of this church in April, 1874.

5. "That in abstaining from evil and doing good we are to act as of ourselves; but we must at the same time believe and acknowledge that the will, the understanding, and the power to do so are of the Lord alone."

To this creed, nothing more and nothing less, is required the assent of those who would become members of the New Church.

It seems almost too absurd to believe, in these late days of intelligence and liberality, that any person can be found who believes that New Church people are worshippers or blind devotees of Swedenborg, yet well meaning and religious people are to be found in our own community who do believe such things, and also the ridiculous and oft repeated calumny, that New Church people " set plates for departed friends." Any one who would learn even a little of the theory of the future life as held by this sect, would find that it is not believed in the New Church that persons in the body are seen or heard by those who have passed into the spiritual world, that their existence is purely spiritual, and that all connection with material things has ceased. No person has yet been found who ever saw a person, or knew a person who "set plates for departed friends." The story has been traced to the ignorance of a servant in a Philadelphia family years ago, and never could have gained such general credence but for popular prejudice against what was new and untried. For modern spiritualism, the New Church has neither sympathy nor sanction. On the other point, worshipping of Swedenborg, or blind faith in a fanatic, whichever it may be called or supposed to be, perhaps the above quotation of the doctrines of the church should be a sufficient answer.

It may not be amiss, however, to state what the church knows about Swedenborg, and why it believes him at all.

Emanuel Swedenborg was born in Stockholm, in 1688, of excellent parentage. He was made a nobleman in 1719. In 1722, he entered upon the duties of "Assessor Extraordinary of the Board of Mines," to which he was appointed by Charles XII. He was admitted a member of the Royal Academy of Sciences at Stockholm, in 1729. He published many learned scientific works between 1710 and 1734, nearly all of which were written in Latin. His society was sought by the most learned men of Europe, and many of his theories and positions on various scientific topics, which were not accepted by the men of his times, have been found by modern scientists to be true. In 1740, he published in a large quarto volume his "Economy of the Animal Kingdom." In 1745, at the age of fifty-four, Swedenborg relinquished his scientific pursuits, and devoted himself to studying theology and unfolding the great truths of the Bible. Swedenborg never preached, wrought miracles, or attempted the founding of a new sect. He wrote his elaborate and voluminous works, published them at his own expense, and placed them in all the principal libraries of Europe. His works are nothing more than a commentary on the Bible; but they differ from those of all other commentators in this, that while others have given their own views of the meaning and design of the different parts or subjects upon which they treat, Swedenborg says nothing as of himself, but constantly says that it was given him by the Lord. This remarkable statement would be enough to condemn the whole thing, were his explanations of Scripture arbitrary, confused, or contradictory; but they are instead, clear and consistent, and founded on a plan of interpretation which is a science in itself, — the science of correspondence.

There is evidence in the old heathen writers and in

Egyptian and other hieroglyphics that the knowledge of such a science once existed. It inheres in the nature of things, and is the invention of neither Swedenborg nor any other man, any more than the truths of mathematics are man's invention; calling it fanciful or visionary does not make it so. Swedenborg was never insane, he lived an honored, useful, and quiet life and died a peaceful death, at the age of eighty-five. He is venerated as a wise and good man, but not worshipped, any more than the old churches worship St. Paul, St. Augustine, or Chrysostom. It is not deemed necessary to any man's salvation, by this sect, that he shall accept the teachings of Swedenborg or any man or body of men. Those who can receive these teachings may do so profitably, — for those who cannot, enough truths of the Bible lie apparent to the simplest consciousness to prove of saving value if followed. Every year the principal doctrines held by the New Church are being more widely disseminated, and are permeating the mass of worshipping Christians of every sect. They are preached in pulpits of every denomination and received as food for the soul by many who would reject them as poison if they knew the source from whence their preacher had gathered his materials, and to whom he is indebted for the consistency of his theology.

The test of a person's religion should be the life which it causes him to live. There are inconsistent professors in all churches, but we think if tested by the standard of life, the main doctrines of the New Church, love to God and good will to man, will be found not a whit behind those held by other churches, in making people fit to live, and thus fit to die.

CHURCH OF OUR SAVIOUR, LONGWOOD, A MEMORIAL CHURCH.

The visitor at Longwood, approaching from Chapel Station, would at once be struck with the neatness and good taste apparent everywhere. The Church of Our Saviour, tasteful in external designs and surroundings, is in its interior appointments and decorations a model of beauty, exquisite in every detail. The parish was organized on the 19th of February, 1868. The church building was the gift of Dr. William R. Lawrence and Amos A. Lawrence, Esq., as a tribute to the memory of their honored father, Amos Lawrence, and is an appropriate and beautiful expression of filial regard for a beloved and noble man, whose character deserves to be held in perpetual remembrance.

The organ, which was built expressly for this church, by the Messrs. Hook, was the gift of Mrs. Amos A. Lawrence, in memory of her mother. The beautiful baptismal font was presented by Mrs. F. W. Lawrence, also as a memorial gift.

The architect of the building was Mr. Esty, of Framingham. Prominent among the members of this society in its organization, besides the various branches of the Lawrence family, were Messrs. Samuel L. Bush, S. H. Gregory, the late Commodore George S. Blake, Mr. William C. Hitchborn, and Dr. Robert S. Amory.

The first public service was held March 22, 1868, at which time the present Rector, Rev. Elliott D. Tompkins, began his work. The church edifice was consecrated by the late lamented Bishop Eastburn, on the 29th of September following.

Although it is not quite five years since this church was organized, there are eighty or more communicants, and the flourishing Sabbath-school numbers over ninety scholars. A sewing circle was also organized and commenced its useful work the first year of the existence of the society.

GOSPEL CHURCH.

Gospel Church, sometimes called "the Sears Church," with its massive walls and square tower, a substantial and beautiful building, is a curious anomaly in church history, having a pastor and a sexton, but no church or congregation. The building was erected by the late David Sears, before there was any other church in Longwood, at his own expense, with the expectation that all sects would unite in common worship within its walls. He prepared a Liturgy or Book of Worship expressing his own ideas on religious matters, for regular use in the church. The well-meant plan was a failure, and the building stands a memorial of the good intentions and fallacious hopes of the wealthy projector whose mortal remains slumber beneath it, and whose design failed, only because it is, or seems to be, a moral impossibility for human beings to lay aside their sectarian prejudices and together worship one God in whom all profess to believe. Worship was maintained for a time, but the attendance was so small that it was finally abandoned.

This completes the list of the eight Brookline churches. Though three are at present without pastors, all except the last mentioned seem to enjoy a fair share of prosperity, and each in its way is a force for good in the community.*

LOCAL INDUSTRIES.

It is customary to record, in the history of a town, some account of its various industrial interests, but Brook-

---

* Since the above was written two of the churches have obtained pastors, and the Methodists are established in the former Congregational church, so that there are now nine churches.

line being but a suburb of Boston has little to offer in that line, though one of the richest towns in the State, for its size and population.

From its settlement, until after the second war with England, it was a region of farms, and no more beautiful or skillful suburban farming was to be found. After the period above mentioned, a number of Boston gentlemen purchased land, and made for themselves delightful country seats here, thus adding greatly to the wealth and attractions of the town. From that time forward there was a steady increase of population and wealth, and farm after farm has been cut up into house lots, until only the remoter tracts of land can be used for this purpose, and the majority of the inhabitants are business men of Boston.

For many years the market gardens of the Wards, Davises, Moses Jones, the Stearnses, Griggses, Coolidges, Coreys, Crafts, Whites, and others, furnished the earliest and choicest fruits and vegetables for Boston market, and the elegant green-houses of Messrs. Perkins, Cabot, Higginson, Gardner, Thayer, and others were the finest in the vicinity of Boston; for then horticulture was not established as a regular occupation, and strangers were admitted by courtesy to admire their beautiful treasures.

The one wharf which gives Brookline any occupation on its river front, has been kept for many years by E. M. Abbott, as a lumber wharf. Of late the Messrs. Cousens have made it also a depot for the storage and sale of coal and wood, its area having been increased. The Boston and Albany Railroad Corporation own an extensive tract of land near this wharf, where a perfect network of rails cover the ground, and the Grand Junction Railway diverges, crossing the river and conveying thousands of tons of produce for export, daily, to their wharf at East Boston.

For nearly twenty years past, until quite recently, the manufacture of knit woollen goods was carried on by Joseph Turner & Sons. The only other business, not merely local, of a mechanical kind, is the manufacture of philosophical instruments, by the Messrs. Ritchie.

In 1868, E. S. Ritchie & Sons removed their manufactory of philosophical instruments from Boston to Panter's Building, Brookline. Their establishment has been for many years the largest manufactory of instruments and apparatus illustrative of physical science, particularly in the higher grades, for colleges, etc., in the country. In later years the principal branch of their works has been the manufacture of marine compasses, particularly of such as are known as liquid compasses, invented and patented by the senior member of the firm, and which are now solely used by the Navy of the United States, and very largely by the mercantile marine of the country. A form of this instrument, specially designed for the purpose, was used on the monitors during the late war.

The Messrs. Ritchie have lately built a magnetic observatory on Gorham Avenue; a neat octagon building, designed by T. P. Chandler, Jr., for the use of the Bureau of Navigation, of the U. S. Navy. It is built of wood and copper, no iron being employed, and is furnished by the Bureau, with the most delicate instruments known to science, for the adjustment and testing of compasses. All such instruments used by our Navy are here inspected and tested by the Superintendent of Compasses of the Navy.

A chair shop, which employs steam power, has within a year been established on the north side of Brighton Avenue; but recent legislation seems to indicate the speedy annexation of this part of Brookline to Boston.

Several florists add the attractions of their beautiful vocation to the embellishment of Brookline, of whom

Mr. Richards, of Clyde Street, and George Craft, Esq., of South Street, have acquired an extensive reputation for the culture of the gladiolus. Miss Tobey, of Linden Place, has also a lovely green-house, which deserves a liberal patronage. The reports of the various horticultural exhibitions in Boston, show that the grapes and pears of Brookline, as well as its flowers, are annually conspicuous among the choice products which adorn the tables on these occasions.

Those who have known and loved the Brookline of the past, cannot but regret the necessity which, in some cases, and the want of a cultivated taste in others, dictates the building of crowded houses so close together that every vestige of rural beauty is sacrificed, and that the chief attractions, which have for years made our town proverbial for its charms, are rapidly disappearing before the march of greedy speculation. The central and southwestern portions of the town still preserve their old time reputation for beauty, and for several years past the elegant green-houses and grounds of Ignatius Sargent, Esq., have been a centre of attraction in spring, when through the generosity of the proprietor the admirers of floral beauty have been freely invited to witness the magnificent displays of azaleas, which have made the place famous.

CHAPTER XIX.

A BRIEF SUMMARY OF THE MILITARY HISTORY OF BROOKLINE.

THE part which was borne by our town in the War of the Revolution, has been incidentally treated of in our account of the various houses, families, and old fortifications.

The second war with Great Britain, so unpopular in New England, was regarded here in the same spirit as elsewhere. It will be remembered that it was during this war that our townsman, Col. Thomas Aspinwall, distinguished himself by valiant services, and lost his arm.

Brookline was called upon during the war to furnish militia for harbor defense, and a company was sent, of which the old muster-roll reads as follows: —

"*Men's names who were detached September* 18, 1814, *by order of Col. Joseph Dudley, for the defence of the State.*

"Lieut. Robert S. Davis, Ensign Thomas Griggs, Sergt. Daniel Pierce, Fifer, Thomas Chubbuck.

David Smith,	Thomas Farnsworth,	Charles Stearns, Jr.
Joshua Loring,	Joseph Goddard,	James Holden,
James Whidney,	Edward Hall,	Artemas Fairbanks,
Charles Leavitt,	Nathaniel Talbot,	William Atwood,
Wm. M. Tenant,	John Graves,	George Morse,
Samuel Townsend,	Jonathan S. Ayres,	Samuel Williams,
Amasa Jackson,	William Otis,	John Warren,
Joseph Whitney,	John Vose,	David Colby.
Eli Hunten,	George Richardson,	

who will report immediately to Fort Independence for three months, unless sooner discharged."

Timothy Corey, afterwards deacon of the Baptist Church, was Captain at this time. He was succeeded in the office by Lieut. R. S. Davis. The sojourn at the Fort was barren of incident, except the occasional firing of a shot across the bows of some foreign vessel, which did not obey the signal to heave to, and report. A Spanish vessel thus arrested, had not a man on board who could speak English, neither was there one at head-quarters at the Fort who could speak Spanish, and after some rather amusing exhibitions of pantomime, the intruder was allowed to proceed.

The Mexican War, hardly more popular in New England than the War of 1812, drew few volunteers from Brookline, and Colonel, afterwards Brigadier-general Mansfield, participated in the events of those times, and at the close of the war took up his residence in Brookline for several years, in the house on the corner of Park and Marion streets, now occupied by Mr. Mann. He fell, it will be recollected, at Antietam, during the Rebellion.

During the years immediately preceding the Rebellion, public sentiment in our conservative community, had kept pace with that of Boston in hostility to slavery, and in 1856 the town was almost unanimous for the election of John C. Fremont, as President of the United States.

BROOKLINE IN THE WAR OF THE REBELLION.

The guns of the siege of Fort Sumter, reverberating through the length and breadth of the land, awakened responsive echoes in Brookline. Groups of pale-faced, resolute men, were seen along the streets, in earnest conversation, in the stores and post-office, at the railroad station, wherever two or three chanced to meet, with defiance in eye and step. The national colors were seen in every man's button-hole, and every school-boy's jacket;

they streamed from every public building and many a private roof, as if dearer and more honored than ever, they might thus be lifted out of their temporary degradation, before audacious and insolent South Carolina.

President Lincoln's call for seventy-five thousand men was flashed by telegraph through the North, and Brookline responded. Companies were forming everywhere, and the nucleus of one collected by Charles L. Chandler, afterwards Lieutenant-colonel of the Massachusetts 57th Regiment, already began to drill, before the town had time to summon a meeting, and take action in the matter; the first volunteer being William, son of Samuel Goddard of this town — since deceased. A meeting of citizens was held, April 22, and a military committee appointed "to take charge of all military arrangements which shall be made by the town." It was also voted "to raise a military fund by a town tax, and that a sum not less than fifteen thousand dollars be appropriated therefor; and to such fund shall be added all private contributions to be expended for such purposes as may be indicated by the donors." The Military Committee were authorized to draw upon this fund "in such amounts, and at such times, and for such purposes, as a majority of said committee shall determine." It was also voted, "that there forthwith be opened a list of all male inhabitants of Brookline, above the age of seventeen years, who wish to be drilled for military service; and that the Military Commtttee be authorized to form the persons signing such lists into such corps as they may deem expedient for the public good." On Monday evening, April 29, 1861, a legal town-meeting, duly notified, was held, and the above votes confirmed.

One of the first acts of the Military Committee was the hiring of the hall in Guild's Block, for a drill hall and armory, and Capt. Edward A. Wild, then a popular young physician in town, with Lieutenants Charles L. Chandler and William L. Candler, commenced recruiting a company.

The old town hall, then standing on the site of the present new one (only nearer Washington Street, which has since been widened at that point), had a piece of open ground in the rear, extending to the Pierce Primary school-house. Here, on the fine days of that memorable spring, the company met for drill, and the rudiments of military science were taught the young heroes outside the school-house, while the young heroes inside took arithmetic and the spelling-book, to the beat of the drum, and listened with eager avidity to the history of their native land, as they saw the sunlight flash on the guns stacked before the windows, or turning in varied evolutions as the drill proceeded. The fingers of the children beat an unconscious tattoo upon their desks as they studied, and their feet marched in a measured tramp as they went to their classes.

The blood of the people was up, and nothing but the war was thought of or discussed. The same week that the drill of the volunteers began, the ladies of the town organized a society to sew for them, and in every house, early and late, the needle and the sewing-machine were plied with vigor, for "our soldiers," that were to be. The best of materials and the best of work were put into the articles made, and though after experience had taught us what was necessary and what was superfluous, and the ladies had learned that a soldier needs no larger slippers, or ampler garments when a soldier than when a private citizen, and all had had their laugh over the mistakes of early enthusiasm, there was left the conviction that at least this purpose was served, — there was a vent thus given to a patriotic fervor of feeling, that was agonizing unless expressed in some way, and the hearts of those were cheered who were preparing to go forth to victory or death. The substantial and excellent garments that were made were far better than those supplied by the government, and a thousand little wants were foreseen and kept provided for from this source during the whole war.

The Brookline Company became Company A, of the 1st Mass. Regiment, and soon went into Camp Cameron at Cambridge. Another company, recruited principally by Wilder Dwight (afterwards Lieutenant-colonel) of Brookline, went into camp at West Roxbury, and became a part of the 2d Mass. Regiment.

The Military Committee appropriated five hundred dollars for use of the men in Company A; one hundred and twenty-five dollars each to Captain Wild, Lieutenants Chandler and Candler, for an outfit; and also furnished the officers with a camp chest. The ladies, who had already been busily at work for three or four weeks, furnished the company with well-made undergarments, the cost of materials for which had been subscribed by various citizens.

In the month of May, Jacob Miller, previously a sergeant of artillery in the United States army, was engaged as drill-master and armorer, and squads of volunteers were drilled at the armory daily and every evening. Two field pieces were also obtained, and artillery drill was practiced by those who preferred that branch of the service. There was scarcely an hour in the day that the drum-beat was not heard in our streets, for the boys, burning with the enthusiasm of the times, must drill as did their elders; and during the whole of 1861–2, the boys of the public schools were drilled at the hall, and in the streets. A fine company of boys was formed, which was designated the "Brookline Rifles," chiefly from the High School. This company was at first drilled by Sergeant Miller, but procured its uniforms and arms without expense to the town. It continued during the whole war, and was so finely drilled as to elicit high encomiums from competent judges, on several occasions. It was invited to many other towns, and was reviewed before the Governor and Legislature. Fortunately, the war closed before the age of the young soldiers admitted of their entering the army. By an enrollment of the town, made by the assessors, in August, 1861, it appeared that there were in the town but six hundred and sixty-seven males between the ages of eighteen and forty-five, — aliens, and persons unfit for military duty included, — and it was apparent that should the war continue two or three years, Brookline would be obliged to procure soldiers, by bounty, from outside her territorial limits.

In February, 1862, our first dead soldier was brought home for burial, not fallen in battle, but accidentally shot by a comrade. This was Herbert S. Barlow. The funeral services were held in the Harvard Congregational Church (now the Methodist), and the crowded house, and many a tearful eye, bore witness of the public feeling. "He was the only son of his mother, and she a widow."

In August of the same year, occurred the second disastrous battle of Bull Run. For two or three days the public mind had been alternating between hope and fear, as contradictory telegrams were flashed over the wires. On Sunday morning came a dispatch from Washington, asking for contributions of hospital stores, and surgeons from Boston and vicinity. Our army stores and hospital supplies had fallen into the hands of the enemy, and our wounded were suffering for every needful appliance. Even surgeons had taken off their own shirts to strip into bandages, and help must have been forthcoming abundantly and promptly, or the results would have been fatal. Governor Andrew and the State of Massachusetts had already established a reputation for prompt, decisive, patriotic action, and the President knew where to look for aid. The dispatch was received in Boston in the night, and before sunrise on Sunday morning Mr. George B. Blake of this town was in his chaise, on his way to arouse the people. He first called on Hon. G. Twichell, then President of the Boston and Worcester Railroad, and a plan was organized for the informing of the officers of the various churches, in order that the regular services of the day might give place to the good Samaritan's work.

Mr. Blake rode till noon, not even delaying for breakfast, and thoroughly posted the people of Brookline, Brighton, and Roxbury, while Mayor Wightman and the police of Boston were active in their department. Mr. Twichell, in the mean time, was telegraphing to all the principal cities on the way, for engines to be in readiness, and carriages to convey the surgeons and others across New York city, and freight cars were provided by his orders to receive the goods, in Boston and in Brookline. The Sunday-schools had assembled at the various places of worship, when the news communicated by Messrs. Blake and Twichell to several other gentlemen was received at the various churches. Before the second bells began to ring, several webs of cotton cloth were on their way from the dry-goods stores to the churches. The congregations assembled in the pews, the news of the morning was announced, solemn prayer was offered, and the people were dismissed to the great duty of the hour. It was the writer's privilege to share in the labors of the Baptist Society on that memorable Sunday. The congregation partly assembled in the chapel, and a part went to their homes for materials. Without any attempt at organization, or any appointed head, everything moved as by clock-work, from the very outset. There was no rush, nor hurry, nor confusion; but there was something for every man, woman, and child to do, for the older Sunday-school children remained, and many were the errands on which they were sent to the various houses of those who were doing work which required their presence, and the quiet and solemn dignity with which the merriest hearted boys entered into the work of the day, showed them worthy of their country. In less than an hour, new cloth which had been cut off the web, in various lengths, carried home, shrunk, dried and pressed, was brought back into the chapel to be stripped into bandages. These were tightly rolled, fastened, and the number of yards marked on the outside of each roll.

In the mean time, various delegations which had been sent out for boxes, came in with shoe-boxes, dry-goods boxes, empty barrels and firkins, from all quarters; others returned laden with shirts, stockings, dressing-gowns, bed linen, slippers, and blankets, and from every quarter every delicacy which sick men could use, and even costly luxuries, unfit for sickness, were poured in. Choice old wines and fine new linen were freely given. Nothing was withheld that could be of use, from the set of a dozen new fine shirts, just completed by one housekeeper for her husband's home needs, to the stock of jellies and preserves laid up for the next winter's use. All were alike freely given, and the only regret seemed to be that there was not more to give, and those who could not contribute goods, freely gave money. Busy little fingers were scraping lint, and aged hands lent their tremulous service in many a useful way. Similar scenes were being enacted in the other churches, and few thought of going home to dine or rest. There was steady, calm, systematic work, and the amount accomplished seems incredible as we look back upon it. By four o'clock the goods were on the way to the depot, where two freight cars, which had been provided by Mr. Twichell, stood waiting. In these cars were closely packed twenty tons of goods from this town. In Boston eight other cars received the contributions of the city and surrounding towns, and the train consisted of ten cars, containing a hundred tons of supplies. Everything was assorted, carefully packed, and every box or package marked. Mr. Twichell volunteered to go on with the goods to Washington, and see them safely delivered, and he was accompanied by Dr. T. E. Francis and others, who went to make themselves useful as physicians, surgeons, or nurses. Twenty-one surgeons gave their services on this occasion, and the Mayor of Boston with a body of police accompanied them. Through some inadvertence the dispatch ordering the carriages in New York had not been received, and on the arrival of the train it appeared as if an inevitable delay must occur, which would prevent the party from reaching the Washington train in time. To Mr. Twichell belongs the credit of securing by his unflagging energy and enterprise the transfer of the forty persons who accompanied him, from the depot of the New Haven Railroad in New York, to the Jersey Ferry, in less than half an hour; and by the coöperation of Mr. Barker, the agent of the connected line of cars and boats beyond New York, the train was detained long enough to admit of the arrival of the party. The physicians, nurses, and those in charge of supplies were thus enabled to reach

Washington a few hours in advance of the goods, and perfected their arrangements there with the President, the Surgeon-general, and the Sanitary Commission, so that the goods which left Brookline at four o'clock on Sunday afternoon, and Boston soon after, were being distributed and applied to the wounded and suffering before seven the next Tuesday morning.

To Colonel Adams of the "Adams Express" is due the honor of having generously and promptly forwarded the hundred tons of goods the whole distance free of charge, and this included the unloading of the entire ten carloads in New York, the transportation on wagons through the city, and the re-loading again in cars at the Jersey Ferry.

Mr. Twichell returned after a few days' absence, and such was the intense interest to know from an eye-witness something of the condition of our wounded, and the true state of things at the Capitol, that a public meeting was called in the Baptist Church, which was then the largest public building in town, and the audience which filled the church to overflowing was addressed by Mr. Twichell, who gave most interesting information, in a clear and satisfactory manner. President Lincoln wrote with his own hand a letter of cordial thanks to the people, which was read by Mr. Twichell; but the good President, fearing he had not expressed himself with sufficient warmth, after giving the letter, added more and stronger expressions of grateful appreciation which he enjoined upon Mr. Twichell to repeat. Mrs. Lincoln, to her credit be it said, took her own carriage and accompanied Mr. Twichell and a gentleman from Boston to all the hospitals in Washington, that they might ascertain just what supplies were needed in each department.

The contributions did not stop with this occasion, but

a steady and munificent stream of benevolence was constantly flowing towards our armies from this town, as well as from the whole vicinity, and the Sanitary Commission never called upon Brookline in vain.

Miss Helen M. Griggs, daughter of the late David R. Griggs, of Harrison Place, early in the war, left the comforts of a beautiful home, and gave her services as a nurse in Armory Square Hospital, Washington, as long as the war lasted, except a short respite which her failing health demanded. When the war closed, she took up her residence in Richmond, as a teacher of the freedmen, until obliged to relinquish her labors on account of impaired health.

In July, 1862, President Lincoln called for 300,000 men to form new regiments, and recruit the old ones.

On the 12th July, a meeting was called by the Selectmen to consider the course to be adopted by this town in procuring enlistments. At this meeting, and at a legal town-meeting, held July 19th, it was voted " to appropriate the sum of twelve thousand dollars for the purpose of paying bounties to volunteers, and for the relief of families of volunteers."

On the 4th of August, the President issued a proclamation, stating that a draft for 300,000 men would be made on and after August 15, and that the deficiency on the call for volunteers which might then exist, must be drafted.

In answer to a call of many citizens, a town-meeting was held on the 9th of August, and the result was a vote " That the Military Committee be instructed to fill up the quota of the town as soon as possible, and to offer two hundred dollars bounty for each recruit." The armory was kept open day and night, and many men enlisted, some even before the town-meeting adjourned.

Many citizens rendered cheerful service in assisting the Military Committee, without compensation. The President's call was for nine months' men only, but the town enlisted none but three years' men at this time. The expenditures of the town during the year ending February 1, 1863, for military matters, was $49,653.24. In all, three hundred and twenty-nine men were enlisted during that year, and the Selectmen passed a vote of thanks to all volunteers, which was duly printed. The Board of Selectmen for 1861 and 1862, consisted of Messrs. James Bartlett, Marshall Stearns, Thomas Parsons, Edward R. Seccomb, and N. G. Chapin. The Military Committee comprised the first three above named, and Messrs. William K. Melcher, N. Lyford, William Aspinwall, James A. Dupee, James Murray Howe, M. B. Williams, M. Stearns, T. B. Hall, and E. A. Wild. Several Brookline men, after drilling in artillery practice, under Sergeant Miller, joined the 10th Mass. Battery, and did heroic service in the field during the rest of the war. This battery went into service in September, 1862.

On the 27th of September, 1862, the Military Committee received a letter from Colonel Thomas Aspinwall (ex-consul to London), inclosing the sum of three hundred and eighty dollars, twenty-nine cents, being two thirds of the proceeds of a lot of land belonging to Colonel Aspinwall, "sold by auction for benefit of our soldiers engaged in the suppression of the present rebellion."

The following year, 1864, the same board of Selectmen served, with the exception of William J. Griggs, who served in place of E. R. Seccomb. On the 17th of October another call came for another three hundred thousand men, and Brookline's quota was seventy-two men. The recruiting office was again opened in Guild's building, and seventy-five men enlisted. It was hoped that this was to be the last call, but the office had been closed but a few days when the summons came for more, and Brookline's quota was forty-eight; making in all, one hundred and twenty men. The work of the Sanitary Commission was drawing upon all the resources the ladies could command, and many soldiers' families were largely assisted by funds appropriated to this use by the Military Committee.

The spring of 1865 witnessed the downfall of Richmond, and the Rebellion was over.

In Brookline, as everywhere else, there was an outburst of jubilant feeling. The church bells rang a merry peal, and every house was gay with flags. A meeting for joyful congratulation was held in the Town Hall, which was crowded to its utmost capacity, with all classes and conditions of people. It was a memorable occasion, and the enthusiastic speeches, the cordial handshaking, the tears, smiles, laughter, and general joyousness, were but a fitting expression of the public feeling. It was beyond words. A few days later, and the national joy was turned into mourning, for a pall had fallen upon every house and heart. The tragical death of the beloved President Lincoln was nowhere more sincerely mourned than in our own community, as all will bear witness who remember that dark episode in our national history.

To many a household, too, here as elsewhere, the triumphant ending of the war was overshadowed with private sorrows, for their brave beloved ones who came not back to join in the gladness of victory, and mingle their tears with the general mourning for the martyr President. They had fallen in camp and field, on sea, and in southern prisons; —

> "On fame's eternal camping ground
> Their silent tents are spread,
> And glory guards with solemn round
> The bivouac of the dead."

The Selectmen, in closing their war report for the last year of the war, made use of the following language: —

"We cannot close this article without referring with deep regret to the many brave men from this town, who have fallen in this fearful struggle for our nation's existence; gladly would we speak of them as they deserve, if it were in our power; but it is not. Their names should be inscribed high on the roll of fame, and held in grateful remembrance by all future generations. We can only say to their bereaved friends, that they have our heartfelt sympathy in this their sorrow; and we, in behalf of the town and their fellow-citizens, gratefully tender our thanks to those who have returned to us, who have survived the fearful ordeal through which they have passed, in discharge of their duty to *our* common country; and to all who are now at the front engaged in defense of law and good government.

[Signed.] JAMES BARTLETT,
MARSHALL STEARNS,
THOMAS PARSONS,
WILLIAM J. GRIGGS,
EDWARD S. PHILBRICK."

From the breaking out of the Rebellion to its close the town of Brookline furnished the United States government with eight hundred and eighty officers and men, in all departments of the service.* Many of these were non-residents, but a large number were not only residents but Brookline boys, brought up in our homes and schools, and who volunteered before bounties were offered, because they were able and willing to do their duty by their country, and not only willing, but would have scorned not to do it. Many young men, natives of Brookline, were residents in other towns and cities. Some of them returned to

* *Report of Selectmen.* Adjutant-general Schouler's report says, "Brookline furnished seven hundred and twenty men for the war, which was a surplus of one hundred and thirty-five over and above all demands. Thirty-four were commissioned officers."

enlist in the roll of their native town, while many enlisted in the places where they were living, and their names honored many a regiment, from Boston to Chicago, and San Francisco.

We had seen our regiments and batteries go, taking their bright banners from the hands of our great "war-governor," with full ranks, new uniforms, and shining equipments. We saw them return, a broken remnant, stained with the soil of dusty marches, bearing the tattered remnants of the flags they had borne through many battles, but they came to a cordial and glorious welcome, whether they came singly or in the ranks. Company A, of the Massachusetts 1st Regiment, which was largely composed of Brookline volunteers, was so depleted by sickness, death, and transfer, that at the close of the war there was but little of the original element left. Its captain had risen to the rank of brigadier-general, one of its lieutenants was wounded, the other lay among the unknown dead in front of Richmond, and several privates, or non-commissioned officers were raised to the rank of officers in other regiments. The 10th Massachusetts Battery had many Brookline men in it, and on their return the town gave the Battery a generous reception.

We copy the following account of the reception, from the " Boston Evening Transcript," June 15, 1865: —

"The 10th Mass. Battery, Capt. J. W. Adams, was received at Brookline yesterday. The battery came up from Gallop's Island at noon, and took the half-past one train for Brookline. On arriving at Chapel Station the veterans left the cars and a procession was formed in the following order: Brookline Drum Corps, Brookline Rifles, a company of lads, Capt. A. L. Lincoln ; 10th Mass. Battery, Capt. J. W. Adams, with 113 men ; Brookline Brass Band ; Engine Co. No. 1, H. M. Hall, foreman ; " Good Intent " Hose Co., G. H. Stone, foreman ; Pierce

Division Sons of Temperance, C. H. Stearns, W. P.; returned soldiers; town authorities and citizens generally.

"The colors of the Battery, inscribed with the names of the battles in which it had been engaged, were carried in the front rank. Moses B. Williams, Esq., was Chief Marshal, and under his lead the procession marched through the streets of the beautiful town. At various points along the route the veterans were showered with beautiful bouquets. The procession proceeded to the rear of the Town Hall, where a bountiful collation was spread in Yale's mammoth tent. Plates were laid for upwards of four hundred, and the collation, furnished by Mr. Aaron Whitney, was excellent in quality, and abundant in quantity.

"After the company had been seated, prayer was offered by Rev. Dr. Lamson, and the edibles were then discussed for half an hour. The company were then called to order, and James Murray Howe, Esq., welcomed the guests in eloquent and fitting terms, to which Captain Adams appropriately responded. Other speeches were made by John W. Candler, Rev. Dr. Hedge, Ginery Twichell, Esq., and Messrs. Atkinson and Dana, of Brookline, and artificer W. Y. Gross of the Battery."

The whole affair was a success, and the veterans were enthusiastic in their expressions of pleasure.

The 2d Mass. Regiment had been largely recruited by Brookline men, and upwards of thirty thousand dollars were raised by private subscription, towards organizing this regiment; but no public demonstration was made on the return of its shattered remnant. The whole amount of money appropriated and expended by the town on account of the war, exclusive of State aid paid to soldiers' families, was one hundred and thirty-four thousand two hundred and twenty-four dollars and ninety-nine cents ($134,224.99). The amount raised and expended during the war for aid to soldiers' families, and repaid to the town by the State, was twenty-one thousand four hundred and thirty-five dollars and seven cents ($21,435.07).

The services rendered by the ladies of the town were acknowledged to be great and valuable.* The amount of money raised by them and spent for the comfort of the soldiers, was not less than twenty thousand dollars. The town was represented in the military hospitals of Washington, by both ladies and gentlemen, who gave their services as either temporary or permanent nurses, and little rills of beautiful unrecorded charities and sweet sympathies never ceased to flow into the camps and hospitals as long as they were needed. Even little children voluntarily contributed their mites, and gave their play hours to the public service.

In closing the record of the war, we would gladly append a roll of honor, which should contain the name of every soldier who was credited to our town, whether a resident or not. They were all residents of our common country, and dear to some home circle, or at least to some human heart, and many names of our own townsmen are lost to us because they were non-residents at the time and enlisted elsewhere. But the attempt would be vain to collect and arrange such a list for this work, and it would be impossible to do anything like justice in speaking of the hardships they bore, and the glorious result of their toils and sacrifices. Many of them have returned to us broken down in health, or maimed and disabled for life; many others still in vigorous manhood are holding positions of active usefulness. We honor them all, from the highest officer to the humblest private, who shouldered knapsack and gun; the noblest man was none too noble for the cause for which he fought and won, and

* See Adjutant-general Schouler's Report.

the least worthy soldier who enlisted, was for once in his life engaged in a glorious cause.

Of those who served in the Navy, we have been unable to obtain a record.

Of those who fell in the infantry and artillery service, we have obtained as full and correct a list as we could gather from Adjutant-general Schouler's reports, and other sources.

Among all our Brookline soldiers we have found but one deserter.

BROOKLINE SOLDIERS

WHO LOST THEIR LIVES DURING OR IN CONSEQUENCE OF THE REBELLION.

ATKINSON, DANIEL W., 10th Mass. Battery, killed at Hatcher's Run, Va., Oct. 27, 1864.

ARCHER, GEORGE E., Co. H, 33d Mass. Reg't, accidentally killed July 6, 1863, at Camden, N. J.

BARLOW, HERBERT S., Co. A, 1st Mass. Reg't, killed at Budd's Ferry, Va., Jan. 31, 1862.

BOGMAN, NELSON, Rhode Island Battery, died in service.

BIXBY, OLIVER C., Co. F, 58th Mass., killed July 30, 1864, at Petersburg, Va.

BURRILL, GEORGE C., Lieut., 59th Reg't, killed May, 1864, in the Wilderness, Va.

BURRILL, PASCHAL, Co. H, 2d Mass. Reg't, died of wounds, May 12, 1863.

BURKE, JOSEPH, Company I, 59th Reg't, killed May, 1864, at Spottsylvania, Va.

CHANDLER, CHARLES L., Lieut.-col., 57th Reg't, killed at North Anna River, Va., May 24, 1864. Son of T. P. Chandler, Brookline.

CLARK, JOHN W., 1st Mass. Battery, died October 4, 1862, at Bakersville, Md.

CUSICK, JOHN, Co. H., 1st Reg't Heavy Artillery, died soon after his discharge at the close of the war, of hardship and exposure.

CLEARY, THOMAS, Co. F, 56th Mass. Reg't, died at Annapolis, Md., April 13, 1864.

COLLINS, GEORGE, Co. B, 2nd Reg't H. A., died March 26, 1865, at Goldsborough, North Carolina.

COLLINS, ELBRIDGE G., Co. G, 2d Reg't H. A., died prisoner at Andersonville, Sept. 1864.

DWIGHT, WILDER, Lieut.-col., 2d Mass. Reg't, died of wounds received at Antietam, Sept. 19, 1862. Son of William Dwight of Brookline.

The intensely interesting "Life and Letters of Wilder Dwight," in our Public Library, has been so widely read, that further remark upon his character would seem superfluous, in a volume which is designed like this for only local circulation. But there is a generation of young people growing up, to whom the events of the Rebellion are as much a matter of past history as the War of the Revolution. To such we can only recommend this attractive memorial, if they would know by one more proof, what beauty and strength of character, what genial traits and deserved popularity in life, and what heroic bravery in battle and in death, characterized this young martyr upon the field of Antietam.

The solemn scene of his funeral, with military honors, from St. Paul's Church, Brookline, is engraven upon the memories of those who witnessed it.

DWIGHT, HOWARD, Capt., killed by guerrillas after he had surrendered, near Bayou Bœuf, Louisiana, May 4, 1863. Son of William Dwight of Brookline.

DILLON, THOMAS, Co. B, 2d Reg't, killed at Antietam Sept. 17, 1862. Son of John Dillon of Brookline.

DALE, JAMES A., Corp., Co. H, 33d Reg't, died of wounds, July 1, 1864.

FOSS, JAMES M., Serg't, Co. I, 59th Reg't, died Nov. 5, 1864, at New York.

FUNK, JOSEPH W., 11th Mass. Reg't, died Oct. 16, 1864, at Washington.

GETCHELL, FRANK, Co. A, 1st Mass. Reg't, died Feb. 3, 1863, at Falmouth, Va.

GETCHELL, LOUIS G., Co. A, 1st Reg't, killed June 25, 1862, at Fair Oaks, Va.

GODKIN, CHARLES H., Co. H, 2d Mass. Reg't H. A., died a prisoner at Andersonville, Oct. 1864.

GRISWOLD, CHARLES E., Col., 56th Reg't, killed May 6, 1864, in the Wilderness.

HARRIS, P. NATHANIEL, Sergt., Co. D, 45th Mass. Reg't, died in North Carolina, June 1863.

HAYMON, JOHN, Co. H, 56th Mass. Reg't, killed at Petersburg, July 30, 1864.

KITTRIDGE, MALCOLM G., Co. G, 2d Reg't, killed May 3, 1864, at Chancellorsville.

KNIBBS, FREDERIC, Co. G, 58th Reg't, died of wounds, at Fredericksburg, May 24, 1864.

KENNEDY, TIMOTHY, Co. C, 28th Mass. Reg't, killed December 13, 1862, at Fredericksburg.

LAMSON, SAMUEL G., son of Rev. Dr. Lamson of Brookline. Samuel Giles Lamson, only child of Rev. Dr. Lamson of Brookline, was in the Paymaster's service, and was stationed at St. Louis. On the 3d of August, 1863, he embarked on board the steamer " Ruth," on his way to Vicksburg to pay off our soldiers.

On the way down the river the boat took fire. (It was said to be the work of rebel emissaries.) The boat was consumed and thirty lives were lost, among them this young man. His body was recovered, and after two weeks was received by his afflicted parents. He was buried in Harmony Grove Cemetery, Salem, Mass. Young Lamson was well educated, highly patriotic, and every way a promising young man.

At the time of his death he was twenty-three years of age.

MERRILL, OTIS S., Co. H, 44th Reg't, died at Newbern, N. C., March 2, 1863.

McCALLEY, JAMES, Co. H, 59th Reg't, died May 29, 1864, at Arlington, Va.

MALONEY, EDWARD, Co. D, 56th Reg't, died June 13, 1864, at Readville, Mass.

MORIARTY, PATRICK, Co. G, 56th Reg't, died Oct. 14, 1864, at Danville.

MEADE, JOHN, 16th Mass. Lt. Battery, drowned Jan. 28, 1865, at New Brunswick, Va.

PHELPS, JULIUS A., Co. A, 1st Reg't, killed June 30, 1862, at Glendale, Va.

ROLLINS, CHARLES E., Co. C, 44th Reg't, killed Nov. 2, 1862, at Little Creek, N. C.

RUSSELL, ALFRED W., Co. G, 58th Reg't, killed July 12, 1864, at Petersburg.

REED, S. S., 2d Heavy Artillery, died at Andersonville, Sept. 1864.

ROSS, HENRY L., Co. G, 58th Reg't, killed May 6, 1864, in the Wilderness.

STEARNS, GEORGE THEODORE, Co. B, 22d Reg't, wounded in Wilderness, May, 1864; died of wounds, in Washington, July 6, 1864.

STONE, HENRY V. D., Lieut., son of Rev. Dr. Stone of Brookline. Killed at Gettysburg, July 3, 1864.

SHURTLEFF, CARLTON A., Medical Cadet, died in Brookline, after return from service, June 26, 1864. Son of Dr. S. A. Shurtleff.

TURNER, JOSEPH, Co. A, 1st Mass. Reg't, died at Fair Oaks, June 21, 1862.

TROWBRIDGE, WILLIAM H., dropped dead at night after Battle of Malvern Hills, July, 1862, while posted on picket duty.

THAYER, JOHN GORHAM, 1st Mass. Cavalry, died of sickness incurred during service, at Sacramento, Cal., Dec. 28, 1864.

WARREN, THOMAS G., Co. D, 22d Reg't, killed June 18, 1864, at Petersburg.

WHALAN, THOMAS, Co. F, 22d Reg't, killed May 10, 1864, at Laurel Hill, Va.

WHITNEY, CHARLES H., Co. A., 1st Reg't, wounded and disabled, transferred to Veteran Reserve Corps, died in Brookline shortly after his return.

WATERMAN, AUGUSTUS, Co. A, 1st Reg't, taken prisoner, May 6, 1864, detained nearly a year at Andersonville, died of effects of starvation before reaching home, after he was discharged.

WELLS, HENRY W., died in the naval service.

Thus closes the record of our dead. If any name has failed to be obtained and recorded, it is a matter of regret.

Let no one say "this one," or "that one was a non-resident." If he was, and our town hired his services, he died that some one, whom perchance we still hold dear, might be saved to us, who might otherwise have fallen in the trenches at Petersburg, or perished by slow starvation at Andersonville.

Allusion was made in the early part of our war record, to Lieut. Charles L. Chandler, who was among the first to recruit a company of volunteers in Brookline. More than a passing notice is due to this brave young officer. When the war began, he at once relinquished his business (that of a civil engineer), and devoted himself to the service of the country. It soon became apparent that he could command himself, and that he had a rare aptitude for commanding others.

He was but twenty-one when he received his first commission, was made 1st Lieutenant in March, 1862, and served with the 1st Mass. Regiment, at the first battle of Bull Run, and through the Peninsula campaign.

In August of that year he was made Captain in the 34th, and in March, 1864, was commissioned Lieutenant-colonel of the 57th (Veterans). Of this he was in command during most of the terrible battles in the "Wilderness," Colonel Bartlett having been wounded in one of the first engagements.

Brigadier-general Ledlie writes of him: "From the moment of his joining his regiment at Alexandria, he attracted general attention by his remarkable qualities, both as a soldier and a gentleman, and no officer in the division was more respected and beloved."

In the advance and terrible repulse of the First Division of the Ninth Army Corps, at the North Anna River, on the night of May 24, 1864, this gallant young officer was mortally wounded. His side received the fatal bullet, but his arm was also shattered, and hung motionless. His officers were assisting him off the field when they found themselves flanked by the rebels. At once he ordered them to leave him and rally their men, and reluctantly they laid him down to die.

He fell into the hands of the rebels, but Colonel Harris, of the Twelfth Mississippi Regiment, kindly cared for him in his last hours, and to him, a gentleman and a friend, as he proved himself, although a rebel, the dying soldier committed his money, his watch, diary, and a photograph.

He had been three years in the service of the country, and had won the highest encomiums for his ability, fidelity, and rare and genial qualities. "Every officer and man," wrote General Bartlett, "that I have been to see in the hospital here, speak of Colonel Chandler's bravery and devotion with filling eyes. I never saw men who, in so short a time had such a feeling of admiration for any man's conduct. His loss was felt throughout the corps."

The kind rebel officer saw the body of the handsome young colonel properly buried, and after the war was over, took measures to let his family know of the mementoes he had kept for them, and delivered them to his brother, who made a journey to Virginia; but the battle-field was vainly searched for the remains of the beloved one. They had been removed, and are now resting in an unknown grave; but the love of friends and kindred, and the honor of his country, long shall keep his memory sacred.

His last letter home expressed firm confidence in the power and love of the Lord respecting him. He had counted the cost, was ready for the sacrifice, and died happy in the noble discharge of his duty.

OUR HEROES

WHO SLEEP IN UNKNOWN GRAVES.

MEMORIAL DAY, 1872.

Bring garlands for each patriot's grave,
  Our dear and honored dead!
Above the brave the flag shall wave, —
  The wreath its fragrance shed.
They bore our nation's emblem hence
  When traitors scorned its name;
Borne homeward from its brave defense
  Wrapped in its folds they came.

Peace to their memories! But for those
  Who went but came no more, —
Who lie where facing rebel foes
  They fell mid battle's roar; —
Who pined in prison and dying wore
  Starvation's martyr-crown, —
Who sleep in fort and trench on shore,
  Or lie where ships went down; —

For them no flag, nor wreath, nor cross,
  To-day above them rest;
But, hallowed by the price it cost,
  In every patriot's breast, —
Is freedom's triumph which they won,
  By the brave blood they shed,
And shrined in story and in song
  Shall be our nameless dead.

Thrice hallowed ever be the land
  For which our heroes died,
Nor the least boon of freedom's hand
  To one who seeks, denied;
By sea and shore, on mountain crest,
  Where'er unknown they sleep,
The God of nations guard their rest,
  And green their memories keep.

ADDENDA.

There have been some local changes in streets and buildings since the proof for this volume was corrected, which it is now too late to notice. An incident illustrative of the difficulty of keeping pace with the march of events even while a book is in press, is connected with the clock now in the new Town Hall, which, at the time an account of it was written and printed, was in the old Town Hall, and seemed to be a fixture there. It has since been removed from the ancient case which had inclosed it for seventy years, and has been fitted in its new location by Mr. John Koch, with an appropriate taste which makes it appear as if a part of the original design of the gallery which it ornaments.

Other changes are going on in the town which are not noticed in this volume because not yet completed, but which will furnish ample material for some future historian of Brookline.

www.ingramcontent.com/pod-product-compliance
Lightning Source LLC
Chambersburg PA
CBHW051736300426
44115CB00007B/582